Praise for *Catharine, Queen of*

"Cynthia Neale has written a wonderfu
narrates the hardships and triumphs of
most remarkable women. Neale vividly recreates the lost world of the early
American frontier, where Catharine and her family navigated an uneasy borderland
between colonists and Native peoples. Along the way, readers will meet a who's
who of historical figures, from George Croghan to Sattelihu, but, above-all,
Catharine deservingly emerges as one of colonial America's most fascinating people.
Grounded in impressive historical research and empathy, *Catharine, Queen of the
Tumbling Waters* reminds us of the human stories at the heart of times of great
change." — Chad Anderson, Author of the *Storied Landscape of Iroquoia: History,
Conquest, and Memory in the Native Northeast*

"Cynthia Neale's extensive research combined with her intuition and creativity
tells an intriguing tale of Catharine Montour and the Native Americans of the
Northeast as the British and French strive for dominance over the land. Catharine's
journey gives us much insight into the relationship between the Native Americans
and colonists, traders, and colonial leaders. Neale tells the story of Catharine,
her romances, her people, and their struggle to maintain their culture and live
peacefully in a rapidly changing world. The stereotypical Indian woman living in a
wigwam dissolves in this stimulating story as we gain a vivid picture of Catharine
and the three generations of Montour women of French and Native heritage." —
Gail Davis, Kanestio Historical Society, Director/Treasurer

"After reading Cynthia Neale's fascinating and meticulously researched novel,
Catharine Montour became very real. Too many historical details can often deaden
a story, but this novel that is packed full of history is anything but dull. In fact, I
had a real sense I was meeting Catharine in the flesh, that this indeed could have
been her life. Queen Catharine lives again . . . on the page." — Charlotte Dickens,
poet/writer; Watkins Glen Writers Group Facilitator; president of Backbone Ridge
History Group

"As a boy roaming Queen Catharine's land, she became a companion in my
burgeoning imagination. Years later, as a volunteer for the library, I became
convinced of her burial site and learned more about her life. Cynthia Neale's
spellbinding novel captures the spirit of Catharine I loved as a boy into my adult
years. I didn't want it to end!" — Norm West, local historian

"Cynthia Neale's beautiful novel is still with me months after reading it. She
depicts Catharine so convincingly, it is as if she is channeling her spirit. To read
this thoroughly researched story is to go back in time and enter a complex and dark
period in U.S. history and get to know one of its heroines who would otherwise be
forgotten. This is an important book." — Haviva Ner-David, rabbi and author of
Hope Valley and *To Die in Secret*

Other Books by Cynthia G. Neale

The Irish Dresser, A Story of Hope During the Great Hunger
Hope in New York City, The Continuing Story of The Irish Dresser
Norah, The Making of an Irish-American Woman in 19th-Century New York
The Irish Milliner
Pavlova in a Hat Box, Sweet Memories & Desserts

CATHARINE

QUEEN OF THE TUMBLING WATERS

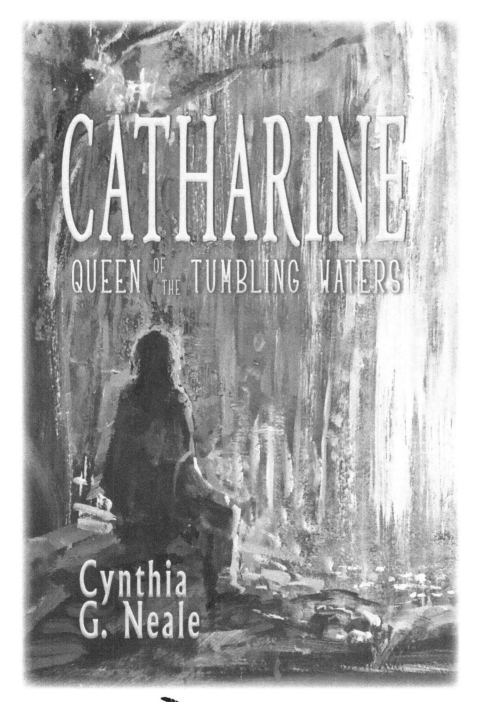

CATHARINE
QUEEN OF THE TUMBLING WATERS

Cynthia
G. Neale

Bink Books
Bedazzled Ink Publishing Company • Fairfield, California

978-1-949290-99-8 paperback

Cover Art
by
Vincent Crotty

Cover Design
by

Bink Books
a division of
Bedazzled Ink Publishing, LLC
Fairfield, California
http://www.bedazzledink.com

For my mother and best friend,
Doris Cope-Filippetti-Force-Huston (1927-2022),
who always believed I would tell Catharine's story

"I have uprooted The Great White Pine Tree. In this cavern we shall toss our weapons of war and bury the hatchets of hatred as we replant the Tree of Peace. On top of this tree we will place an eagle to watch for any dangers that may come to endanger this peace. I will also send out four white roots of peace. If anyone seeks peace, they can trace the roots back and find shelter here." — Peacemaker to the Mohawk, Oneida, Onondaga, Cayuga and Seneca

Author's Note

This is a work of imagination, inspired by the life of Catharine Montour, also known as Queen Catharine, born in Pennsylvania possibly around 1729 and who lived in what is known today as Montour Falls, New York. She was a métis, which means *mixed* in French, and was French and Iroquois. It was said of her that she was handsome, possessed more than ordinary intellectual powers, and meted out justice to all. She was regarded by Europeans as a superior woman. Please see the Character Index to know more about her lineage.

Queen Catharine Montour's name is perpetuated everywhere in Montour Falls, New York and the surrounds. There is a memorial, a street, a park, a creek, a trail, and many businesses named after her. History describes Queen Catharine as the leader and matriarch of a Seneca tribe and village, She-O-Qua-Gah (there are different spellings), a Seneca (Iroquois) word meaning *tumbling waters*. The village was later called Catharine's Town, Catharine's Landing, Havana, and eventually Montour Falls to honor Catharine Montour. In my novel, Catharine names the area Eagle Cliff Falls, which is the name of one of the waterfalls in Montour Falls.

In 1779, nearing the end of the American Revolution, General George Washington initiated a campaign led by Major General John Sullivan and the Continental Army (also known as the Clinton-Sullivan Campaign) to destroy all Iroquois villages, whether they were enemies, allies, or neutral to the Revolution. Congress approved Washington's plan, "directing him to take all measures necessary to protect the settlers and to punish the Indians." Washington wrote to Sullivan, "The immediate objects are total destruction and devastation of their settlements and the capture of as many prisoners of every sex and age as possible. It will be essential to ruin their crops in the ground and prevent their planting more." (Founders Online/Archives.gov.Home)

Queen Catharine Montour heroically gathered the people in her village in She-O-Qua-Ga and led them away from Major John Sullivan's approaching Continental Army to Fort Niagara to be sheltered by the British.

The campaign ended and forty Indian settlements were burned to the ground, thousands of bushels of corn, fruits, vegetables and livestock were destroyed, but most egregious were the thousands of Iroquois who sought refuge under the British at Fort Niagara. The winter thereafter was brutal and severe and many Iroquois died from cold and starvation. It is not known whether Queen Catharine returned to She-O-Qua-Ga, but I believe she did. After the American Revolution, the great Iroquois Nation and Confederacy scattered and has never been the same, but their spirit has always remained and today, there are many Iroquois museums, writers, artists, and organizations celebrating this indigenous history and their place in America.

I've often said my writing career includes working with the dead and although this sounds morbid, it is not. We all carry the blood and stories of our ancestors and there's a thin line between here and there if we attune our hearts to listen. I wanted to be a writer at a young age, but it took years to learn to listen. And when I did, I encountered many unusual experiences and synchronicities. This is not the place to talk about my other novels and their strange incidents, but before you put your curious and discerning nose into this novel, I want to tell you about some of my Catharine visitations. No, I didn't just channel Catharine's story, but through grueling, ardent, frustrating, and thrilling research, and with her spirit and various encounters, I have written a Queen Catharine Montour story!

I grew up in the Montour Falls, New York vicinity and was intrigued by Queen Catharine, but there was little known information. Historians have puzzled over Queen Catharine Montour and the Montour family for years. The Montours were elusive, famous, but obscure, and have been difficult to track down. Historians have disagreed over the life of Catharine Montour and her various family members for years. Her grandmother, Isabel Montour (Madame Montour), was born in New France in the 17th century. She was complex, a go-between, interpreter, and told a couple of different stories about her life. It was Simone Vincens, author of the wonderful biography, *Madame Montour and the Fur Trade*, who instructed me to learn about Isabel Montour and her son, Andrew Montour, if I wanted to know Catharine Montour. After uncanny and astounding Catharine nudges and reading local history articles, I delved into Simone Vincens' book and it became the skeleton that eventually led me into fleshing out Catharine's life.

In 2006 while visiting family in Montour Falls, I walked the Catharine Creek Trail as I usually do. Off the trail is a memorial to Queen Catharine with the Seneca and English words, "Every One of You Always Remember This." I quizzically pondered this memorial because I didn't remember much of anything about her. Suddenly, an emphatic voice within said, "Write my story!" I stomped my foot and said aloud, "No, I'm still writing Norah's story!" That evening, I pulled out my mother's couch bed and found a book on the Iroquois on her bookshelf. I read about the Three Sisters (corn, beans, and squash) and fell asleep. In the morning, there was a kernel of corn in my bed! It was May, not autumn, and there were no dried corn arrangements in the apartment. Two big nudges, but I ignored them.

I took the Iroquois book home to New Hampshire and read it while continuing my work on a novel in The Irish Dresser series. The next visit to New York was in autumn and one morning I walked the trail and stopped at

Catharine's memorial. No voices, but as I continued my walk on a gorgeous day, I hummed and then incoherent words tumbled out in song. When my husband called, I jokingly said, "I'm singing in Senecan!" Later, my mother and I went to the Wind Mill Farm & Craft Market in Penn Yan, New York. Mom sat with a coffee and I went off to browse. Suddenly, I heard music that reminded me of my earlier crazy singing. With goosebumps and excitement, I followed the music to a Native American store where Seneca music was playing. I shared my experience with the owner and he gifted me with an owl necklace and I bought the Seneca CD. He strongly encouraged me to write Catharine's story.

Thereafter, for years while working on The Irish Dresser Series and writing a screenplay series, I researched and wrote Catharine's story. I found many books, rare books, journals, and ordered out of print books that cost me a pretty penny. Some of the print in the reprinted books published in the late 1800s or early 1900s was so small, I wore reading glasses over contact lenses and used a magnifying glass! I would find Catharine peeking out here and there in three volume history tomes and gradually, although painstakingly slow, her life was pieced together. In the empty spaces in this hide and seek research, I took creative license and used my imagination. However, I must say that even then, it seemed Catharine was telling me what to write. For instance, George Croghan, the Irish-born fur trader and a key early figure in colonial times, kept popping up in my research. And when I learned he became a good friend of Catharine's uncle, Andrew Montour, it seemed natural for Catharine and George to have a dalliance. Well, if they did . . . You will have to read the book to find out. But George Croghan matters a lot in the novel although I kept saying no, no, no . . . he's Irish and I don't need to bring this Irish fellow into this story.

I felt at times I was in over my head and on many occasions decided to quit. Well, I had said this with my Irish novels, too, but this was different. It was difficult writing about a real person of history and a Native American, at that. The voice of doubt, at times, was stronger than the voice of Catharine and the characters' voices in her story. But each time I was going to quit, peculiar things happened.

Once, after stating it was over with Catharine and I felt briefly unshackled, I was at an Irish festival in Boston to sell my books. The authors were gathered together in a tent and we introduced ourselves to one another. One of the authors had written a book about General John Sullivan and I asked him if he knew of Catharine Montour and he responded, "how do you know Queen Catharine?" Another time, my husband and I were driving through Newmarket, New Hampshire when we came upon The John Sullivan House! I hadn't known this general who led the campaign against my protagonist and her people was from New Hampshire. I had only known him through New York history and hadn't known he had been attorney general, federal judge, and a governor of New Hampshire. Was I getting the message to keep writing?

I continued to work on the novel, but at times, reluctantly. A few years later, at the beginning of the pandemic, I was walking on a remote deer path in the woods. I looked down and there was a kernel of dried corn, bigger than life. I put it in my pocket and decided there would be no more quitting. I finally finished the novel in 2021, but then my mother went into hospice and I traveled from New Hampshire to New York to help care for her. She was my biggest fan and encourager and repeatedly said she didn't want to die until she held Catharine's story in her hands. Fortunately, I was able to read her an edit before she passed in May 2022. During these difficult times, my publisher for my last two novels indicated publication for 2023 would be non-fiction and they would not be publishing Catharine's story. At this point, with my mother in hospice and knowing my best friend was soon going to leave, I quietly decided not to pursue publication and laid aside this story. Around this time, while back in New Hampshire on a reprieve, my husband and I went to dinner at Ambrose Restaurant located in the Inn by the Bandstand in Exeter, New Hampshire. While dining and talking to one of the owners, we learned that the inn was originally the Sullivan-Sleeper home, built in 1809 for George Sullivan, the son of Major John Sullivan, who was a lawyer and statesmen in New Hampshire. Of course I would have to continue to pursue publication for this story! After saying goodbye to my dear mother and less than two months after she passed, I had an offer for publication from Bedazzled Ink Publishing, a publisher who represents authors who shine a light on under-represented women. And that is what I have sought to do in this novel—to shine a light on an under-represented Native American woman. But did I really have a choice not to?

Montour Falls, New York 2005

HO-DE'-NO-SAU-NEE LEGEND STATES that, as for Owl, he remains as the Everything-Maker had shaped him. He was created with large eyes, a short neck, and ears sticking up on the sides of his head. He was made to sleep during the day and come out only at night. One autumn in 2005, Owl flew into a black hole of the night where the stars had covered their faces, unwilling to shine. There he saw the spirit of a man flying away from his body parts that had been hacked into small pieces and floated down Catharine's Creek. A woman with fire in her belly had long ago cursed this landscape because it mocked the empty bowl of her life. She had raged and murdered this man.

This land absorbs the blood of the slain and creates beauty from ashes. Otherworldly melodies sing over sandstone and shale in the caress of waterfalls. A verdant land with meadows, hills, and gorges emanates a timeless grandeur. It is the land of the Ho-De'-No-Sau-Nee and memories of the three sisters—corn, bean, and squash still sustain and nurture one another in the intertwining of give and take.

Catharine Montour, a Ho-De'-No-Sau-Nee of mixed blood, is buried nearby in an unmarked grave. From this hallowed place, her spirit watches as human fury rises up again to leave another scar on the majestic imprint of the Great Spirit. Owl, night messenger for death, wisdom, and healing, flies out of the dark hole, screeches, and scatters her feathers nearby. Feathers that carry Ho-De'-No-Sau-Nee prayers to the Creator and possess great healing powers, but they are never seen among the severed limbs in Catharine's Creek.

Painting of She-Qua-Ga "Tumbling Waters" by Cynthia G. Neale

The Beginning

Otsonwakin, PA, Home of Madame Montour, 1742

HUNGER GNAWS THE inside of my hollow belly as I try to sleep. My sister, Esther, is curled up against my back and breathing like a windstorm. From time to time, her legs kick involuntarily against mine. When hunger and Esther finally take a break from badgering me, I fall asleep, but then I get a kick from Esther and the hunger that coils like a snake rises up and bites me.

"Wake up, granddaughters, wake up!"

I ignore Grandmother and pull a blanket over my face and inhale her mysterious scent in the scratchy wool. The old perfume given to Grandmother by her adoring governor of New York many years ago lingers. There is none like it I have smelled in the flowers of the field.

Flowers, I imagine wistfully, as I try to return to sleep. This is the bloodletting season when vibrant life drains from the earth. The time of year when the sun withdraws the colors of our land and leaves it barren; gray and brown merge into one and the earth becomes listless. Between autumn and winter, I lie down on the earth to listen, but this mother hardens herself against my bony body, waiting for the snows to cover her. This year when the first snow arrived, my grandmother gave me her blanket. She spoke in somber tones when she presented me with the scarlet blanket that smells like some other world's flowers.

"This was a gift from Corlaer, a great man in Albany," she said proudly. "I was his interpretess. I was Madame Montour who brought wisdom through many languages. I want you, my granddaughter, Catharine, who has been given the meaning of snow, to have this garment not just for warmth, but also for honor. You are the great-granddaughter of an esteemed French governor."

I didn't ask what the meaning of snow was. I also didn't ask how I happened to have a French governor as an ancestor. Why then do we live like we do in winter?

On the day Grandmother gave me her blanket, I danced in the first snowfall and asked to be blessed by Ga-oh, the Spirit of the Winds. It was twilight when day cavorts with evening and they become one. As the violet sky swirled above the field, I felt more than hunger crawling around in my belly. My mother said my years were fifteen or sixteen and I was a woman now and shouldn't be dancing alone in the dark. I skipped around the oak tree, kicking up snow that sparkled under Grandmother Moon who smiled at me from behind clouds. I prayed to the Great Spirit and became aware of the spirits of the dead who come to visit at night. I hurried back to our crowded cabin with cold, wet feet. Grandmother sat at our table making wampum and wearing her scarlet blanket across her shoulders. She laid aside her work and asked me to sit with her by the cook fire. We sat down and she removed her blanket and gently wrapped my icy feet in it. All the while, my mother made disapproving clucking noises.

"No, Grandmother," I whispered so my mother wouldn't hear, "don't give me your special cloth. It's for you, it's a queen's garment, this blanket. Don't soil it with my smelly feet."

Grandmother smiled, caressing my feet beneath the blanket.

"Your feet are special and they need honor and warmth, for they'll go many places. Do you think I live like a queen? I'm not a queen. I'm just an old moccasin of the house. And someday you'll be an old moccasin, too. But first you'll be filled with wondrous love and live many years."

Grandmother had been blessing my life and preparing me for the threshold of marriage, a threshold I was unsure of. I'm curious about marriage, but I'm in love with the handiwork of the earth—the soothing streams that caress my body, the summer trees that woo me with their sighing green leaves as I sit beneath them. I think of that special day as I close my eyes and nearly sleep, but then Grandmother yells again.

"Wake up, Esther and Catharine! I'm going out and when I return, you'd better be up and dressed."

The door shuts and I try to fall back to sleep. Esther hasn't stirred. I love my grandmother, Madame Montour. Her first name is Isabelle and she is both a French woman and an Indian woman, and that means that I, too, am French. I don't want to learn this language of the French even if Grandmother and my mother insist we learn it and others. Grandmother says we are to live like her mother, my great grandmother, an Algonquin, and my grandfather, Carondowana, an Oneida chief. And we must believe in the Great Spirit and adore the white man's God tucked away in the special chambers of our hearts. My great grandfather was French and Grandmother says little about him, except when she tells the white people he was a governor. My mother, French Margaret, loves to speak the words of the white men and she loves the Christ Jesus more than the Great Spirit. My mother's Christ Jesus is full of rules, as is my mother, but I believe they both love me, my mother and this Christ Jesus. My grandmother loves me as real as the sun in springtime loves the earth. My sister, Esther, and the other children are also loved by her, but I'm the singular vessel she places her secrets in.

I roll over and Esther still doesn't wake. My mind gallops into the past and how it is living in this family. The spirits cavort in our home when it becomes a resting place for travelers of every peculiar tongue. There is oftentimes confusion because of the different tribes, fur traders, and missionaries. At the crossroads of the Shamokin Path, our lives are a mish mash of chaos and inspiration with every person of the rainbow traveling here. Europeans seek land and power, the fur traders are greedy, and the Indians want respect and dominion over their hunting grounds.

My mother took hold of Esther and me one day and declared a prophecy from God for us.

"These two daughters will carry the spirit of their grandmother and are destined to see great change in this country. They will flow like rivers carrying the wisdom and messages of their people. If they become like the beaver and stop the flow with a dam, they will suffer."

I didn't want to carry wisdom or stop the flow of anything. I have heard squabbling and anger in various tongues and listened to Grandmother's voice bring harmony to the sour notes and grating languages of the raucous voices of men. I would like to be admired by men and women, Indians and whites, but I don't wish for the life of my grandmother. I don't want to travel to Philadelphia or Albany to bring understanding between men. I don't want to interpret the words of a white man for my people. I wouldn't be able to ignore the unstated words of the heart that wanted power over the Indian. There is less heat coming from the Ho-De'-No-Sau-Nee's Council fire now and their longhouse is in need of repair, but let Grandmother and Sattelihu, my uncle who is also called Andrew, bring salve for healing, not me.

All these thoughts keep me awake, but when I finally sleep again, the scarlet blanket is pulled off of me.

"Out of bed now!" Grandmother yells. "Sattelihu and our friends have traveled many days and are coming home. They've walked in snow that is trying to bury us all. They'll be weary and hungry and the village is preparing to greet them. Get up and prepare food and make your beds for them."

I hate to give up my bed, the bed Esther and I share. This bed I keep clean, made up each day, and scented with dried flowers. None of the Indian children in our village have a feather bed like ours, a bed bought from Grandmother's stash of money she keeps hidden somewhere in our cabin. When the goose feathers started coming out, I put straw in with the rest of the feathers and sewed it up.

Esther and I climb out of bed and hurry to dress to help our grandmother and mother. Shivering, I quickly fold my blanket and hide it in a basket. I don't want the lice of the travelers to find a warm home in my special blanket. Our guests will sleep in our bed and we'll sleep by the fire on our table that we make into a bed.

My mother, my sisters, Esther and Molly, Karontase, my eldest brother, and the younger children quickly prepare for more bodies to fill our cabin. My mother stirs the ashes and builds up a strong fire, uttering to herself, "No rum will have touched the lips of Peter Quebec, my Katarionecha." She has been on a mission to keep rum out of our home ever since the missionaries first came to visit. My father is her first convert, but who knows what he does when he travels with Sattelihu who likes his rum.

The bark barrel kept in the pit for our corn behind our cabin is empty, as empty as my belly feels. We still have five braids strung with twenty ears hanging in our cabin. Esther and I take down the white flint corn first because my mother instructs us to make hominy. The rest of the children assist us shelling the corn and then we take turns pounding it with our wooden mortar. After, we sift the corn in our sieve basket to remove the chit and coarse particles. The rest of the white corn braids will be used to make bread tomorrow. There will be soup from chestnuts saved in our storage loft. I'm thankful, but I can't live life in one color, no matter how bright it is, and I don't like eating just one food, no matter how many dishes we make from it.

Long ago, my brave grandfather died in a battle with our eternal enemy tribe, the Catawba. It is now my father, Katarionecha and my uncle, Sattelihu, who go on special missions with other men, the white man, Conrad Weiser, and our friends, Chief Shikellamy and Chief Allumpapes. They have been gone for so long that our cache of venison and bear meat buried by our cabin is empty, as is our corn bin. But soon they'll be home and there'll be hunting. My stomach growls as I think of meat cooked over the fire.

I look at my grandmother who is wrapping a beautiful beaded band around her forehead. Tears flow down her face and when she notices me, she turns away. Grandmother is hungry. We are all hungry because we have only eaten corn and chestnuts for weeks. I know her tears aren't only for her own hunger, but for our guests who will have traveled far in harsh weather and will not have enough food to fill their bellies. I'm not as goodhearted as Grandmother and I'm anxious about my own belly and resentful that our guests will eat the little food we have.

Chapter Two

Sattelihu

SATTELIHU AND HIS companions are journeying on the Shamokin Trail over the Blue Mountains toward Otsonwakin to his home filled with women. Other men in the village will have looked in on the women to see if they needed anything. His mother doesn't easily receive help from others. His wife, Sally, is the granddaughter of Chief Allumpapes and will be in disagreement with his mother over many things and he fears she will have left again and walked foolishly to her own mother's home miles away. He's always glad to have time away from this wife, for she is argumentative and rarely happy.

Sattelihu Montour is a son, an uncle, a husband, and a father all under one small roof. He often feels divided being half in one world with the white man and half in the other. He looks at Katarionecha, his brother-in-law, walking next to him. He's a good man, a good hunter, but he has married into the family and doesn't carry the weight of responsibility that is for Sattelihu only. Sometimes he wonders what his life would be like if he only had duties to his family and village. The white man's obligations are honorable, but burdensome. He thinks of these things as he walks with a white man and the Indians. He won't allow the small stream of white blood that runs through his veins to become a river that overflows. His French ancestors are as far away from him as the moon, even when full, except when his mother talks to him about his grandfather, Pierre Couc. He has never asked her why she tells the white officials that her father was a great governor of France. Pierre Couc, his grandfather, was a simple farmer from Trois-Rivieres, Quebec. He smiles thinking of the look he gets from his mother when she's engaged in eloquent conversation with Weiser and others. It was his brother, Lewis, who moved to the Ohio region from Quebec, who told him that his grandfather was Pierre Couc, a simple French farmer. His mother has other children living in Quebec, but she speaks little about them. *His mother is a mystery.*

French or English, they are both white to Sattelihu, but his mother will only ever be loyal to the English. She has said many times that it had been the French government who killed her brother and his uncle, Louis. Does he have a say in being loyal to the English? His mother is the queen of peace and because the English have given her great respect and have provided for her, it is the English she will be faithful to and so will he. He is proud of his mastery of roping people together for peace, for conquest at times, and for order. But this day as he travels in the blinding snow, he thinks the rope is fraying and isn't as strong as it once was. This long peace in the Pennsylvania colony is beginning to fragment and dissolve into the night of European discord and native confusion.

Sattelihu and his companions have spoken little to one another on their journey back to Otsonwakin. Each day the wind has leapt about them, kicking up snow into their faces like a bully. They're traveling from Onondaga where they met with the Great Council of the Ho-De'-No-Sau-Nee, the Iroquois, as the French and British refer to them. They had been greeted with flutes, violins, and hospitality, but the trip now feels futile and bereft of meaning. Brother Onas, the governor of Pennsylvania, sent them on this arduous journey and instructed that he and Conrad Weiser speak to the Council and ask them to reprimand the Shawnee and Delaware and bring them back into the English fold. Many of the tribes are weary being underfoot of the English, as well as the Ho-De'-No-Sau-Nee and are fleeing over the Allegheny Mountains to settle and trade with the French.

Sattelihu has his own opinions, but in the end, it's his mother's voice that restrains him. No one will really know his thoughts. He's a vessel, a channel for languages and this vessel has to be free from the clogging of his own thoughts. It isn't easy, for a word spoken in French is very different from the word spoken in English and native languages. And now this weather they should have never traveled in is costing them dearly. He tried to convince Weiser they should wait until late spring, but Conrad Weiser, like his mother, always has the final word.

Sattelihu was appointed to the Great Council of the Ho-De'-No-Sau-Nee, the Six Nations, and has become indispensable to both the Council and Pennsylvania. Although he can function in the white man's world and is as close to a white man he'll ever be in his relationship with Conrad Weiser, other than the fur trader, George Croghan, he also distrusts him. Weiser came from Germany as a child and lived among the Mohawks as a young man and learned their language. Sattelihu senses superiority in him and this he despises. Weiser has a big farm in Tulpehocken and has been an interpreter longer than himself, so Sattelihu defers to him.

Sattelihu looks back at Weiser struggling in the snow and his thoughts become more gracious. *The man is a just man. If it wasn't for him, I might have been ignored by the Pennsylvania Council.* Weiser took Sattelihu under his wing and introduced him to the Pennsylvania Counsel and is proud of his command of five languages, as well as his ability to be comfortable being white and Indian. But Weiser's wing isn't broad enough for Sattelihu who quietly clings to his own ways. He knows this perplexes Weiser because Sattelihu is comfortable sitting at a meeting in Philadelphia dressed as a European or dressed as an Indian sitting at council in Onondaga. He is sure-footed with one foot planted in Iroquoia and one foot planted in Philadelphia's Council chambers. He has proven his worth and is recompensed well, traveling hundreds of miles on missions for Pennsylvania and her sister colonies.

Sattelihu goes back to see if he can help Wesier as he struggles in the storm. *This just man is becoming a burden around my neck. And now this failed journey to Onondaga and losing our horses in this snowstorm.*

The wind crescendos and the snow whips and chokes them. They wrap cloth around their faces, covering all but their eyes, but shut their eyes against the icy wind and can't see where they're walking. A foot of snow covers a bed of ice and it had been impossible for the horses to walk without stumbling. The great beasts shook their grand heads and snorted, sometimes falling to their knees with the men sliding down over their heads into the snow. The men listen to icebergs clashing against one another on the Susquehanna. Their provisions have been exhausted and most of the Indian villages and cabins they stopped at had no food to spare. At one cabin, armed men flew out the door and fired their guns. Shots flew all around them, but not in them, and Sattelihu felt the protection of the False Face ceremony he had attended at the Great Council. Yesterday, they gave up their horses and left them at a farm, hoping they can return for them in a few days. Now they're nearly home, and as long as they travel alongside the tempestuous and faithful Susquehanna, they will not lose their way. Sattelihu walks between Weiser and Chief Allumpapes, whom he loves.

Chief Allumpapes's Delaware nation has been subjugated to the Ho-De'-No-Sau-Nee for many years. Although their land was unjustly confiscated by Penn's descendants and given away by their uncles, the Ho-De'-No-Sau-Nee, Delaware dignity is still intact and their presence is felt in Pennsylvania, New Jersey, and beyond. Sattelihu touches Chief Allumpapes on the shoulder, assuring the old chief that he is next to him. Sattelihu wishes he could have spoken the truth to the Great Council about their treatment of their brothers, but it would be futile. He misses his own father and this chief has become a source of solace for him.

"We're nearly there, Sattelihu, my son. I can smell the meat on the cook fire and hear the women singing for us."

"And your granddaughter's voice is the most beautiful of all," Sattelihu replies. Allumpapes is wise enough to understand Sattelihu is unhappy with his granddaughter, but he knows Sattelihu will do what is right. He pities Sattelihu for having to endure this granddaughter who is his own flesh, but burdensome.

Sattelihu puts his arm across Allumpapes's shoulder to assist him as they walk through the deep snow. There will be no meat on the cook fire and none of their women are singing, but Allumpapes is always an optimist and a dreamer. Sattelihu fears this trip has taxed Allumpapes too much and may bring his death much sooner.

When the exhausted and weary travelers arrive at the village of Ostuaga, they fire their guns. Two young Indians come to greet them and help carry their baggage across the icy creek to Otsonwakin.

Chapter Three

"IT'S TIME. I'M going to meet Sattelihu." Grandmother is readying to leave the cabin.

"I'm coming, too, Grandmother!" I leap up from a crouch around the stone pestle with my sisters, Esther and Molly. It's an honor to greet travelers, sing a song, and play instruments for them. I rush to the corner of the cabin where there are flutes and drums and pick up my hickory flute that was given to me by one of the Seneca warriors passing through on his way to fight the Catawbas. The Senecas are the fiercest of warriors and Telehemet, a handsome warrior, asked my mother if he could visit me again. He lives seasonally in a small Seneca hunting village a short distance away and his family dwells far away in the New York colony. I often listen to his dramatic speeches about the hunt with his big doe eyes staring deep into my own. He is older than me by many seasons and has many scalps and honors. Telehemet hides his warrior spirit when we walk together and when he touches my hair. This is not his warrior spirit, but another spirit that is new to me. I also like Telehemet's flute playing that makes me want to be with him and listen to his dull speeches. When I saw him last, he gave me his flute as a gift and said he'll make another one for himself.

"You must stay here and help us with the food," Esther says, interrupting my thoughts about Telehemet. My sister is always worried she is doing more work than I am.

"I'll return to help, but our father and Sattelihu must be greeted properly!"

"You only want to get his gifts before the rest of us!" Esther states angrily.

"Enough, Esther. You can greet them, too, if you like. Catharine will return and work extra hard," my mother says.

I throw a fur over me, step into my snowshoes outside the cabin, and wait for Grandmother. I hope my uncle will have gifts for me and all the children. Ceremoniously, he will touch his heart with his tightened fist that often holds a burlap bag of trinkets. And then smiling, he will place the bag of trinkets in my hands. My father never has gifts for us, only small items for my mother that she won't let us touch. They have their secrets together and no one, even their children, will ever be as loved as they love one another. Each time my uncle returns from a journey, he places the bag in Esther's or my hands. The younger children chase after one of us as we run around the outside of the cabin clutching the coveted bag. Eventually, I sit under the beech tree, or if it's wintertime, I'll rush into the cabin to sit by the fire. Carefully, I will open the bag and pour out the beads and bracelets. As much as I wish to choose my favorite piece, it is understood that I must allow each child to choose first.

My grandmother holds onto me as she steps into her old deerskin moccasins that have faded to a yellowish brown. The cuffs are adorned with blue and green beads she sewed onto them. She lifts one foot at a time, admiring them. Her leggings are plain leather, un-beaded, but her skirt is made of royal blue broadcloth that is harmoniously beaded into an intricate design of a tree with flower-shaped leaves. The beads are light blue and green with white beads between them. This is the work she has created during winter months, but it is in the summertime that she gathers the patterns from each flower and tree in Pennnsylvania to create needlework that adorns the clothing of her family. Esther once asked if she could learn to bead animals into her clothing, but our mother said to leave the animals in the forest and so Esther's skirts are adorned with patterns of daisies and wild roses. A year ago, I sat with my grandmother in the woods and asked her to teach me. I'm enamored with every flower, even the light blue wild-eyed onion in springtime, but it is the ox-eye sunflower I especially want to adorn my clothing with. As we walk to meet Uncle and the travelers, I think about our conversation last summer.

"You must make small flowers, Catrine, for you will use up all our beads and we'll have to wait for Sattelihu to bring more," Grandmother said. "Sunflowers are the biggest and brightest flowers of all. Sew one special one so it doesn't dominate. Sometimes the brightest things in life must stand behind the others. It doesn't diminish the brightness, but harmonizes all."

Does Grandmother think I'm too bold? Sometimes it's confusing trying to understand her as she often lapses into French or other languages. I've learned languages quickly from her and my mother, as well as the Europeans and other natives who visit our home, but mostly I'm learning the more naked an Indian is, the less important he or she is. I've watched Conrad Weiser frown and his cheeks flush when the Indians dance and sing half naked around him.

When Count Zinzendorf, the great Moravian, visited us when our friend, Chief Kakowatchey, was a guest at our home, the chief said, "I believe in a God who created both Indians and Europeans, the former praying with their hearts and the latter with words, a difference God clearly sees. I am satisfied with my condition and have no desire to be European, for God is more pleased with the Indians than with the Europeans, who are for the most part bad people."

I'm pleased the chief said, "for the most part bad people . . . for the most part." I have French blood, but it's the Indian part in me that is the strongest. I was proud of the old chief's wise speech to the Count and how it made the Count's bushy eyebrows rise to the top of his head and his fat eyes bulge. This Count is a big important man who would not baptize us after Grandmother pleaded with him. I didn't want his reptile-like fat hands clenching my head and pushing me under water.

My thoughts fly around just like the snow that swirls ghost-like while Grandmother and I walk to meet the party of travelers. Soon we see Sattelihu, my father, and the rest standing a few feet away. They are snow clad and wear weary countenances. I take out my flute and play a series of notes that travel through flying snowflakes. Uncle approaches me and with his customary greeting, taps his chest with a burlap bag and hands it to me. He clasps his mother to his broad chest that is covered with heavy blankets and holds her for a long moment.

He releases her and places his large cloth-covered hands on her shoulders and looks into her face. "The Grand Council wants to bring the Delaware and Shawnee back from the French who have built a fort in the Allegheny Mountains. The Delaware and the Shawnee are our brothers, but they're weary being underfoot of the Ho-De'-No-Sau-Nee. How, Mother, can I convince them to return to us?"

Chief Allumpapes and Chief Shikellamy stand with Uncle and nod in agreement, but Mr. Weiser, takes a few steps ahead of the rest to speak.

"Madame," he says and bows to my grandmother before speaking to my uncle. "We are indebted to the Council's vision and wisdom, Andrew. The Onondaga chiefs are the most diplomatic of all the Iroquois and they're loyal to the covenant chain with the British. We must convince the Shawnee and Delaware to return."

My teeth chatter and I try to be still and listen. Grandmother won't wait for the warmth of the cook fire to hear the news from Onondaga. She's also waiting to hear if they have brought back food, for our entire village is in want because of this harsh winter. Some of the Indians who live near us have gathered to meet the returning men, hoping for food.

Uncle addresses the Indians coming to greet them and speaks delicately in the Delaware language to these old Indians, the few Delaware, Shawnee, and Chief Allumpapes, who all stand rigid and tired in the snowstorm.

"My father and my friends. You know the Shawnee and Delaware are loved by me, by their uncles, the Ho-De'-No-Sau-Nee, but you have seen that they and the British act like parents who need to discipline their children. Parents and children are not always right and sometimes the children suffer at the hands of their parents. I promise that you will not suffer at my hands and I will try to keep the British from bringing suffering to you. If you see it right that your people, our brothers, stay in French territory so they can hunt and gain back respect, I can let it be so and will not persuade them to return, as the Council has asked."

Grandmother nudges Uncle's arm and speaks to him quietly, but firmly. "You will do as instructed, Sattelihu. You will do the bidding of the English and the chiefs of the Grand Council."

Grandmother's words sting my Uncle, but he won't disrespect her although he's embarrassed by her insistence to override his leadership.

Grandmother continues to speak to her son in earnest. "I have dreamed you will go to the Shawnee in Ohio. We will all go to them, for we need to watch out for them as if they were our children who need to return to the fold. Worry no more about it now. Let's go to the cabin to be warmed with food and fire."

After my uncle gives burlap bags of dried corn and other foodstuffs to the waiting Indians, we trudge back to the cabin in the darkening day. I suddenly spy movement in the woods and immediately recognize Telehemet and his small war party. He comes into focus for only a few moments and my heart leaps. I feel excitement, but like a deer seeing a hunter. Why is he here? If Telehemet has triumphed in war, he would have killed an elk or buck and would be proudly displaying it in the clearing, waiting for us to invite him. And then he disappears as if he was merely an apparition. No one else has noticed him, but me.

I look again into the woods, desiring to go to him. Will Telehemet survive? He won't come to our cabin uninvited or without food for our table. He will still have a journey to the Seneca hunting camp in the Wyoming Valley and this storm is unfriendly to all. Telehemet, a Seneca warrior! I'm warmed just thinking of him. And I'm anxious for him! If only he was a warrior of any of the other Ho-De'-No-Sau-Nee nations, for the British are coming to distrust their Seneca brothers. It's grave knowledge that the Seneca responds to the embrace of the French and their promises and gifts. The Seneca nation has lived closest to them than any of the other Ho-De'-No-Sau-Nee. Grandmother always welcomes Telehemet into our home, but only when my uncle and father are hunting or traveling to Council meetings. Grandmother won't allow them to disapprove and my mother closes her mouth to criticism. No talk has been spoken about my marriage to Telehemet. Grandmother and my mother will select a husband for me one day and I will accept it, whether it is Telehemet or another. He is treated as a friend and visitor in our home that welcomes all.

"Who is there?" Uncle stops walking and shouts into the woods.

Two loud sharp cracks that sound like ice breaking on the river fill the air and Grandmother is suddenly lying on top of me nearly suffocating me with her furs. All I can hear is her heavy breathing and the muffled sound of the pounding of her heart meeting my own. We were both surprised by the gun shots.

TELEHEMET HAD FIRED twice and the second shot claimed the life of an old buck with tough sinew, but even the leather-like taste of this animal greeted our hunger with satisfaction and gratitude. He and his party of three stay the night and it's not merely a hunting party but a wooing party. No one in our cabin understands this except Grandmother and me. As we sit around our fire late into the evening, Telehemet speaks of his good traits and deeds. He speaks forthright and his mooning, soft looks he usually has for me disappear. He speaks not of love. I'm not disappointed because Grandmother believes Indians live love more than they speak it and this is more important.

My father's countenance is stiff and unfriendly, but he's tired from the journey. My uncle doesn't utter a word, but his face reveals he's disquieted with my Seneca warrior and with his journey. Telehemet is talkative when he speaks to the men, but why is he not when we are alone? His eyes, the closeness of his body, and his flute music have spoken to me of his interest. No words. My own father speaks little to my mother and yet there's much affection. I look into Telehemet's eyes now and long to scatter my thoughts on his heart and have him water them with his wisdom, for he's many years older. His wife died before children came and this will lessen the awkwardness of our union as he'll be experienced and I am not. How will my life change? We've not followed many of the customs of the Ho-De'-No-Sau-Nee, for the Montours live differently. It's most common for the mothers to bring together couples in marriage and we have brought ourselves together. Grandmother's ways of long ago in New France have covered us with new ways, like the colorful blankets she received from the British.

Grandmother nods approvingly with a smile, passing her pipe to Telehemet. She is remembering her many loves, I'm certain. She has had many husbands and not just my grandfather in marriage. She is different than the other Indian women, for she speaks eloquently to me of love. "I've had lovers," she whispered to me conspiratorially one evening. Another time she spoke to me of a friend she had in New France. "My first dearest friend was Judith Rigaud who was fiercely independent, although she came from France to the new world as a servant. She told me it's good to love a man, but we must do so without submission and illusion." I wish I could be like Grandmother, so free about love, but I don't have room in my heart for many lovers. I wonder if even one warrior will fill my life with too many children and little time for my childish ways, as my mother calls them. My grandmother openly speaks of love and whispers intimacies to me of her many lovers. Indians living among us don't usually talk of love this way. Love is done quietly, with dignity, and is not sloppy, passionate affection.

My mother, not wishing to disrespect her mother, but desiring to keep her children from expressing feelings of this nature, said to me one day, "Catrine, your grandmother is to be held in esteem, but her ways of love are unique. Do you know how you walk in the snow in springtime when the sun is melting the icy earth? This mushy snow becomes trapped in your shoes and clothes. That's how your grandmother has been with her husbands. I want you to show restraint in the expression of your passion. This is our way and also the ways of our Christian friends who stay many days with us."

Telehemet plays his flute and I watch his lips form to breathe his spirit into song. I hear the melancholy cooing of the male mourning dove lovesick for its mate. All the other children, but Esther, drift into sleep as he blows notes of love at me and the wind sings snow loudly against our warm cabin. Esther grimaces and squints at me, her knees folded up to her chest and her arms around them. I ignore her moodiness.

When he stops playing, Grandmother says, "In the summer, Telehemet, Catharine, her mother, and I will meet your family in the New York colony. I lived many seasons there with my husband, Carondowanna. We lived in an Oneida village on the Mohawk River when I was interpretress for Governor Hunter."

Telehemet smiles at me and Grandmother. "My brother is head chief of Caneadea, a Seneca village on the Genesee River. My mother and father are with the ancestors, but I have many aunts who will be devoted to Catharine."

I've never been to this land and Grandmother tells me it's like Pennsylvania, but even more beautiful and majestic. Although I don't want to leave my home, I'm eager to go to this Caneadea to meet Telehemet's family.

Later, when everyone is asleep and the guests snore in our beds and the children sleep uncomfortably on and under the table by the fire, Telehemet and I walk out in the silence of winter. The snow and wind have withdrawn from their dramatic performance and all is still. I spy a jack rabbit springing forth across new snow. The earth sleeps peacefully beneath this blanket of sparkling white, as if tiny stars have fallen and are beaded into this icy cloth by the Sky Mother. The clouds have parted and Grandmother Moon smiles at us as if in agreement to our marriage.

Telehemet embraces me and I feel his strength and a slight tremble. I'm aroused with love and apprehension. How will it be to become as the earth and receive love as the earth receives blankets of sparkling snow?

Chapter Four

WINTER TARRIES AND reminds me of the guests who stay in our home too long. They arrived in late February when icicles hung like spears from our roof and spring was invisible. The somber, dark-clothed Moravian missionaries walked into the warmth of our cabin like a flock of hungry, bold crows. We were mesmerized, at first, by these mysterious people coming to tell our village about Jesus who came to earth to give us rest for our souls. I already knew about this Jesus because Grandmother had taught us about him and my mother loves him. In the beginning, there was novelty and excitement as they read from their large black book that matched their clothing. A book! I could speak English and other languages, but I didn't know how to read and was captivated by the orderly black marks on the pages of the Bible.

Shortly after they arrived, I was making the bed for Anna, one of the missionaries, and beneath the mattress I found a small book. Inside, there was a drawing of a white woman dressed in flounces of cloth and petticoats. Standing beside the woman was a white man wearing a wig and dressed in a scarlet lapel, waistcoat, and breeches like my uncle wears at important meetings. I was curious and wanted to hear the story about this man and woman. I put the book away and waited for the right time to ask Anna. Anna is young but older than me, with curly blonde hair she pulls into a tight knot in the back of her head. She places a simple head-covering over her hair that is lacy white. Anna calls it a haube, or a sister's cap, that the women in Germany wear. The women look alike except for the color of their hair and eyes. They don't wear the elaborate dress of other European ladies. There is little embroidery on their dresses, no beads, or fancy stitching. Anna's cap has a pink ribbon tied beneath her chin. Pink is for unmarried women, dark blue for married, and white is for widows. No colorful and bold colors on any of these people! I tried to give Anna a red ribbon to replace the pale pink one, but she smiled sweetly and shook her pretty head no. I asked Anna if I should wear somber clothing and she said we all must honor God with our modesty. I don't want to wear black and pink or even black and blue, so I asked Grandmother.

"Why should a carpet of bluets be covered, Catharine? They are vibrant and delicate, put forth from the Sky Mother. You are as beautiful as these flowers. Don't listen to the ladies hiding their beauty. They fear much of God's creation, especially themselves."

Anna's spirit is as sober as her clothing, especially when I find her near the forest walking alone. She stands out from the other missionary women because she's not married. I have seen her wiping tears from her eyes. One day all the women were busy cooking and the men were hunting. I asked Anna if she would like to help me prepare the maple trees for tapping. Our village will soon be preparing for the Maple Festival to give thanks to the maple and Ha-Wen-Neyu for the return of the maple and its sweet waters. Ha-Wen-Neyu is our god of goodness and light.

We trudge through mushy, gray snow together and I think of the struggle going on beneath our feet in the earth.

"Winter is proud, Miss Anna, and each season he resists rolling off the earth so the earth can blossom again. Winter reigns over her for many months each year and never wants to leave her. Grandmother says it's like a man who spends too much time lying on top of his woman."

I giggle and think of Telehemet. I hear Anna's sharp intake of breath.

"Why is it, Catharine, you speak of winter in human terms and that of being a man?"

"Everything has a spirit. And winter is as strong as our warriors."

Anna sighs and looks at me strangely, so I change the subject.

"Grandmother creates stories on blankets and our clothing. Not like the dark lines in the Bible, but they're like words that give messages. Do you create with words, too, like the writing in books? I've seen you with a quill pen and I'm curious. I'd like to learn about your book . . . not the big one, but the smaller one you hide beneath my bed."

Anna blushes and looks surprised. "I'm a handmaiden of the Lord and in my devotion to Him, I create songs of praise. I write them down as poetry and later, I sing them to music I hear in my head."

"Will you sing one of them now?"

"Do you have your flute?"

I pull out my flute from my bag and she smiles and takes my hand to lead me to a clearing in the woods where we find a large rock to sit on.

"I'll sing my simple hymn to you and after, you can try to find the music to accompany me. Do you think you can do this?"

Anna's face colors with excitement and it's the first time I've seen her lively and happy. So it's music she loves, as much as I love the forest, wind, snow, and flowers.

Anna and I sit in the woods creating stories with sound and we forget the time. We never visit the maple trees. When the sun says goodbye to the day in a flourish of pinks and reds, we return to the cabin. I'm relieved no one asks us about the maple trees. Both of us quickly assist the women in the cabin with making our evening meal.

There are many times Miss Anna and I go to the woods together and I ask her to teach me to read the book beneath her bed. She hesitates, but agrees if I promise not to tell anyone. It's a wonderful romance about a poor peasant girl who marries a duke. We speak to no one about our music making and reading. It's our time alone and I come to care for Miss Anna like a sister.

FINALLY, IT'S THE season of new life and I'm in love with the courting songs of birds, including the sweet chortle of the bluebird. The sun's rays fall on new young grass and entices the crocus and snow drop to come out to dance in the soft breezes. The ghost-white cloak of father winter has departed and brother maple is waking up. The Keepers of the Faith in our village announce the maple sap is flowing and our village spends many days carefully collecting it. We boil it in clay vessels and it's used as a sweetener and stabilizer of our moods and health.

There's always much work to be done, but each day I go to the forest in the mornings and today it's most important before the maple festivities begin. I'm up early and deliberately wear no moccasins so I can wash my feet in the dew and purify my thoughts. The trees and I are beginning to feel crowded out by new settlers and their ways. These settlers tramp through the woods, their eyes seeing through the trees, imagining them cut and cleared for their homes. They don't come to the forest to commune with the spirits of the trees and flowers and to give thanks to the Great Spirit. They resemble hungry hawks diving for their prey. They're desperate and greedy the way they come rolling into our village with wagons loaded with their belongings, hoping for more, and disregarding those who already live here. The Moravians come to teach us about God and help us plant our corn, but the settlers come to take from the Great Spirit, and their countenances reveal superiority to the Indians. They don't know what to think of us, whom they refer to as "those Montours!"

Yesterday, I sat near a few women who had come to the river for water. I was listening to the conversation of bluebirds in the tree above me. And then I heard a woman say to another in a loud whisper, "The family of Montours are a promiscuous bunch and difficult to understand."

I left wondering what this meant and asked Anna when I returned home.

"How is it we are immoral people who indiscriminately join our bodies with others? Do you think we are promiscuous, Anna?"

Anna's face reddens and says it's not of her mind to judge anyone. It is God who sees all and judges righteously. I make my own judgment. The Montours don't aimlessly engage in uniting their bodies with others. We purposely and decisively live our lives. We're not like the dogs that mate outside our doors and what we do is of our choice and in private. Once, after an old Delaware chief's wife died, Grandmother went to his bark house and didn't return for a few days.

She said she was consoling her friend and missed his wife, too, who was also her friend. Grandmother might have joined herself to him, but she didn't do it without consideration.

In the forest this morning, I put away my thoughts and stand between two tall pine trees, placing my hands firmly on each one. The air is refreshingly brisk and my feet tingle from the wetness of the earth. I close my eyes and ask the Great Spirit for peace and for the greedy trouble makers to leave us be. And then I rush further into the forest to dip my fingers into a sap-tub of the maple waters that has been left. I lick them and thank Brother Maple and the Great Spirit for such deliciousness. When I turn to go back to the cabin, there before me is a pale-faced young man clutching a rifle. I know his name is Tom and he's the unhappy son of a family that came bumbling into our village seeking a new life. They're a quiet family, but this Tom is morose.

"I ain't going to hurt you. I was up feeding the chickens and saw you run out half naked into the forest."

"It's the Maple Festival today and I've come to see how the sweet waters are doing," I answer, a chill going through me.

Tom comes close and grabs my skirt and pulls it up. "I want to taste your sweet waters, Catharine."

I push him away with a force that comes from my tree brothers. Tom tumbles backward and his gun goes off when he falls to the ground. I rush back to our cabin and my father and uncle hurry toward me. I tell them that Tom Miller was acting indiscriminately toward me and they stare at me with puzzlement. They go off into the woods to look for the unhappy boy.

My uncle explains that European men sometimes treat their women disrespectfully and this means the Indian woman will be treated worse by them.

"Tom Miller won't be bothering you again. We dragged him to his home and woke his family to tell them of his disgrace."

I wonder. By the look of that boy's eyes, he doesn't care about disgrace.

"There are many white people living among us now and you must carry a gun when you go into the forest."

I agree, but feel the threads of my freedom beginning to unravel. Sattelihu shakes his head at me.

"If Telehemet is going to be your husband, you should be less child-like."

Until today, I hadn't been conscious of my looks and how much my body had changed. Later, I seek out Anna and ask if I might see myself through her looking glass. I look into a distorted image of myself and although I'm pale compared to my sisters, I can see how wide my eyes are. They're shaped like small dug-out canoes and I can't tell their real color. They're not brown like my sisters and mother, but neither are they blue or green. They seem to be a mixture of these colors. My lashes are pale and my nose is small like Anna's and my lips are large.

This face is my own and I'll kiss well with my full lips. Looking into this mirror makes me feel a little dizzy.

"Can I put your hair in a crown atop your head, Catharine? And then I'll weave flowers throughout it. It will be special for the maple festivities."

"Will you do the same with your hair, Anna? It's the color of corn and will look beautiful."

Anna shakes her head no and continues to smile as she brushes and arranges my hair. My hair is the color of my sisters and brother's hair, a deep, rich brown, nearly black. It's thick, but unlike their hair, there are waves in it. Telehemet told me when the sun shines on my hair, he sees flecks of golden light.

This season, the sap has run powerfully through the maple and through us all and some of the waters are sweet and some are bitter. Mine is sweet, but only for Telehemet and soon Grandmother and my mother will take me to meet his family in New York and we'll be joined together, but not indiscriminately.

Chapter Five

IT'S TIME TO give thanks to the Maple. We gather at the Council House nearby the home of the Oneida chief, Shikellamy, a home that Conrad Weiser built for him. The time before the festivities of feasting and dancing is a somber time of confession and repentance for our people. Our wrongdoings must be acknowledged while we each hold the wampum and pledge our sincerity to live with goodness. The wampum records our deeds and marks our sincerity. This festival is a Ho-De'-No-Sau-Nee tradition, but many nations have similar rituals. These are times to bring people together in celebration and renewal. This year, Anna and the Moravians are with us and although they're curious and respectful, they don't always participate. Count Ludwig Zinzendorf put up a large tent to hold services and requested we have our Maple Festival inside it. None of the chiefs agree and I'm glad.

Count Zinzendorf also declared we should touch the Bible when we hold the wampum and acknowledge our evil deeds, asking God to forgive us.

Chief Shikellamy was quiet for a moment and then lifted his beautiful Manitou necklace he wears around his neck and said in a proud voice, "As an infant, I was baptized by a Jesuit, but I believe in the Great Manitou, the Great Spirit, and we would like to believe that your God is one and the same as our Great Spirit. Whoever would like to touch your Bible while confessing may do so, but the Keepers of the Faith will not insist on our people adding this to our honored ritual."

Very few of our people touch the Bible this day and when they do, they don't linger over it. It's the wampum they caress as they speak solemnly of their wrongful ways and promise to live better. I enter the circle and don't touch the Bible, but hold the wampum up before me and acknowledge impatience with my two mothers and speaking harshly to them. I look around for Tom Miller, for I'd like to drag him into the circle to confess his evil. Anna and my mother call our wrongdoings sins, but they're one and the same. Do we believe in the same Spirit? The Christians listen to their God speak to them from a book and we listen to the forest, the animals, and all of nature.

MY FATHER, KATARIONECHA, also known as Peter Quebec, was born of the Mohawk nation and is a Keeper of the Faith. He was appointed by his nation many years ago and because he is faithful and trustworthy, he continues to hold this office. Wise Crow is his Keeper of the Faith name and he is going to deliver the speech for the Maple Festival. The Keepers of the Faith watch out for their people, admonishing them and even censoring them at times. Women and men are appointed for this special position and are equal in arranging all festivities, as well as the mourning ceremonies. My father will drink no rum and become a fool as many Indians do when they drink rum. My uncle has nearly fallen into the fire after he has come home from a treaty conference and drinks to forget his precarious position among the white people.

I stand on this celebrated Maple Day and listen to the dignified, booming voice of my father!

> Friends and Relatives:
> The sun, our ruler of the day, is high on his path and we must hasten to do our duty. We are assembled to observe an ancient custom of our people. It has been given to our forefathers by the Great Spirit. And he has ever required of his people to return thanks to him for all blessings received. This season when the maple tree yields its sweet waters has again returned. We are all thankful that it is so. We want everyone to join in our general thanksgiving to the maple. We also want you to join in our thanksgiving to the Great Spirit, who has wisely made this tree for the good of all people. We are thankful you are all gathered here and we expect order and harmony to prevail. We thank the Great Spirit that he has been kind to so many of us, in sparing our lives to participate again in the festivities of this season.
> Na-ho!

The women of the village have made a feast they started early in the morning. I helped with the preparations of the food that we'll eat after my father's speech and the other speeches made by the Keepers of the Faith. We have a cache of cured venison, elk, and bear that have been buried in a pit covered in bark bottoms and lined with deer-skins.

We made two varieties of corn bread, soup, succotash, charred corn, beans, and squash dishes. There are many kinds of tea and my favorite drink is made from the tips of the hemlock boughs that are boiled in water and seasoned with the maple water. We all delight in the maple tea and I think of swallowing the Great Spirit's sweetness each sip I take.

By the time we partake of the bounty of our feast and give thanks, I'm sleepy, but eager for more festivities and this includes the games. Anna has come to sit with me and we watch young men in our village play the Ball Game, a favorite amusement. It's played with a small deer-skin ball and a ball bat. There are usually six to eight players on a side and each set represents its own party. The game is divided into several contests, in which each set of players strives to carry the ball through their own gate. In preparation for this game, the players have undergone a course of diet and training, just as they do for the foot-race. They have stripped themselves entirely except for the waist-cloth. I helped sew the waist-cloth for Chief Shikellamy's son, John. I took a strip of deer-skin about a quarter side and two yards long and ornamented it at the ends with bead and quill work. John looks quite handsome in his waist-cloth, and so do the other young men. Their brown skin glistens in the sunlight from their exertion and they're all in excellent shape. Suddenly, I see Tom Miller standing by a large oak tree watching our games. A few white people have come to the Maple Festival, but only the Indian men play the games. I feel sorry for him, in spite of his horrid behavior this morning. He's always alone and I've never seen him with the other boys in the village.

"That boy needs salvation, "Anna says. She, too, has seen Tom Miller lurking.

Of all the missionaries, Anna is most gentle and doesn't preach to us at every opportunity. But, of course, in her eyes, who else might help such a lost boy as Tom Miller, but Jesus. I think maybe she's right and someone should take him to Zinzendorf's big tent so he can be properly saved from his evil ways.

After the games, the Feather Dance is performed, a favorite of the Maple Festival. I'll participate just as I am, for the women don't have to wear a costume to join in the dance.

I have always danced alone to the wind and bird song, but at the festivities, the ceremony of thanksgiving in our dance joins our hearts and feet together. We become one with the music and with one another. The Great Spirit knows we cannot live without dance. We believe the Great Spirit has given us this dance and so we give back to the Great Spirit in our dance. It's a time we become the most pure, spirited, and graceful in our lives.

The Great Feather Dance, O-sto-weh'-go-wa, is our consecrated worship and is also for the faithful in the future life. All of our dances are of this nature, but this one is particularly holy. Mothers of the village select men to perform who possess distinguished powers of endurance and spirit. The men wear full costumes and the largest article of their apparel is the kilt (Ga-ka'-ah). We were surprised to learn that some white people wear kilts. There is a group of settlers who live north of us who came from Scotland. They laughed when they saw our men wearing kilts, for they had brought their kilts over the sea and once they wore them for us to admire.

There are singers with turtle-shell rattles seated in the center of our Council House and they close their eyes and sing supplication to the Great Spirit, marking time with the rattles. I stand with some other women against the wall of our lodge to wait until it's time for us to dance. Someone is playing a drum and I wish Telehemet was here playing his flute. I close my eyes to feel the Great Spirit in the rhythm of the rattles and sung words. I prepare myself to receive the Spirit into my mind and into my feet so I can dance freely. I do this for a few minutes, but I don't want to miss delighting my eyes with the array of copper skinned dancers who exhibit dignity and give themselves to the Great Spirit in dance. These are warriors who kill in the hunt and war, but here in the dance, they become graceful and gentle. There is no distortion in their countenances as there is no violent passion coursing through them now. Here they can let down their inhibitions and forget they are as sly as a fox or as fierce as a bear.

They're arrayed in costume, nude to the waist, except for the many ornaments on their arms and necks. They file into the lodge and dance slowly around the council-house. The rattles quicken the time and as they advance around the room, there is gesture with their arms as they place their bodies in a variety of beautiful positions, but still remain erect. I watch as each foot is raised a few inches from the floor and their heels brought down with great force to the beat of the rattles. Every muscle in their bodies is strung to the highest degree of tension and I hold my breath watching, for it stirs the deepest parts in me.

The dance continues and endurance is tested amongst the men, for this also is their purpose. When there is ample applause given for an earnest and spirited dancer, he is called out to stand at the head of the column and lead the party. This is an honor and all eyes are upon him. When this happens, John Logan is chosen and his face is lit with pride. Our eyes meet and our spirits are one in joy. The dancers move around the room and there are two other men called to lead the dance before it's time for the women to join at the foot of the column of dancers. I'm delighted for my body to finally be able to respond to the music, for I'm brimming with my soul's fire. Our women steps are entirely different from the steps of the men, as we move sideways and simply raise ourselves alternately upon each foot from heel to toe. Then we bring down our heels upon the floor with each beat of the rattle. We keep pace with the advancing column and are quiet in our steps. As I move around the room, I try not to be too enthusiastic, for then I will disrupt the flow we have together as dancers. I focus only on my feet and the music, lightly feeling the swish of my sisters' skirts before me and behind me. After a few minutes, I look up to see Anna standing inside the doorway, her head aglow from the sun shining behind her. And then suddenly there is darkness in the doorway and the light is gone. Anna disappears.

Sattelihu, Conrad Weiser, and George Croghan step through the doorway and block out the light. Anna moves from the door and sits on the floor with the other women. We keep dancing, but my feet feel heavy instead of light as feathers. George Croghan disturbs me when he's in my presence. Once we met alone in the woods, but my brothers, the trees, protected me from his strong medicine. There is something I like and don't like about him. And now he's here and I must finish the dance and believe the Great Spirit is greater than George Croghan's medicine.

We file out the door to the sound of just one rattle and I look into his fierce blue eyes as I pass him, challenging him. He smiles and walks beside me as I dance. He places forget-me-nots in my hair and they feel heavy, although they're delicate. I continue following our column out of the Council House and George Croghan falls away from me and the dancers. The setting sun is golden peach and splashes across our column, as if in gratitude for our dance. I feel weak in my legs and hurry to sit beneath a large willow. Maybe I didn't eat enough at the feast or this man's medicine has worked on me. I tug at the flowers in my hair and as they fall out my hair tumbles out of its crown. I'm not a queen like Grandmother.

The Maple festivities continue and there will be more feasting and dancing late into the night. We prepare to leave with my sisters, mother, Sally, and Grandmother to return to our home. The men stay to drink more rum and some will become foolish devils on into the night. The missionaries left early to go to Bethlehem and Anna went to see them off. I'm happy she's staying on with us for another month. There will be less food to prepare, but now that my uncle has returned from another journey to the Onondaga Council with Conrad Weiser and George Croghan, there will be work. The men will sleep at Shikellamy's cabin, but they'll be at our home early in the morning. They probably won't sleep much, having to keep an eye on the Indians who become deranged from rum. Conrad Weiser doesn't drink much rum and George Croghan seems to be able to drink barrels of it without it altering him, although I've heard he sometimes becomes belligerent. Sattelihu won't drink too much in the presence of the two white men. Sally is pleased for this, but she'll harangue him nonetheless for having been gone so long from her.

I gather bowls and leftover food and put them into a large basket to carry on my back. The evening breeze wraps around my head and cools my heated thoughts. I walk with the other women slowly, contented with the day's festivities. Sattelihu comes to say goodnight to Sally and alongside him is George Croghan who sees the burden I'm carrying. He asks if he can take it from me. While removing it, his hands touch my shoulders that creates a curious sensation.

"Your dance was a delight for the likes of a poor traveler's eyes such as mine, Catharine."

"It was danced not for travelers such as you, but to give thanks to the Great Spirit," I reply, removing myself from his side and turning to find Grandmother to walk next to her.

She leans in as we walk and whispers in French, "He's a good friend to the Indians, Catharine, and he's well respected by them and Sattelihu. He assists us in many ways and this evening, he's being helpful to you. You should not be rude to him."

I sigh and look not at George Croghan, but at the crescent moon cupping a few stars in the sky. Grandmother thinks too highly of George Croghan and Conrad Weiser, but I understand why. These men have made it possible for her son to become well respected and successful through his negotiations as an interpreter for Pennsylvania, New York, and Virginia. George Croghan is also becoming a wealthy man, opening trading posts, and building houses for himself everywhere. But why does Grandmother not care how he looks at me when he comes to visit Sattelihu? As if she knows my thoughts, Grandmother walks more slowly so we fall behind the others.

She whispers again in French, "George Croghan is a man who charms men and women, Catrine. He's a good talker and very humorous, and he doesn't like the French. You're not the only young woman he has noticed. As long as he's not improper toward you, you can delight in his attention. You are no longer a child, but a woman now. You'll soon be married, but all women enjoy the admiration and respect of other men, even if they're married. Don't be so cold, my sunflower granddaughter."

Later, I don't sleep well lying next to my sisters, Esther and Molly, and think of Grandmother's words about George Croghan. I can still feel his hands upon my shoulders. It's the first time in a long time I don't think of Telehemet as I fall to sleep.

The next morning I'm busy sewing, cleaning, and talking with the other women. I have not had any time to think of Telehemet or George Croghan. But then when it's time to prepare our meal, thoughts of both men occupy me so much that I drop the kettle of succotash into the fire. As I try to salvage it, my mother scolds and says I've ruined our food. I leave and go into the woods, forgetting my moccasins and my flute. I want to be free again! I don't want to be a woman, for I can see it's a big burden. As I run into the woods, I hope for the sun's declining rays to fall upon me and give me wisdom.

The gloaming is upon the land and the trees have already received the blackness of night as the sun's red glow says farewell behind them. The sky has not yet given itself up to the night and is threaded with light turquoise and blue. The trees shimmer as if in a dance. As I watch, the sky changes and becomes a deep violet and star jewels begin to shine. I forget my mother's anger, George Croghan, and Telehemet. Here is the true queen in the sky and I give thanks.

But as the night descends, I feel the spirits lurking in the dark. The blackness of night can hold the wisdom of the day and it can also hold the evil of the day. When I turn to go back to our cabin, a large hand is placed over my mouth. I bite down on a finger and the hand falls away. I scream to the queen in the sky as she disappears into the night. I smell the sour odor of rum breath and fear Tom Miller has come again to try his lust on me. As I'm being dragged into the woods, there's a loud crack and my captor and I fall to the ground. This evil falls over my body as I lay on my back and look into the face of Tom Miller. And then my mind becomes as dark as the night.

Chapter Six

THERE IS NOTHING as startling as new red blood, whether it's animal or human blood, but especially when it flows from someone onto you. Inside our cabin, I wake and see my skirts are covered with blood. I think my moon time has arrived and there will be the usual rituals. I can't remember anything at first and tell everyone I'd been watching the sunset on the hill by the forest. After my mother removes my clothing and sees I'm not injured, she gives me maple tea and prays to Jesus and the Great Spirit to bring forth the truth. Slowly, as I drink the warming tea, everything that happened in the forest becomes clear.

Tom Miller had followed me to have his way with me, but someone else had also followed and shot him before his foul body could enter mine. I don't know who it was who saved me from Tom Miller, for I fell into unconsciousness. I was left outside our cabin door for my family to find me after my warrior knocked loudly before retreating. I woke when Grandmother cried out to the Great Spirit and my mother invoked prayers to Jesus. They saw my bloodied skirts and legs and assumed I had been grievously injured. My father and uncle immediately left to learn of the whereabouts of this boy and whether he had been killed. None of us wished him dead, for the Pennsylvania Council would deem it more egregious to kill a white man than to violate an Indian woman. No one said this, but in our quiet nervousness, we knew it would be so. Anna prepared our bed and after I drank my tea, she lay down next to me and this brought me much comfort. My mother was unable to console me, for she was wringing her hands with worry over my father being gone so long. I gradually fell into a deep sleep and dreamed I was in a new land and there were many meadows and lakes, but no forests.

The next morning, my father and uncle meet with the men in the village. In our cabin, the women talk about the upcoming planting season. The cabin is filled with nervous energy and no one says a word to me about what happened the night before. I need to know if Tom Miller is dead and who killed him! I turn to Anna to ask, but she puts her finger to her lips and shakes her head. I go to Grandmother who is kneeling beside the cook fire preparing breakfast, but she ignores me when I tap her shoulder. Finally, I can stand it no longer and shout, "What happened to Tom Miller?" My mother comes to me from across the room and places her hands on my shoulders.

"He's recuperating in his home after a medicine man removed gun shot from his leg, Catrine. He will heal and live to carry on his evil ways unless he's stopped.

His family has great shame and we'll do what we can to cover this terrible deed. We must pray to Jesus for his salvation."

"Who shot him?" I ask.

"No one has come forward to confess and so we leave it to rest. His family has agreed to say nothing, for they know their son wanted to do evil to you. They're grateful their son is alive, in spite of his dark soul."

So Tom Miller will live to stalk me like prey, I think, surprised that I hoped he had died. I'm overcome with dread, for the forest will no longer be safe for me and hatred is stirring my thoughts.

A FEW WEEKS later, my uncle announces we're moving to Shamokin, although it's uncertain when it will be. I feel it's because of what happened with Tom Miller and I don't want our lives controlled by this evil. Sattelihu assures me it's because of his business as an interpreter. He soon leaves with Conrad Weiser and George Croghan to go to Ohio country and my father leaves for a long hunt. Grandmother is proud of her son and will move without much questioning and my mother and father will not object and will go with Grandmother and Sattelihu. Although the incident with Tom Miller frightened me, I'm saddened with this news of moving. I've made friends with the forest, streams, and lakes. And it is here I have grown into a woman and met Telehemet. I wonder if Telehemet will move with me, for it's our Indian way for a husband to move in with his wife's family. But we're the Montours and sometimes we don't follow the traditions. Will Telehemet still marry me? Will my marriage be delayed? And why do I think so much about George Croghan?

George Croghan was born in Ireland and came here a few years ago. He's become a successful fur trader with many trading posts in Indian villages in Pennsylvania and a store on the Cuyahoga River in Ohio country. He's a threat to the French traders and this, of course, is exactly what the British desire, for they want to be the only ones trading with the Indians. Always there's fighting between the British and the French and now we have their King's war across the sea that comes to harass us here in our country. I saw puppets once at a fair and enjoyed the make-believe of the wooden people and their stories. They were controlled by the strings attached to them and at times this is how it is with our people. The Indians, especially the Ho-De'-No-Sau-Nee, have strings attached to them and they're puppets, either to the British or to the French. But these days, mostly it's the British puppet masters who control them.

King George's War is making King George Croghan and fur traders rich men, for the King's men have kept the French trade goods from reaching Ohio country and if they do get in, these French goods are too expensive for the Indians to buy. The English goods have become more prized and plentiful and George Croghan has become a cunning puppet master with the Indians.

IT FEELS AS if our Maple Festival was only yesterday and now it's time for the Planting Festival. Anna left for now, but we have no lack of missionaries, for Sattelihu returned with Martin and Jeannette Mack, Moravians from Bethlehem, Pennsylvania. They wish to live like Indians and bring the gospel to the Indian souls among us who are deprived of Christ. I cannot help but like Jeannette, for she's sincerely kind and speaks fluent Algonquin and other languages. She, like Anna, is friendly and intelligent. These strong women who are dominated by their husbands and the men in their community are interesting. Listening to them speak and listening to their men speak is as different as the sound of thunder and a soft rain. Most of their men grunt, nod, and make loud statements that no one would want to refute. Some of our men do the same, but they're much more eloquent and tell stories with their words. I notice the white men grow weary with Indian stories. Like the Indian men, the white women tell stories with many words, as if they're strolling through a garden describing all that is in it. They're very descriptive and I hang on to their words, but notice their men look far off when they speak. The Macks are going to build a cabin and a school for the children of the village. But for now, they will stay with us.

WE INVOKE THE Great Spirit at our Festival to bless the seeds we plant. It's a special time to give thanks for the return of this season and to ask for the earth to become abundant. We assemble to observe the day and like other festivals, there are speeches and the Feather Dance and other dances are performed. The ceremony of mutual confession is conducted before the day's activities begin and there is tension among us because of the Tom Miller incident. If one of the Indians injured Tom Miller and hasn't confessed while holding the wampum, there is fear our crops will fail and not be blessed. Rain might be withheld from our crops. The ceremony of confession ends and no one confesses shooting Tom Miller. I sit nearby and feel guilty for this has happened because I enticed this boy to follow me into the forest. And then I close my eyes and invite a flock of crows to come and shoo away these thoughts, for I have done nothing wrong and it is Tom Miller who has brought a bad spirit into our planting festival.

We return thanksgiving to the trees, plants, and all of nature and ask the Great Spirit and the invisible spirits to help us because of wrongdoing in our midst and to be assured of the prosperity of our crops. It is the Keepers of the Faith who appoint someone to sprinkle a few tobacco leaves upon the fire while addressing our Manitou, the Great Spirit. After this is done with much solemnity, we all ease into the rest of the day's celebratory events.

Then it is time for planting. The men clear the land and go off in a hunting party and the women prepare the ritual for planting. I have always liked tamping down the seeds during the spring planting, for it is a dance of its own if one makes it so. I find that my feet are heavy during this planting season and fear I'm pushing the seeds too deep into the earth. Am I angry? I'm not prone to anger, but it seems to have made a home somewhere in me. The sun is blistering hot and I keep turning to see if there is evil lurking behind me. My bleeding time has ceased to flow, as if my body is confused by the blood that had been spilled onto my legs. Anna promised me she would return and help me prepare for my wedding to Telehemet. Telehemet! I haven't even thought much of him since the ordeal with Tom Miller.

Grandmother is next to me in the field telling stories about her life in New France, but they echo from a faraway place. I only hear birdsong, wind song, and the laughter of children. When it's time to plant sunflowers, I lift my seed-filled hands to the sky before planting. The sunflower will give me back my cheerfulness in late summer. Can I wait? It isn't long before the spirits in nature soothe me during our planting days and my feet feel lighter as I work in the fields with my mothers and the other women in the village.

OUR PLANTING WAS blessed and we gather much corn and squash in autumn and then move to Shamokin, not far from Otsonwakin. Shamokin in the Iroquois language means *place of eels* and these slithering dark fish are in the waters where I bathe. I'm now able to love other parts of the Great Spirit. It's a new beginning and my heart is less heavy with woman worries. The Macks decide Shamokin is the best place for their ministry and are living with us until their cabin is built. Although our home is larger, it feels small with them here.

Winter doesn't bother us with much snow and then spring arrives with eager hope. We are busy with another planting season and there is tension in our village because of Indian raids on white settlers not far from us. I hope Indians in our village haven't participated because our planting won't be blessed. The days pass and windstorms visit us with ferocity. The Great Spirit must be angry and our seeds will be carried away from the soil and into the streams and river. Grandmother says we must wait for the storms to be over and then accept what has been wrought.

"We'll be given what we need, Catrine, and if we have lack, it's for a reason. I've lived through both lean and fat times."

We huddle together in the cabin and the Macks pray morning, noon, and night and assist us in our duties in caring for a big household. I'm trapped in this crowded home and miss the forest, but Sattelihu has mandated I not go alone into the forest again. Tethered to our home, I tuck my longing feet beneath me and sit with Grandmother to sew colored beads onto the fringes of our skirts. These are beads that my uncle brought to Grandmother and me after returning from Philadelphia on his last trip. He went to Ohio and then to Philadelphia with Conrad Weiser and George Croghan. When he returned, he didn't touch his chest with the bag of gifts before giving it to me, but handed the bag to Grandmother without any ritual. Later, when we walked outside together, he gave me another bag and said George Croghan had bought the beads just for me. I told him I didn't understand and he smiled and said his friend, George, is a generous man and often gives gifts. I tried to give them to Grandmother, but she shook her head and said I should make something very special. Finally, I accepted this gift and tried to be like Grandmother and be grateful for this man's attention. Sitting here now with Grandmother while the wind roars and the rain assails our roof, I sew the gift of beads onto my skirt.

Chapter Seven

THERE IS GROWING tension and distrust among the fur traders, Indians, and colonists who have lived together in Pennsylvania for many years. The peace of the past is spilling out like the blood in Tom Miller's leg. Maybe it was a sign of things to come.

The spring storms end and we survey our fields to find that our planting has not been disturbed! I give thanks to the Sky Mother and I'm refreshed like the earth after a summer rain. I hadn't realized how parched my mind had become and soon I find myself walking into the woods again, in spite of Sattelihu's warning. My freedom has been nearly lost and I cannot be constrained and kept from the forest.

Grandmother is respected and admired by the colonists for her long ago role as an interpreter for Governor Hunter of New York, and for her travels to Philadelphia and Lancaster to attend council meetings. When white people visit, she tells them her work has been given to her son. Sattelihu is also respected, but feared when he paints himself in angry war colors as all Indians do in their fight with the Catawba and others. When they see him dressed in fine European clothing looking like an Englishman, they're at ease. They've told Grandmother this and she graciously explains he's not to be feared, only respected and honored. The white women are fascinated with Grandmother and sometimes come into our home poking around for information to cast around the village for their amusements. Many are weary from their house and farm work and serving their men day and night. I thought they would find common friendship with the Macks and other Christians, but although the colonists believe in the same God, the Moravians approach God in a way that is different from other Christians.

The days fly by and my peace becomes short-lived. I'm unsettled about the colonists and the Indians in this village, for they both have lost sincerity. The colonists' speech is harsh and not as friendly. They try to accept the Indians, they tell my grandmother, but they're repulsed by their ways. My grandmother slyly answers them, for as they speak, they often forget that she, too, is an Indian. At times they catch themselves and are embarrassed in apology, "Oh, not meaning to offend your goodness, Madame, for you are different!" They come knocking on our door out of curiosity and also for Grandmother's fever medicine. When the Indians come to visit, they are keenly inquisitive to look upon some of the clothing and items Sattelihu has brought back to us from his many trips to Philadelphia. They also know of the many gifts Grandmother has received over the years from the governors of New York and Pennsylvania. One evening, Grandmother and I sit around the fire after everyone is asleep and Sattelihu is away again on business in Philadelphia.

Grandmother speaks to me in a whispering voice. "The Indians believe the gifts from the Europeans are symbols of being blessed by the Great Spirit. Some think these goods have come from a magical and mysterious realm. They all desire the cloth, fancy pistols, and beautiful china, Catrine. Having many of these things makes us special, but it also makes the Indians want everything we have. I'm not one to turn away these gifts, but the coveted European goods are making the Indian's mind turn away from one another and the Great Spirit."

"We've never really been like the others," I tell Grandmother, "and it's not because of what we have. Look around and see! I'm pleased with our cloth and the few pieces of furniture, but we've given so much away that we don't have as much as we've been given. Our friendship with the missionaries and Sattelihu's white friends who visit and stay with us covers us with invisible cloth, beautiful cloth that our Indian brothers see in our demeanors. Our own white blood is quiet amongst them and we have wished it to be so. But when white people are with us, this blood is no longer still. Now that I've become a woman, I've changed my mind. I only ever treasured my Indian blood, but now, I would like to experience my French blood, too."

Grandmother glances at me with puzzlement and continues sewing, her head down. She says nothing for a long time and I fear I've trodden on the soil of her soul that is soggy with loss. I'm quiet and must wait for her to speak. In the dim light, I look over to the far corner and see the Macks entwined with one another as if they are one body, not two. There is no movement or sound and I wonder about my own marriage with Telehemet and if we will sleep like the Macks who during the day say little to one another, but at night, sleep as one.

Soon Grandmother's head falls onto her chest and she is asleep. I listen to her quiet snores and to the cry of a lonely wolf in the distance and soon, I fall asleep and dream of Telehemet. In the dream, I become him and he becomes me as we dance a harvest dance together. In the dream, I look into Anna's cloudy mirror and peer at my face that is part wolf and part Telehemet's. I wake with a pounding heart and hear howling and hope wolves haven't come in a pack to dig up our cache of venison and other meat. But soon I realize the howling comes from men. Men who have become part wolf because the demon rum has possessed them. I get up to retrieve a rifle, but before I reach it, the front door is pushed open and two Indian men enter who are deranged by rum. Their faces are painted black and they roar like wild beasts and shout that they have come to remove all whites from our cabin and village.

"Then you must take me, too, for I am also white," I say to them.

The men say nothing, but toddle back and forth in their moccasins, drool collected in the corner of their mouths. One of them holds a bludgeon in one hand and a jug of rum in the other. The other man is carrying a torch and I fear he'll burn our cabin down. The Macks have risen from their bed in the corner of the cabin and stand in the dark clutching one another, quietly praying. My sisters and brothers have risen, as well as my mother, from the opposite side of the cabin. My mother has gathered them all to her in a huddle. They, too, are silent, waiting. And then Grandmother comes to stand by me.

"You must take me with our white friends and granddaughter Catharine. You forget I am not only an Indian and carry white blood."

Both men, too drunk and startled to know how to respond, turn and leave the cabin. I rush to bolt the door and my mother coaxes the children back to bed. The Macks come to sit with Grandmother and I build up the fire, for it has grown dim. When I get up to look out the window, I see the men, along with two others, open another cask of rum and begin to dance. It's an insult to say that they have become wolves, for wolves have more dignity than these Indians. None of us sleep this night, for we listen to the incessant dancing and howling as they prowl menacingly around our cabin. Grandmother is distraught unlike I've ever seen her. My mother gets up to sit with us and hugs Grandmother while she weeps.

"These Indians are cold and apathetic. They only know how to drink and dance," she says between sobs. "I'm ashamed to be among them. They've become something other than who they were born to be. They cower before the colonists during the day, coveting their homes and lives, and at night after they drink to excess, they become fearless with hate and want to destroy all the whites. Many of them have lost their nobility and respect for the Indian way of life. They're weary, but mostly, they've become empty vessels only to be filled with rum."

"I'm saddened that your home has been attacked because we are here, Isabelle," Jeannette Mack says, sitting down beside Grandmother.

"We must leave as soon as possible. Our own cabin should be finished soon and we can move. We're putting you in danger," Martin Mack chimed in, sitting next to his wife.

"You yourselves are in danger. They will not harm me or my family, for no matter how drunk they become, they understand the curse that would fall upon them if they hurt their own. You must move to Shikellamy's Oneida village, thirteen miles upstream. You'll be safer there. But I will miss you both if you leave."

Grandmother weeps and I'm concerned for her, but also for myself. Grandmother's spirit has spread large wings over my life. I've always lived under them and felt protected, but this night I feel her wings have folded in. Grandmother's wings have slowly weakened while I've become a woman soon to be married. She has been worried over the Shawnees and Delawares leaving Pennsylvania and turning to the French in Ohio country. She has been worried over her son's reluctance to bring them back, and the increasing anger the Indians have toward the colonists. She is also anxious for my marriage to Telehemet, a Seneca warrior, whose family enjoy visits with French officials from New France. And what of her grown children and grandchildren who live in New France? Grandmother is a mystery even to me. I gaze at her and fear that when she dies, I'll not be able to live without her. She wipes her eyes with her shawl and looks over at me with grave sadness.

"Yes, Catharine, I believe you'll experience your French blood as you desire to do."

SATTELIHU RETURNS THE next day to find us exhausted and huddled inside the cabin, although the summer weather is perfect for working in the fields. Strewn around the outside of our cabin are the remains of an elk's bones and innards, old blankets, pewter cups, and empty casks of rum. The embers in the fire the drunken Indians made outside our cabin are still glowing and there is a rancid smell of meat and ash.

"Where is Sally?" he asks.

"She left to go to her mother's home many days ago and it's a good thing. She would have been hysterical if she had been here last night," Grandmother says.

"Tell me, Mother, what has happened."

"I'm tired and I'll lay myself down to sleep now that I know we are safe because you are here. Martin will tell you everything that has happened."

While Martin tells Sattelihu about our grievous night, Jeannette and I leave the cabin to get water for the household. As we walk, Jeannette tells me that she and her husband will not live in fear, but trust God and build their own cabin nearby to continue their work for the Lord.

I stop walking and Jeannette stops walking, too.

"Does God believe white people are better than Indians, Jeannette?"

Jeannette is quiet for a moment, her red-rimmed blue eyes denying what she has said about not being fearful. I see them darting around, looking for the drunken Indians.

"God loves all people equally. I believe this. The Bible speaks this and also that there is only one way to Him through Jesus Christ. We believe that God has sent us to tell this good news to the Indians who have not known this."

"I've heard this said many times by the missionaries. I know some of the Bible. But just because you read this book, how do you know it's true? These stories in the Bible are like many stories. The Indians have many stories they haven't written down. They've given us signs and symbols. It's up to each of us to take meaning from them. I want to believe in Jesus, but not if I must give up our own stories. This angers many of the Indians, Jeannette, for you believe your ways are better than ours. Is your God better than our God? This makes us feel as if you are being God yourselves."

I sigh and Jeannette puts her arm around my shoulders. I don't feel this gesture is comforting, but that she is trying to replace my truth with her truth. I squirm away from her to walk ahead, agitated that I'm acting inhospitable and angry because I don't know who God is.

DURING THE NEXT few days, the drinking party continues and increases in number, but they stay away from our cabin. They rail against the colonists with yelling and curses that keep us up each night. Sattelihu finally prevails upon them to leave and never return, threatening to drive them away with force. When the two Indian instigators from the Ohio country finally leave, the Indians from our village sober up and become peaceful again. Calmer days ensue, but I can feel the undercurrent of anxiety and strain in all of us. My uncle leaves again and the Macks move out to build their own cabin. My grandmother clings to them and begs them not to leave. I've never seen my grandmother so fawning toward anyone before and I'm relieved to have them gone. Since I spoke honestly to Jeannette, our friendship soured and we've been tip toeing around each other. I'm surprised Grandmother hasn't noticed, nor has Jeannette said anything to her about my questions. I'm unsure whether Grandmother would have scolded me. I like to think she'd be proud of me standing up for our Indian beliefs, but these days I'm thinking even Grandmother is losing the Indian ways.

And then a hideous murder terrifies not only the white settlers of Pennsylvania, but the Indians, as well. We are shocked to learn that Mushemeelin, a Delaware who lives near us, has killed a fur trader named Jack Armstrong. These men had known one another for years and there had been a certain trust between them. It wasn't the first time an Indian killed a white person, but this was an aggressive, planned murder. Mushemeelin is of a volatile temper and many are afraid of his black art and conjuring ways. No one wants to cross him and when Jack Armstrong took his horse and gun for not paying his debts in beaver or bear, Mushemeelin took revenge. Indians cannot live without their horses, especially those involved in the fur trading business.

The body of Jack Armstrong and his two servants were found and the rumors and questioning has begun. Our lives are filled with more distrust, anger, and fear than ever before. A knife has been thrust into the back of our village and is now being twisted again and again. When I look into the forest, I can sense the presence of evil lingering and I don't visit during this time. The stars are hidden by clouds at night and there are high winds and much rain with hail. It's like this for days, and all the while our dear Shikellamy is the recipient of angry letters asking why the two Delaware young men, John and Jemmy, are not in jail, as is dark Mushemeelin, the culprit who claims proudly he murdered in self-defense. John and Jemmy are just boys and had only thought they were going bear hunting, not men hunting. Mushemeelin had not declared his intentions of killing Jack Armstrong and the two boys believed their elder that they were only going hunting. They claim they didn't participate in the horrendous slaughter and I believe them. And the village believes they're innocent because they've been known here since they were babies. Our village also knows that Mushemeelin is full of dark spirits.

Sattelihu, Conrad Weiser, and George Croghan meet at our home and announce there will be a special council meeting in Lancaster. The Onondago Council declares we must all attend, including those who aren't on a hunt or in a war party. There will be envoys from Maryland, Pennsylvania, and Virginia, as well as the sachems of the Ho-De'-No-Sau-Nee Six Nations and as many of us that can be there. I don't want to go. We're sitting around the fire after a delicious meal when my uncle tells us this. Grandmother, Mother, Esther, and I prepared food all afternoon and now we've eaten and feel the fullness of a day's work and sustenance. George Croghan sits next to me, his thigh touching mine. Grandmother looks over at me and I see a glint in her eye. She looks at her son and indicates she wants to speak.

"We'll send a messenger to Telehemet's family in Caneada to say Catrine and Telehemet's marriage will be postponed until after the Lancaster Council."

I stare into the fire and don't respond. Does this fire suddenly flame high and increase the warmth between George Croghan and myself?

Chapter Eight

THE YEAR IS 1744 and here we are at the Lancaster Treaty Conference in this strange and fascinating place. Sattelihu, with all his declarations about our attendance, isn't here with us. He has gone with my father and a war party to fight the Catawbas. Grandmother, my mother, Esther, Molly, the children, and I have journeyed miles with Chief Shikellamy and other Ho-De'-No-Sau-Nee to come to Lancaster.

There are over two hundred of us who journeyed to this town that has a main street with a market and a large court house. There are side streets and many churches with different faces, both welcoming and foreboding. When we arrived in very good order on horseback and walking, I felt proud. It was later said that we were a beautiful sight to behold. The people in town stopped to stare at us as we followed behind our great Onondaga chief, Canassatego, right up to the steps of the court house. And then our chief sang in our language a song of renewal of our treaties and for the new ones that will be made. After, Mr. Weiser led us to the back of the town and instructed us to build our temporary cabins. And then began a fury of activity, in spite of our exhaustion, to gather tree boughs and boards to build our temporary wigwams and cabins. I ask Grandmother why we are not invited into the homes of the townspeople. In the past, she stayed in wealthy people's homes during important treaties.

"The Montours, and you especially, old Grandmother, should be offered an honorable place to stay in their homes."

Grandmother looks sharp at me.

"We'll live like our brothers and sisters, Catrine. Most of the Ho-De'-No-Sau-Nee do not like to dwell or stay in a house built by white people."

"But will you take me inside one of their homes while we're here?"

"I don't want to bring it to our Indian family's attention again that I've been treated differently."

"They hold you in esteem for your work, Grandmother."

Grandmother is tired and flustered. She waves me away and shakes her head. Later, after I've worked to help create our paltry dwelling, I escape from them all—the Montours and my people. I don't walk into town, but further away from everything and everyone. I wander alongside a stand of trees and soon find myself at a stream. It's hot and I'm sticky with sweat and a coating of dust from the roads we've traveled on. I would like to strip down to my naked body and soothe it unencumbered in the inviting waters, but I'm in a new place that doesn't know me. And I'm feeling heavy with new growth everywhere in my body. I look down at my breasts that have swelled in just a few months. I want to feel light as a feather again, but Grandmother said this will come when I've learned to carry my womanhood correctly so as not to break under its weight. I look around, pleased no one is here, except a blue jay squawking at me loudly. I step out of my moccasins and into the cooling stream and sigh with relief. I sit down among the pebbles and wiggle until I've made a comfortable place to settle into. I undo my braids and slowly lean back into the water and close my eyes. The blue jay has gone away and I listen to the twittering of small birds and the background noise of my people building their temporary dwellings. I open my eyes and peer at the late sun rays sparkling through the leaves of trees. I smile, knowing I can find home anywhere where there are trees, water, and birds. I stay in the stream until I feel refreshed and then slowly return to my family for an evening of rituals and noisome activities.

When I'm back at our camp and ready to explore this new place, my mother tells me I'm not allowed to leave our cabin.

"But Grandmother will be called upon to interpret and she'll take me with her. She's preparing me for her work," I say in protest, although I don't desire to be an interpreter.

"No, Catrine," Grandmother speaks from across the room, "I'm no longer a voice at these treaties, nor do I wish to be."

"Then why did we come all the way here to sit in this hot, dirty place?"

"Our presence is strong here. There are many of us and it's important we are here together. We show strength in our unity so the white men will not take advantage of us."

Mother grabs my arm and looks into my face with her hard demeanor.

"Your Grandmother is highly regarded and her reputation is known far and wide. We'll be receiving many guests come to speak to her. You'll make this temporary home a place of hospitality."

I glare at Esther who never seems to incur wrath from our mother. I was supposed to be married by now. Why should I be treated like a child? Other Indian mothers don't discipline and harangue their children as my mother does.

"Start the cook fire, Catrine, and we'll eat and rest. And then you'll help with the wampum belts."

I turn to Grandmother and she smiles at me. She has always liked making wampum belts, but I don't. Their stories I've loved, but now the mostly remind me of the constant struggle between people.

"It's customary we rest after our long journey before taking council, Catrine," Grandmother says. "This is your first time at a treaty. It's an honor to be here and don't despise it. Remove your child's whimpering and perhaps you'll be treated as a woman. There'll come a time at this treaty you'll sit at a council meeting with the mothers and children and listen to the flair and gallantry of our chiefs debating and discussing our land. But if you continue to run into the woods and remove yourself from everyone, you'll miss the growth of your wisdom."

I sigh and leave the cabin to prepare our cook fire. I gather a few rocks and place them in a circle and then go to the edge of the woods to gather branches for kindling. As I pick up branches, I sense a strong presence behind me. I turn around and gasp, dropping my armload of branches. A tall, brawny, old man stands before me and on his enormous chest are tattooed black patterns. His skin is dark, but his tattoos are even darker. I can hardly keep my eyes off the designs that are bold and intriguing. His face is painted with white and red stripes and his countenance is solemn.

"I'm Catharine, daughter of Margaret and granddaughter of Madame Montour," I say, nervously.

"I'm Chief Tachanuntie of Onondaga."

The chief picks up the branches I dropped.

"I'm from Shamokin . . ."

"Yes, I know your Uncle Andrew . . . Sattelihu. He is most respected at our Onondaga Councils."

"Will you be speaking . . . ?"

"I'm always ready to speak, daughter, but mostly I'll observe and later give my council to the chiefs at our fire in Onondaga."

I walk toward our makeshift village and the chief walks alongside me.

"Grandfather, you are different."

The strange man laughs. "I'm both African and Indian. My life has been questioned since my birth."

"But you're a chief and a warrior . . ."

"I'm called the Black Prince of Onondaga. When I began to live proudly out of both parts of me, the questions about my worth ceased. You must respect the seed that planted you to become Catharine. Your blood is both white and red. On the journey, I watched you from afar and saw the struggle in your countenance. Look at your grandmother, Madame Isabelle Montour! Her blood has been stirred into wisdom and beauty. She is loved by all who meet her! The most elegant aristocratic ladies enjoy your grandmother, but she remains humble. She may hide some truths about herself, but she's at peace with who she has become."

Catharine looks up at this strange Indian and smiles. He returns her smile with a firm hand upon her shoulder for a moment.

"The Indian blood in your grandmother we respect most! You may not become the mediator she once was, but in the clouds and light in your eyes, you'll have an important path to follow."

"But I don't want anything out of the ordinary. I'm to be married to a warrior soon . . . a Seneca warrior. I only wish to be his wife and already fear I'll miss cavorting with the spirits in the woods after we marry. I love simple things."

Catharine hesitates and continues, "But one not so simple thing is that Anna, my missionary friend, taught me to read. I'd like to read the white man's books and if any women have written books, I'd like to read them, too."

Chief Tachanuntie laughs and continues walking. Catharine sighs and walks next to him. In the distance, she spies her mother waving frantically at her.

ON THE EVENING of the next day, I convince Grandmother and my mother I must go for a walk. I walk alone on Main Street and ponder this place. My spirit is dizzy from the quickened pace, smells, sights, and sounds of Lancaster. I sense that the old earth spirits have been trampled on by ravenous and strange new ones. Mr. Weiser said this town only sprang up a few years ago. The mighty Susquehanna, Ga'-wa-no-wa'-na-neh, wildly flows near, but is not heard. There are many houses built of wood and a few of brick and stone. I'm surprised how closely they stand together. Why not have one longhouse rather than many walls separating them all? I'm pleased not to live in a longhouse, as our home is already crowded with love and travails, but living with all the sounds and smells of others and not being able to see faces would be strange. There are heaps of animal leftovers and skins of fruit in front of the houses and I cover my nose. Certainly vermin, fleas, and bugs are their close companions. How can they accuse the Indian of being slovenly.

Many white people who have come from across the sea live here. I asked Grandmother what the French look like and she said most of the French here are fur traders and their look isn't French.

"Catrine, there are English, French, German, Dutch, and then there is the fur trader," Grandmother said.

"But the fur trader can come from all nations. George Croghan is Irish."

"Oh, Catrine, the fur trader gives up his people's blood when he comes across the sea to become a fur trader. And then he speaks one language only . . . mostly the language of money and greed."

"But you said your brother was a fur trader, Grandmother. And your father, my great-grandfather."

"Granddaughter. Do you not understand me? My father and brother didn't leave their people to become fur traders. They never drained their blood and filled it with greed. They honored the animals they hunted."

I won't argue with Grandmother. I'm a woman now and not a child who sees only one color or one way. I love my Grandmother, but she sees what she wants to see and believes what she wants to believe. She is Madame Montour.

There are many tongues spoken in Lancaster. I think most everyone, including my people, have come with good intentions to make treaties to live in peace. My people are greedy for cloth, tools, and horses from the white men and give too much away for these things. They don't understand maps and words on paper and this is one reason I want to read.

I continue my walk and listen to the languages, mostly the English that is clipped with tiny gasps and flares. In the distance, I hear music made with string instruments. I follow the sounds to the Court House, an enormous white building with large columns. Did Grandmother sit in important meetings here? I see many well-dressed gentlemen and ladies entering and I'm curious. It's a very warm evening and the windows are opened wide. No one has noticed me and I walk to the corner of the building to stand near a window to watch the dancing and listen to the conversations. I smell the sweat of the Europeans, different from our own that has bear grease and plant scents. I sniff and smell lavender and roses, along with faint skunk. I inhale so much that I sneeze and a burly looking bearded man sticks his head out the window. I quickly lower myself down so he doesn't see me.

After he leaves, I continue to look inside and watch people being merry and dancing in a circle. One man plays an instrument with strings as large as himself and another man is playing a small wooden instrument with strings. Their music is not very pleasing and I'd rather dance to bird and wind song and to our drums and flutes. The men's voices are loud and thunderous, like irregular drumbeats, and the women's voices are shrill. I see a young Indian poorly dressed in an old red, ragged match-coat and wearing the usual deerskin leggings. He's laughing with another man dressed in a frilly shirt and a white wig. How silly is this white wig on such a hot evening. I then realize the Indian is Chief Shikellamy's son, John Logan! I didn't know he was in Lancaster. He's the chief's oldest and most respected son and he and I have sat together in many gatherings with our families. We have exchanged interesting words and he thinks much like I do about the strange behaviors of people. As children, we were unable to keep ourselves from smiling and when our mouths were overflowing with many smiles, we covered them with our hands. Sometimes we had to rush outside to let all the smiles turn into laughter that caused us to fall to the ground.

I haven't seen John Logan in a long time, not since Telehemet began coming into our village. I have missed John Logan and here he is in the white man's ball doing what he does best—laughing. I long to be inside with him and to experience this joy and freedom.

The musicians stop playing and begin another song. This song is lively and suddenly John Logan grabs the man with the wig and they're lifting their feet and dancing together. The people in the room clap for them and I recognize it's an Irish jig that George Croghan once showed me how to do. I had laughed as he hopped up and down while singing a song.

I move away from the window to the side of the Court House in the shadows. I try to dance, for the music isn't as displeasing to my ears as the other songs. I tap my toe on the ground and bring my knee up to my chest and then kick out my leg. I do so with my other leg and take turns with each one, all the while trying to keep in rhythm with the music. I'm sweating and giggling to myself when there's a tap on my shoulder. I turn, surprised and embarrassed to see John Logan. He laughs and I laugh and soon we are laughing and leaning against the court house so as not to fall to the ground. We are no longer children as we once were and should show restraint. But we can hardly stand it to be adults on this night and soon give way to more laughter until we see Mr. Weiser and Chief Shikellamy walking toward us from the street. We quickly become sober Indians and greet the two men.

"Why are you dancing secretly in the dark, Catharine and John?" Shikellamy asks.

"I wasn't dancing in secret, Father. I was inside dancing with the white men, but I left to go back to camp and saw Catharine."

Mr. Weiser laughs aloud. "An Indian dancing the bog dance at a ball?"

"Bog dance?" John Logan asks in a whisper.

Mr. Weiser continues laughing and Chief Shikellamy turns his back on him, crosses his arms, and nods at John Logan and me. We immediately walk by his side to head back to the camp. Mr. Weiser stops laughing and scrambles quickly behind us.

"I'm sorry to offend you, Chief, but it's so unlikely. It would be extraordinary for me to dance in the midst of your war dance, as well. I think you might also laugh."

The Chief stops and we stop, too. He turns to face Mr. Weiser. "And so now you will have opportunity to become an extraordinary Indian dancer, for we will go to the dance at our campfire and we'll see who laughs now."

Mr. Weiser protests, but we ignore him and walk in silence to the camp. We hear the drums and sounds of the war dance as we get nearer. I'm looking forward to seeing Mr. Weiser dance. He's a solemn man and believes he understands Indians more than we understand ourselves. He hungers for honesty, but his pride must be fed all the time.

Earlier this evening, I heard him talking with low tones to a Maryland commissioner outside our cabin. He didn't know I was in the doorway listening.

"Whilst we're here, don't talk much of the Indians, nor laugh at their dress, or make any remarks on their behavior. It will be much resented by them and it might cause some differences to arise betwixt the white people and them. Most Indians understand English quite well, although they'll not speak it when they are in treaty."

And tonight Mr. Weiser broke his own rule and thinks our behavior and dress ridiculous. We'll see how he dances.

Chapter Nine

THERE ARE TIMES I'm ashamed by some Indians because of their drunkenness and desperation for the white man's gifts. Their dignity disappears when they become whimpering dogs at the splendid doors of the Europeans or howling wolves when they're full of rum. But tonight, as the stars glimmer in the sky, I'm proud when I see over thirty young men in a circle around a large fire. Near this fire, there are three elders beating drums that the young men dance to. There are vigorous hops and leaps and a rush of excitement comes over me. From time to time, the men cry out, "Yo and Bugh!"

Grandmother and my family are sitting with women from our village and I sit down next to them. Grandmother reaches for my hand and I look into her eyes. They're glistening with tears and I know she, too, is pleased this evening. There are many white people, especially young men, standing near the dancers and clapping from time to time. Their smiles are wide and I know they're pleased with the music and dancing. Some of their elders aren't quite sure and their faces don't reveal much of anything.

John Logan and his father sit outside the ring with the other chiefs and Mr. Weiser stands next to them nervously. Chief Shikellamy is talking rapidly to the chiefs and suddenly one of them stands up and shakes Mr. Weiser's hand. He leads him through the ring of dancers inside to the fire. Mr. Weiser's face is calm, but his eyes are wide and focused. The chief demonstrates a dance and then with a nod and a gesture of his arm, he indicates to Mr. Weiser to do the same. Mr. Weiser looks around to see who is watching and then moves side to side, from one foot to the other, but it's barely noticeable. He has no spirit, this man. The chief laughs loudly and Mr. Weiser turns to leave, but when he tries to go through the ring, a young man grabs his arm and shows him how to dance with the others. Mr. Weiser finally gives up his sobriety and dances with much more ease. I look over at John Logan and catch his eye. We want to laugh aloud but only smile at one another. I lean against my sister, Esther, and she whispers to me that I cannot marry both John Logan and Telehemet and I should save one of them for her marriage. We giggle like girls, not like women, and I'd like to stay like this for a long time. Just being girls together and not women who have to marry warriors and chiefs and become like our mother and grandmother.

A few days later, in the afternoon when the sky is lingering with ease in its blue canopy, Chief Shikellamy comes storming over to our makeshift cabin in the Indian camp. Grandmother and I are sitting on blankets in front of the cabin enjoying the stillness of the day, for most of the Indians are at the court house or in their cabins resting. We are making wampum and for once, I'm not irritated doing so, for the rhythm of our work is calming. And Grandmother, for once, isn't trying to instill wisdom into me. Our conversation is as light and airy as the day and we speak of the peace that Lancaster might bring to all of us.

The chief looms over us with his arms folded and a large shadow falls upon us. Grandmother stops her work, sighs, and looks up at her good friend.

"We'll go inside and have refreshment and you'll tell me what has happened."

The chief nods and helps Grandmother up. She looks down at me.

"It would probably be best if you continued making wampum, but since you are now a woman who will someday listen to the chiefs in your village and give sage advice, come inside. You can serve and listen, but what is said is not to be shared with anyone else, even with your sister, Esther."

I'm pleased to listen to their conversation, but I'm uneasy. I don't want to hear about the grievances of our people with the white men. I'm disappointed this songstress day with blue peace and bird singing has seduced me into believing there is hope for this treaty bringing peace. I follow Grandmother and the chief inside and pour cups of wild grape juice for them. I also give them succotash I cooked in the morning. I sit down with some juice and quietly listen, trying not to drift off into dreams of Telehemet and what my life will be like after I marry. I feel strong urgings for Telehemet, especially on a day like this when the wind caresses me with gentleness and the sky is full of happiness. Chief Shikellamy finishes his food before speaking. He sighs and speaks loudly.

"We're being asked to give up lands in Maryland and Virginia! Our people are being lured and tempted by rum and gifts! Our chiefs think they're important because they make marks representing their names on papers! Feathers on pens soften our cheeks and manhood as we scribble. We do not drink the rum when we are in treaty, but the fire in Indian bellies from the night before, along with the cheerfulness of a summer day, and all the goods the white man puts before us, seduce us to give too much away."

"Greed and fear in our own people," Grandmother replies.

"I refused to sign and walked out."

"Were there others?" Grandmother asks.

"Only two and I've broken peace with everyone."

"Chief Shikellamy, are you in there?" Mr. Weiser stands just outside our cabin.

Shikellamy and Grandmother are quiet for a moment. Grandmother nods to the chief and then to me. I rush to welcome Mr. Weiser, the man who is all business all the time. He barely greets me and walks quickly to stand before Shikellamy and Grandmother.

"You must sign and get the others to sign this deed to give the land to Lord Baltimore. It was already agreed to and twenty-four chiefs of the Six Nations have looked over all the goods and gifts given to them. Not only looked, but they've already taken them."

Chief Shikellamy shakes his head.

"What were the goods given?" Grandmother asks.

Mr. Weiser pulls out papers from the satchel hung over his shoulder. His hands shake as he looks through them.

"Ah, here it is. The list of goods—4 pieces of stroud, 200 shirts, three pieces half thicks, 3 pieces dusssle blankets, 47 guns, 1 pound vermillion, 1,000 flints, 4 dozen jews-harps, 3 half-barrel gun-powder . . ."

Chief Shikellamy stands up slowly while Mr. Weiser reads. He grabs the paper from him and throws it down.

"None of it is worth what our land is worth!"

"But you have been given more land in Pennsylvania that has restricted use for only your people. This is also part of the exchange. It has already been decided upon. As you are well aware, there's been much conferring with the chiefs and drinking of health to all and it was agreed to now have the ceremonial signing of the deed to transfer the land in Maryland."

"Thousands of acres for a few guns and blankets! And you know well that this land, our land, in Pennsylvania is not being protected from people coming across the sea."

"It's already been agreed, Chief. I implore you to tell the other two that we'll have the final signing tomorrow morning at the house of George Sanderson, the clerk to record the deed."

Grandmother stands up and faces Mr. Weiser who is red in the face.

"No amount of wine, sangree, bumbo, stroud, and guns can be equal to the land of the Great Spirit. Give our esteemed chief this night to ponder this solemn exchange. Many of the chiefs of the Ho-De'-No-Sau-Nee have not seen the land in Pennsylvania and they sign like dumb oxen you use to plow fields. They don't understand ownership of land, but only the sharing of the land, for the land is owned by the Great Spirit and allows all of us to honor it by living on it. We share land in common and we have offered to do so with white men. But many white men are greedy and don't want to share. Like children fighting over playthings. To these chiefs, the marks they make on your papers is giving you permission to use the land as they have used it. It is not understood that it is your land only."

Grandmother turns to Chief Shikellamy and places her hand on his shoulder, smiling. "But this chief knows much more and knows the lies that hide invisibly beneath the words on the deed. Leave him be until tomorrow and then he will have an answer for you."

Mr. Weiser quickly leaves and Chief Shikellamy places his hands on Grandmother's shoulders. "You have been a close friend to me, Isabelle, and I'm grateful for your wisdom. You explained what I could not because of my anger."

"Remember, too, Chief, that peace is more important than the squabbles over land and we must not allow these white brothers to destroy the peace among us all. Chief Canassatego is a wise man and we must listen to him. It has been my experience that there are some white men who have been true to their word. I was honored and always given pay for being an interpretess, even if it took a long time to receive it."

Chief Shikellamy drops his hands to his sides and Grandmother whispers to him. "I've been told by my son, Sattelihu, that he has been given more land that is near the land given to the Indians for their use only. He will soon move there to watch out that squatters and breakers of our treaties from across the sea don't move to this land. Maybe you need to sign and make good peace with all. But let Mr. Weiser take back what I said to the commissioners. They'll know my words are not to be ignored."

Chief Shikellamy leaves and Grandmother looks at me solemnly.

"We'll return to our wampum making, Catrine, for it will be needed more than ever."

I think with satisfaction and sadness that I'm not wrong in believing that the spirits of men and nature seduce us. But men do so with shining objects and nature seduces us with perfect summer days.

I stand in the doorway of the cabin and look into the sky. Before the chief came, it had been clear and wistful and now it has darkened with rain clouds forming.

LATER THAT EVENING, fires roar and my people dance furiously around them. Young warriors are painted with fierce designs and wear headdresses full of colorful feathers. They hold tomahawks and arrows in their hands while they dance around the fires. They shriek and run out of the camp and down the street until they meet commissioners from Pennsylvania, Virginia, and Maryland. There they circle and make noises while brandishing their weapons. The commissioners know to be still, for they have been told beforehand that this would happen. The war dance is a patriotic demonstration and is danced for council meetings and prominent occasions.

I follow the bands of warriors dancing down the street displaying their strength and pride. They glisten with sweat and roar like bears. I watch each commissioner stand in the center still as stone with eyes of steel. Each one clutches his hands to keep them from shaking. This was supposed to be the night they would have celebrated the signing of the treaty and now this war dance has a different meaning for them.

I grow tired of following the warriors and slowly make my way back to our cabin. I glance into the sky just in time to see a falling star and maybe it's a good sign. As I walk by Chief Shikellamy's cabin, he comes out and smiles at me. I think he'll sign the treaty in the morning and I hope it will bring peace. We value this more than war. I trust that Sattelihu's presence on Pennsylvania land will be safe, but this means another move.

THE NEXT MORNING, Chief Shikellamy, Mr. Weiser, and the chiefs who had not signed the treaty, come to our cabin to tell us we must all go to the final signing of the treaty. Then we can go home and be finished with all of this noise and tension. Mr. Weiser doesn't seem relieved, but he's never at ease. He speaks nervously to Grandmother.

"First, all the chiefs who are signing will go to the house of George Sanderson to address any problems or specifics before meeting at the Court House. Then they'll go to the Court House and celebrate with more speeches and wampum. I'll take you, Madame Montour . . . and children, to the Court House now."

Grandmother is already ready, dressed in her finest cloth and moccasins. My mother is also wearing clothing only worn for feast days. The rest of us have done our best to get the mud off our moccasins and clean our faces. Our clothing is everyday working in the field clothing. I wish Grandmother and my mother had told us we'd be a part of something important.

"Will we feast with them?" Esther asks.

"Yes, but we must wait for their customs while we're there," the Chief responds.

I don't want to eat with these men. I have seen the rolling of eyes and surprised looks of the white men when they visit Grandmother and share meals at our home. They don't approve of the way our men eat their food, but they say nothing. Although I'm curious about the Court House, I don't like being mixed together inside their building.

THE TWENTY-FOUR Iroquois chiefs have been invited to dine with the honorable commissioners of Maryland, Virginia, and Pennsylvania after the signing of the Treaty. Also attending are other gentlemen of importance from the colonies, Grandmother, mother, Esther, Molly, myself, and the rest of the children. I see the surprised looks of some of the other mothers and children from our camp as we enter the Court House. I fear this honor given to the Montours will only distance us further in their hearts.

As I enter the Court House, I become dizzy and note the smell of wood that has lost its original scent from the forest. I slowly adjust from going from bright sunshine into a dark entryway. The floor creaks and I look down. It's made of wood and there are eyes looking up at me. Pine knots. The wood on the floor and around the building is shiny and as I walk next to a railing, I rub my hand over it and sniff. This is what has altered the forest trees! Some kind of oil to make the wood shine.

"Over here, Isabelle, Margaret . . . children. Over here, please." Mr. Weiser ushers us beyond the big bench in front and to smaller ones to the side. They look like stairs, each raised above the other. These benches circle around the room.

"Please sit on the left side. This is where spectators and auditors are allowed to sit during proceedings, so this is where you'll quietly observe the final treaty signing and exchange of gifts."

"And where will our chiefs be seated, Mr. Weiser?"

Grandmother doesn't wish to be cast aside, even if she won't be part of the proceedings. If Sattelihu was here, he would make certain she sat with the chiefs.

Mr. Weiser gestures to the other side of the room.

"They'll sit on the right side to make treaty."

"I'll also sit on the right side."

Grandmother strides confidently to the other side of the room and sits down alone. She folds her arms in front of her and looks toward the bench and table in front. I hear my mother sigh as she plops down on a bench and pulls me down next to her. Esther, Molly, and the children also sit down, wide-eyed and curious.

Soon the commissioners file in and sit down in the front. One of them sits at the bench alone. They all wear black robes and white wigs and faces without color. They are such a sight. But we, I imagine, are also a sight to them. The Ho-De'-No-Sau-Nee chiefs march in behind them. They are much more radiant and dramatic than the white men, although many of the chiefs wear a mishmash of ragged European clothing, as well as Indian clothing. It must be said that we like our colors in paint and clothing. The colors of feathers and the chiefs' footwear are bright and expressive. I wonder why so many insist on wearing the white men's clothing at all. Grandmother said it's a trick of the spirits the white men bring to us.

"Our chiefs think if they wear the white men's clothing, they'll become esteemed in their eyes and not be overpowered," Grandmother explained.

While the chiefs march in, I'm again proud of my people. They don't smile, for smiles are reserved for festivities and not to be given to the somber spirit of the Treaty. Their heads are held high and it's obvious they're warriors, for their strength is revealed in their muscled arms and the paint they wear depicts their feats in battle. After they file in, the commissioners, Mr. Weiser, and others seated in front rise to their feet and greet the chiefs. They shake their hands, their mouths trying to smile, but most of them fail to do so. This is an important treaty and they're nervous. Mr. Weiser leads them to the right to sit on the steps next to Grandmother and each of them acknowledge her as they sit down.

Mr. Weiser stands and announces the order of the day. The tall and brawny Canassatego, Chief of our Iroquois nation, stands next to him. He's most esteemed by the white men. He's been instructing the commissioners to create a government similar to the Ho-De'-No-Sau-Nee. He wisely told them they don't have unity and are under a great threat of France.

Unlike the other chiefs, Chief Canassatego does smile. He's the star of this treaty and speaks eloquently. "Our lands have become more valuable: the white people think we don't know their value, but we're sensible that the land is everlasting and the few goods we have received for it will soon be worn out and gone. For the future, we'll sell no lands but when Brother Onas is also with us; and we will know beforehand the quantity of the goods we are to receive."

"Jo Ha!" the rest of the chiefs reply, except Chief Shikellamy.

Mr. Weiser speaks to the commissioners. "Yesterday we were threatened with a storm in our relations with the Iroquois, but today, the storm has passed and the deed of release for a hundred thousand acres in Maryland from the Iroquois has been now signed."

"Huzza!" the commissioners cry out.

Mr. Weiser has never referred to us as the Ho-De'-No-Sau-Nee, only as the Iroquois. Is it too complicated for him to say it? We are the Ho-De'-No-Sau-Nee, the Iroquois, and the Six Nations.

The chiefs appear somber and one chief is wearing two silver bracelets he keeps touching. Their faces wear the doom for what they are doing. Grandmother said it was acres of land rashly given for flounced skirts, calicoes, dressing gowns, ribbons, silks, scarves, silver brooches and bracelets. These items are in addition to the usual necessities given to Indians in treaty. But never has so much land been given at one time. The gifts presented to them are beginning to fade in their minds as they realize the land will now not only be their own to hunt and fish on. They had conquered other nations who had lived on this land, such as the Susquehanna, long ago, and their own blood had been lost. And now this land is signed over to the white men to use. Will they truly live as brothers on this land together? I can read their thoughts from their lined faces. The casks of rum given to them the night before have already been drunk. It is over. We can all go home, I think, with sadness and relief.

Chief Canassatego speaks loudly. "Our wise forefathers established union and amity between the original five nations. This has made us formidable. This has given us great weight and authority with our neighboring Indian nations. We're a powerful confederacy, and by you observing the same methods our wise forefathers have taken, you'll acquire much strength and power; therefore, whatever befalls you, do not fall out with one another."

"Jo Ha!" the chiefs yell.

"Huzza!" the commissioners reply.

Can the colonies unite and be one as the Ho-De'-No-Sau-Nee have been? I think on this and how eloquent Chief Canasstego's words are. As the strings of wampum are being exchanged, I'm overcome with sleepiness and drift into sleep. I lean on my mother's shoulder and dream of golden fields of abundant crops. Corn, beans, potatoes, squash pumpkins, cucumbers, and watermelons grow in unbelievable plentitude. The cornstalks are over sixteen feet high and I see myself walking between the rows, caressing their leaves and lifting my head to give thanks. And then I see thunderous clouds and hear men's voices shouting in English. I run from the corn and stand in a nearby woods, watching men in uniforms slashing and destroying the corn, burning the fields, and tromping on all the abundance the Great Spirit had bestowed upon the earth. I look to the side of a field near a large hill and see a number of Indians lying dead, their scalps taken. These soldiers have warred against the Indian and the Great Spirit's bounty.

My mother gently pushes me away from her shoulder and I wake from my dream. My heart beats so loud in my head I hardly hear her tell me we must all leave. I sit stunned by the dream and visions I've had.

"Catrine, it's time to pull down and travel home."

I continue to sit and close my eyes, trying to capture the dream that has just left me.

"No, Mother . . . I've had a dream. We must not trust these white men, for they'll destroy all the bounty the Great Spirit has given us."

I open my eyes and Grandmother is standing before me looking sorrowful.

"Your dreams may help in the future, Catrine, but they're of no use now. You must be strong and set them aside for another time."

Why has Grandmother said this? Dreams are always taken seriously, perhaps too seriously at times. I stand up, but sit down again in a swoon. I close my eyes and hear the thunderous pounding of horse hoofs and terrifying snorting and screaming that comes from their nostrils and throats. I faint and after waking and being given water, I walk from the Court House through Lancaster to our makeshift cabin. My family lets me sleep while they prepare for the trip back to Shamokin.

Chapter Ten

IT'S JULY AND we have faith our harvest will be blessed. Anna and a few missionaries return and stay with the Macks. Anna and I have many happy afternoons on the edge of the forest talking and making music. She sings sweetly as I play my flute, but speaks too much about Count Zinzendorf, the old missionary chief of the Moravians. His wife died and soon he'll be desirous to have another wife by his side. I think Anna wants to be this wife, but she's young and beautiful and she'll be diminished next to the old badger with the sharp tongue. I heard Count Zinzendorf say to one of the missionaries that the Montours are an immoral population of French Indians all under the protection of the English. He would never say this to our faces and Anna would never say this, nor do I believe she thinks it. He's not as true and loving as she is! Her joy will be smothered if she marries him, but I think it's too late, for her eyes look soft and dreamy each time she says his name.

It's time, Grandmother, says, for my wedding to Telehemet and this means a long journey to New York to meet his family. His family live where the cascade of waterfalls speaks loudly.

"Some fear the truth in the language of our waterfalls, Catharine, and so we're not visited by many whites as you are here. And for this, we are thankful."

Sattelihu, Grandmother, my mother, Esther, and I travel on horses with our bundles, baskets, and dried food. My father doesn't travel with us and trusts that Grandmother and my mother will make the right decision for me. We stop often because of the roughness of the narrow trail along the Susquehanna and I'm given time to ready my heart for this union. July bathes us in the rich greens and yellows of the earth. We must have only dreamed of the stark, blinding snow-ghost of winter and every summer I feel as if winter will never come again.

I'm excited about marrying Telehemet and the fear of losing my independence has left. My heart is bursting with love and I want to shout it out to the forest and to everyone. But I don't, for the show of this kind of emotion is not part of our customs. Maybe it's my French blood making my feelings as full and round as the moon. I've spoken of my feelings with Telehemet and he was surprised by my words. His eyes and touches have said much, but he's never told me he loves me.

It's rained only twice during the many days of our travel, but it was light rain each time and didn't burden us. I don't want the baskets we've made to become sodden. It's true that Indian women excel at basket-work, although it saddens me that white men laugh at Indian women and refer to us as silly basket makers, as if this is all we're good for. Basket making is a skill I've not learned well, but my mother and Esther possess skill in their work. They not only use corn husks, but black-ash splint and white flag iris. I'm impatient with this kind of work and prefer sketching and sewing. But now I'm pleased that a few of the corn-husk baskets have been made by me and contain the dried meat and other food we'll give as wedding gifts to Telehemet's family. We also have a basket net that is made of black-ash splint to catch our fish. Esther and I stand near the Susquehanna where the water ripples over the stony bottom and with a stick we direct the fish into the submerged basket. Later, all of us sit in the twilight and watch the sun say goodbye to the earth in her dance over the horizon as we eat corn-meal coated fried fish and some gathered nuts and berries we found in the woods. I play my flute freely and Grandmother tells us stories of New France. Sattelihu soon sleeps soundly after eating and drinking. I hear wolves in the background talking to one another and wonder if they speak of us. Grandmother made us gather our food scraps to leave nothing for them to desire.

SOON THE CLAMOROUS Susquehanna River changes her tune and sings softly while flowing into New York. We leave walking her gentle banks and travel through a swampy area and our arms and legs become swollen from insect bites. The horses are tired and we stop often to help them through mud and weeds. We're hot, exhausted, and there's no sight or sound of any human life. I complain that we've gotten lost, but Sattelihu assures me we are close to the Seneca village. He eventually leads us out of the swamp and back to the path alongside the river. It's no longer the familiar Susquehanna, as this water is smaller and quieter. Sattelihu calls it the Chemung, which means horn-in-the water because once a Seneca warrior was fishing and found a giant tusk that looked like a horn. He said it was from a time before our creation came from the sky. My imagination is fired up and I keep watching the river for a giant horn to come floating alongside us.

We're all weary and soon there's sickness in my stomach and I need to rest. Esther accuses me of being frightened of marrying Telehemet and says I'm not really sick. My mother and grandmother insist we take time to rest, but Sattelihu says we're close to our destination. As always, my grandmother's wishes are carried out and I'm glad for it. We spend the night in the strange woods so thick with pine, white birch, and oak that I feel one giant tree spirit. There's also a strong warrior spirit dwelling here and a mystery that beckons respect. It's dark in the forest even before the sun sets and I shudder not just from fever, but from the spirits here. In a small clearing between a few pines we stop and make camp. We don't make a fire or eat anything but the dried venison we have carried with us. I only take a few bites and drink some water.

My uncle tromps through the woods around us, but the rest of us are soon asleep before the sun leaves the day behind.

The next morning, I wake when a vibrant ray of sunshine slants between two pines that are merged together near the earth. The trees look like legs of a giant with his head in the ground. I hear the cooing of melancholy mourning doves and the shrill voices of blue jays. I sit up and my strength returns to me. My fever has lifted and my clothing is soaked with sweat. Everyone slowly wakes, but Sattelihu is already up. I peer at him through the trees in a clearing where he has made a cook fire for our breakfast next to the river. The smells coming from the fire tell me that he's used our basket to catch fish. My mouth waters, but I must cleanse myself first from the evil spirit of the fever and any that dwell here in this forest. I slide down the banks of the Chemung and when I go under, I open my eyes and see shining bones sitting on the bottom. I surface and climb out of the river and although I'm refreshed and ridden of sweat and grime, I'm frightened of its power. I say nothing to my uncle and all of us are very quiet as we sit around the fire and eat corn bread and a yellow bass Sattelihu caught and Grandmother cooked. Soon we're ready to travel and as we walk and ride our horses, there are daisies, blue cornflowers, and other wildflowers alongside the narrow trail. I pretend they've been planted by the Great Spirit to guide me to Telehemet and our marriage ceremony.

We travel unencumbered for two more hours and when the sun sits directly over us, we swelter under its heat and intensity. Grandmother shouts it's time to stop for rest. It's clear to all of us that the path we trod is not well traveled and it's been very difficult for the horses and all of us.

"Can we rest here at this creek, Sattelihu?" Before he answers me, I get off my horse, drop my bundles, kick off my moccasins, and walk into the water where there are flat, smooth rocks. The cool rocks send strength up my legs and soothe and refresh my weariness. Esther does the same and Grandmother and my mother follow us into the creek. My tired uncle stands with the horses, looking around him, ever alert to danger. There's no one here but the spirits and what kind of spirits they are, I don't know, except that the ones in this creek are nurturing and not evil.

We sit in the shallow creek and splash and laugh with one another. After a few minutes, we get out of the water to sit in the tall grasses and don't feel the need to talk. There's tranquility and stillness and the wind has lowered her voice to a mere whisper. Sattelihu, too, stepped into the water and now sits with us in the serenity of this new place; a place full of the Great Spirit's presence. Blue jays, cardinals, and crows call to one another in the distance and a robin sings in the grasses near us. We unfold our bodies and lay down in the grasses after applying grease to keep the biting ones away. Closing our eyes, we sleep soundly while the sun slides down Sky Mother. Time stands still until a small wind gathers other winds to come and wake us, as if curious about why we are here. I'm first to wake, startled by wind sounds. I don't think human beings breathing their dreams and tromping these grounds has happened much in this place. Moments pass and the wind gathers strength and brings to my ears water singing in a sonorous roar. I jump to my feet, eager to follow this voice of the Great Spirit.

"Wake, everyone! Wake and listen!"

My family get up from their slumber and Sattelihu says he doesn't know where we are. The path we took out of the swamp was merely a deer path and it took us in a different direction he hadn't planned for. He assures us we are walking north and we'll find our way. We'll arrive at our destination, sooner or later, he states with contrived confidence. I tell him I'm glad we have gone off the trail because I want to go to the singing waters. I walk in the direction of the sound of the water as if I'm being pulled by an invisible rope.

"We don't have time. We need to travel north so we can find our way back to the main trail to reach Telehemet's village before the sun sets."

The power of the singing water overtakes my good senses and I run, my heart racing faster than my feet.

I'VE NEVER TRIED to imagine the Great Spirit with a face like one of us. I've found comfort in the secret and unseen presence of this Creator. The Ho-De'-No-Sau-Nee believe every animal and tree has a spirit and I believe that these spirits are children of the Great Spirit. Then there are spirits who have abandoned the Great Spirit who dwell in places where men and beasts invite them. They're like rebellious, evil children. This is my own belief. The Indians have many stories about the spirits and I've taken some of them to make my own. When Anna showed me a book with a picture of what God looked like in his son, Jesus, I admired his countenance, but he was sad and appeared weak. I cannot help but love him, too, for he's part of the Great Spirit, but I'm pleased to not have an image for the Creator. I want to allow the Great Spirit to be just that, a Great Spirit unseen.

But now, standing at the foot of this thunderous, light-filled, waterfall cascading into a pool, I'm altered in my relation with the Creator. This place is the essence of the Great Spirit and as I stand before and behind this waterfall, I'm home. It is the nearest to an image of the Great Spirit I can imagine. When Sattelihu, Esther, Grandmother, and my mother follow me and stand in awe before the waterfall, I remember with solemnity this isn't my destination and we'll soon leave this sacred place. I'm overcome with a sense of having arrived where I belong.

We stand on the flat shale rocks facing the flowing water and are baptized and renewed by water spray. My uncle is telling us we must leave, but I hardly hear his voice. It's drowned out by the waterfall's voice, the king and queen of all voices. Grandmother moves near me and wraps her blanket around my shoulders and turns me away from the white veil of flowing water. She points to the steep rock cliff to the left of the cascade and shouts into my ear.

"Do you see the eagle, Catharine?"

There is an open-winged and majestic imprint of a giant eagle within the structure of rocks next to the waterfall. Although I've seen symbols in the trees of the forest, I've never seen nature reveal something this resplendent and majestic. Sattelihu, my mother, and Esther gather around Grandmother and me to ponder this magnificent sight. Certainly, the spirit of Eagle has made a home in this place. I wonder if we are the only people to visit here, but as soon as I think this, Sattelihu turns to look up into the trees on the cliff. Our eyes follow his and we see two Indians standing above us. No war paint. Friendly? Seneca? They wave at us and then disappear. I wonder if they will come down from the top of the cliff to find out who we are. I'm immediately possessive of this place and wish I could stay. Sattelihu signals for us to leave and we turn away from the fervor and voice of these waters to continue our walk north to Telehemet. The wind changes direction and the waterfall sends a mist over us that becomes a shroud of grief for me. We remain silent as we travel. The Indians we saw on the cliff never come to greet us, but I feel their eyes on us for a long time. We travel on, but the sound of the eagle cliff waterfalls continues to resound in our ears. Its voice then becomes a murmur and we walk a long time and rest once more before our arrival at Telehmet's village. After we water our horses and sit down to eat a few corn cakes, Grandmother speaks of the waterfalls.

"The eagle is a protector of peace and for you, especially, Catharine, it gives meaning and is a gift for your upcoming wedding. You'll have peace in your marriage and you'll be a peacemaker for your people."

My mother and sister nod in agreement, but my uncle's eyes are closed and he's silent. He is the peacemaker and although he brings peace through his words for others, oftentimes there is no peace for himself.

Chapter Eleven

THE SENECA NATION dwells on land extending westward to the Genesee River and they are the keepers of the western door of the Ho-De'-No-Sau-Nee. They have also been known to adhere with a dogged obstinacy to the French and this is why my uncle has been cautious about my marriage. We arrive at Caneada where the heavens rest upon the earth. The sun setting over this small and pleasant village on the Genesee River casts golden highlights causing it to appear restful and serene. I wonder if I'll find happiness here in my new marriage or will Telehemet return to Pennsylvania and live with us. I'm hopeful he'll follow the custom of our people and we'll live with my grandmother and family in Pennsylvania.

The river is narrow and Sattelihu calls it Gen-nis'-hee-yo, which means beautiful valley. Since my time at the singing eagle cliff falls, heaven has not stopped dancing upon this land. I'm in love with another part of the Great Spirit and think there must be other places in the world I'd like to see. Sattelihu is tense as he walks ahead of us, leading his horse.

Esther turns around and says jeeringly, "Are you excited about your union with this old Seneca chief?"

"Telehemet is not an old man like Allumpapes or Shikellamy, even if he's many years my senior." I'm angry at her and lash back.

"You, Esther, want a boy for a husband, so you can teach him to be your love slave."

Esther, unmarried, has been hungering for a well-muscled boy in our village on the Shamokin Path. I've seen interest for him in her eyes and watch as she tries to be near him at festivals. She must wait for our mothers to decide for her and I doubt they'll choose him, for he's not seasoned and is too careless about many things. I should be patient with my sister who is probably jealous of me. She's my sister no matter our differences and I want to give her my affection.

I'LL ALWAYS REMEMBER walking behind my grandmother and mother into Telehemet's family's cabin and feeling more excited than nervous. We had our simple ceremony there in the twilight of our traveling day after we bathed and briefly rested. Esther stood behind me as Grandmother and Mother presented Telehemet's aunts with a few cakes of unleavened corn bread and dried venison, which is an earnest display of their skills over the cook-fire and the caring of their families. In return, Telehemet's aunts gave large gifts of cured bear and elk meat. If Telehemet's mother was alive, she would have presented these gifts to my family. These gifts demonstrate to my grandmother, my mother, and me that Telehemet has the ability to provide for his household. His two aunts are aged old moccasins with smiles circling half their faces and the light from the candles casts an appearance of glowing rings around their heads. There is warmth and love emanating from these two wise women. Sattelihu is visiting the men in the village and isn't needed for the exchange of gifts that concludes our binding contract. It's the responsibility of the mothers of our tribes to conduct the marriage ceremony. These mothers are responsible for harmony and concord not just between us, but for the entire tribe.

After the ceremony, I'm taken to another cabin to ready myself for Telehemet. I hope I'll be respected by my husband. I think of Anna and how white women must always submit themselves to their men and wait for their respect. While waiting for Telehemet to enter the cabin to be presented to me, I become more excited than worried.

And then there he is, my Telehemet. Tall, rugged, and somber, but in his eyes I see brightness of love and affection. He is resolute about this union and I know he'll always love me, even if he doesn't say so in words. We've already had friendship and the notes of our flutes have brought harmony and pleasure that often doesn't come until after being married a long time. I smile at him and immediately his serious demeanor disappears. He returns my smile with one so wide I see he has a few missing teeth. I've never noticed this before, but I'm not disappointed, for his big smile reveals he's pleased to become my husband. I laugh nervously and know that in years to come, I'll remember this wedding day and my Telehemet's trusting smile that showed missing teeth. We come together in an embrace that is tender and strong. We kiss lightly and then passionately, and soon we lie on the floor among the herb-scented blankets. I give myself to Telehemet in trust and excitement. When I feel pain, I'm unafraid, for Grandmother told me it would visit as an initiation to pleasure. "After this, Catrine, there'll be waves of joy that can come again and again." On our third night together, this suffering lessens and there's sweet measured tempo as our bodies move as one. No wonder Grandmother laughed so heartily when she gave me instruction for our union. I cannot help but feel this is only for me, this pleasure. I can't believe that all women experience this, too, for if they did, the women I know would be wearing much happier faces!

I'm relieved that Telehemet travels with us home to Pennsylvania and although Caneada is a beautiful valley, I want to live with Grandmother, Mother, my sisters, and family. As we journey back, I ask Sattelihu if we can stop at Eagle Cliff Falls, for this is what I have named them. He sternly says no as if they don't exist. He states proudly that he has to meet George Croghan and travel to Ohio to confront the rebellious Delawares and Shawnees who are always flirting with the French. I beg him to let us stop and Telehemet gives me a light swat on my backside. I'm surprised and look hard at him, but he only nods his head to indicate we must keep traveling. Grandmother's eyebrows rise when she sees this, but she turns away. I sting from his slap, although it was light. He has only been gentle with my body, although he's very lusty. Eagle Cliff Falls is where I go each night in my lovemaking with Telehemet and before I drift into sleep. And now I wonder if I've only dreamed of this powerful place.

After we settle back into our lives at Shamokin and Sattelihu leaves for Ohio, Telehemet tells me he's leaving in two days to go to the Seneca camp.

"Why not hunt with the Indians here, Telehemet?"

"I must visit my Seneca brothers."

"Are you going to hunt with them or are you going to war against the Catawbas?"

"I'm meeting my Seneca people and you don't need to question what I'm doing, Catrine."

He eventually returns from this trip and we are as close as before. One day when we're alone in a field behind the forest, he turns me over and gently slaps me on my backside. Again. Tears come to my eyes and I want to challenge him, but I don't want him to be angry with me. I trust him and desire him. He is not rough, but he hurts my dignity. Grandmother hasn't told me anything about this kind of behavior. Most Indian men never hit their women, but this is not really a strike against me, I tell myself, and it doesn't hurt. It's playful and the sting is from my pride and confusion. Telehemet laughs heartily and turns me over again to kiss and bring our bodies together in lovemaking. Again and again. Gentle and strong, my warrior. I forget about this odd behavior and only remember the delight of his hands now.

After, we sleep and when we wake, the afternoon sun is preparing for the day's end with a celebration of colors.

"When winter comes, I'll play my flute and you can read to me. You'll be warmth for my winter soul, Catrine."

I have told no one but Telehemet about the books Anna gave me. One was a very silly romantic story I had begged Anna to read to me. I could not imagine being dressed in layers of heavy clothing and being so simple, waiting to be wooed by a man of riches who wore a white wig. The other one is a small poetry book and this is the book Anna taught me from. I learned to read words that sang to my heart. I have no other books to read and I'm gratified for this one, although there are words I cannot understand or pronounce. Sometimes I play with words in my mind that tumble down my throat and out the door of my mouth. These are English, Indian, and sometimes French words that dance and sing to the Sky Mother. No one knows and sometimes I wonder if my words are poetry, too.

I think Telehemet is pleased to have me read from the poetry book because he knows no other Indian woman who can read.

"You are my heart's song," I reply, "I'll warm you with my own words when winter comes and not just read the ones from my book."

"I'm almost an elder, my years are advanced. You can see I wear the elder's colors in my hair," Telehemet said, laughing. He leans over me, his coffee-colored skin smooth and muscled with scars tattooed on his forearms.

August is hot and full of butterflies that flit from wildflower to wildflower. A painted lady butterfly lands on my arm and we watch it closely. How delicate. It flies away and Telehemet gently traces the path the butterfly landed with his tongue.

"I'm jealous of the butterfly who kissed you so sweetly and I must do the same!"

What woman is as loved as I am!

"Every day of the summer you must crush flower blossoms and rub them onto your cheeks to keep them pink and creamy. Your skin is not like mine or the other women. You shade is light and as soft as flower petals."

I close my eyes, inhaling summertime and Telehemet's scent that is not offensive. It's a mix of bear grease and the sweat of his labors from early morning work.

"We must enjoy music and words now, for soon children will come and occupy my time," I say to him. I've been dreaming a flower grows within me and since there has been no visitation of blood this month, I must be carrying Telehemet's baby. And now it's a good time to tell him this happy news.

Telehemet sits up and smiles, pulling me up, too, and onto his lap. He places his hands over my breasts and looks into my face intensely. I feel tenderness and I lean in to kiss him. He responds, kissing me back and searching my mouth with his tongue, wanting more. He pulls back and then places his hands on my belly and looks at me again with the same seriousness.

"You carry my child, for I feel it in your breasts and your mouth," he said, "for you have twice the heat than you had when we first joined together. I'm pleased, Catharine, and we'll teach the child to play the flute and read your words."

We embrace for a long time and I hope I'll have joy in bearing new life, for I crave the fullness of our love together and don't know if I want to share it with anyone.

THE YEARS PASS and Sattelihu and my family move again near Logstown in the Ohio Valley. My uncle is appointed an agent for Conrad Weiser and watches for the French coming into the Pennsylvania colony from Ohio. It's my third journey away from the land and village where I was born. My journey to

Lancaster a few years ago gave me a taste for adventure and the New York colony gave me love for a waterfall, but this trip to the Ohio Valley is exhausting and unpleasant. Even the trees seem to be ill at ease as they sway in the wind and we are always on the lookout for danger.

Telehemet continues his visits to the Seneca camp near Shamokin to hunt and from there to war against the Catawbas. Now that we're living in the Ohio Valley, it takes him longer to return to me. His visits are less and less. I'm disappointed my husband is gone more than he's at home, but when he's with me, there is much love making and conviviality. He's also tender and playful with our children and the children living in our home. Although our bodies come together as natural as water touching the shore, we aren't communicating well. Telehemet no longer asks me to read to him, nor does he play his flute. He's preoccupied and when he's here, he senses the dangers lingering nearby.

I birth two children and name them Roland and John. I've been so in love with Telehemet I thought it impossible to have any other love. My heart, quite the contrary, has expanded to welcome and love my children. I give thanks to the Great Spirit for my husband, children, and life. I cannot imagine loving as many men as Grandmother has loved.

Although Indians don't often profess love, Telehemet said to me, "I love my Catrine with the strange ways." He believes that the best blood is Indian blood and only mildly admires white people and so he thinks my strange ways are from being French. His first wife had opened her heart and legs for him, but she had been silent and there were no children. He laughs when he says now he has a wife who never stops talking and who is always ready for lovemaking. He doesn't know I talk little to my family, except to Grandmother. Telehemet makes me want to open my heart and let it bleed out in words only to him. But since our move and my children were born, there's been little time for us to be playful and talk together. I miss my visits to the woods to commune with Ga-oh and the Great Spirit and I've not been playing the flute. I'm very busy with our home, village, and children, but I'll always make time for Telehemet when he comes home to me. There are nights I can't sleep, fearing he won't return or will tire of traveling so far to me and our children.

Our buoyant happiness lasts only a few years and while it did, we didn't pay attention to the radical changes taking place around us. The long peace that had been in the colony of Pennsylvania between Indians and Europeans has ended. Since moving to the Ohio Valley, my family has been immersed in one another and the tasks at hand. We wished to ignore the conjuring and warring spirits swirling around us, but soon it becomes impossible.

Chapter Twelve

AFTER A LENGTHY separation, Telehemet comes home and we're as close as when we first married, but it's brief. Today, he took me to the edge of the woods and played his flute and said goodbye. He has only been with us for three days. There has been a re-kindling of our intimacy and I regret he has to leave again. He said Chief Shikellamy's son, John, and he have become close hunting brothers. Maybe because Shikellamy and his family have accepted my husband, he'll return more often. Shikellamy, like my grandmother, has had experience traveling in New York and Pennsylvania. They have understanding minds and tolerance for many kinds of people. My husband has become more accepting of white people, as well, after spending time with us and the missionaries. Sattelihu and Telehemet seem to never fully trust one another and my uncle doesn't speak many words when Telehemet is with our family. Sattelihu has become quieter and only speaks privately to Grandmother. Grandmother said he has to cleanse himself from activity so the flow of words can come and help bring understanding and signed treaties.

"We wash our vessels, do we not, Catrine? Likewise, your uncle needs his mind cleansed sometimes, too."

This makes sense, but I'm sorry my husband and uncle don't talk. Telehemet is tense when Sattelihu is home. I wonder if he is ill at ease when Sattelihu brings George Croghan to stay with us. Telehemet must sense my nervousness, for George looks at me with doe eyes and speaks to me when he gets a chance. But Telehemet never asks me about him or voices any judgment about my uncle or George Croghan. He knows George is well respected by the Indians and is skilled in their ways and languages. And if the chiefs believe he is a man of integrity, Telehemet believes it, too. My Telehemet is a peaceful man and sometimes I wonder how he can also be a warring man, but his many scars tell me otherwise.

Dark spirits prevail and although wampum was given for the terrible Jack Armstrong murders years ago and treaties are signed, distrust grows like fungus. Our Delaware and Shawnee neighbors continue to abandon the English for the French and these two European powers try to persuade the Indians to take sides. Many believe too much land was given away by the Ho-De'-No-Sau-Nee at the Lancaster Treaty and this will someday come to haunt us.

A YEAR PASSES without a visit from Telehemet and I become melancholy and fear he won't ever return to me. Grandmother sleeps too much these days and my children don't interest her as they once did when they were born. Her eyes don't see well and although she doesn't know who is near her, she always knows me. George Croghan has been at our home many times since Telehemet left a year ago. He and Sattelihu are like blood brothers, traveling together, interpreting and trying to keep the Indians from siding with the French. He doesn't make me uneasy now, but I don't know why we are always doing an invisible dance together.

And then Sattelihu declares we must move again. It's become unsafe, he says, to live in the Ohio Valley, and he's planning to take Grandmother to live in a special place in Pennsylvania. My mother, father, my sisters and brother, and my children and I will continue to reside with Grandmother and my uncle. I'm pleased to move away from this place and return to Pennsylvania. When we move, we'll have supplies from George Croghan's farm at Pennsboro. It seems I'm meant to have him nearby and I come to enjoy his company, but continue to hope for Telehemet to return.

Time passes and I'm lonely for the days of my girlhood with Grandmother and the dances in the forest to the Great Spirit. My simple dreams were only beginning then and now I fear they've gone by the wayside. I feel the loss of a husband, as if he's been taken to the ancestors. My children give me only so much contentment, as children should, but they cannot be a replacement for their father. I have no one to confide in and the Great Spirit and Sky Mother feel as distant to me as the sun, stars, and moon. In this state, I slowly respond to George Croghan's Irish charm as I wait for my husband to return.

THIS SUMMER'S BOUNTIFUL harvest removes from our minds the travail of the times and the upcoming move. My Roland has grown four or five years and plays with the older boys in the village. They're constantly swimming, running, climbing trees, and looking for adventure. He is tall and his skin is lighter than my own. My mother, Margaret, has insisted he learn French and he speaks this language, our Indian language, and English. He looks different from most of the village boys and when he speaks French, I try to imagine my French great grandfather. I'm proud of Roland. My uncle and I believe he'll someday be a mediator, a go between, and a real diplomat with the Europeans. George Croghan gives him special attention and Roland has warmed to him. Grandmother, I believe, has given up on me to do the great things she has done. I see her often squinting at Roland and asking him to sit beside her to listen to her stories. But I also fear for Roland, for there's an angry spirit about him.

One late hot August afternoon in the year 1749 I sit by the cool stream near our village to rest. Along with the other women, I've been harvesting our crops and the week has been busy with turning cornhusks into mats and dolls. I made a large pot of succotash early in the morning that we'll have in the evening and now I'm resting and thinking too much. Grandmother is now only able to see shapes and shadows. Sattelihu has taken time off from traveling with George Croghan and Mr. Weiser to take her on horseback to Venango to visit her grand-nephew, Nicolas. She's an old moccasin at eighty-one and her blindness affects me because I've been unable to see through her eyes the purpose for my life. I feel she's very disappointed with me. I've only wished for a happy union with Telehemet and a family life, not a life of adventure. Recently, Grandmother grabbed my leg as I walked by and said to me in a loud whisper, "You'll go to other places, Catrine, so ready yourself." When I sat down beside her and asked where I would go, she shook her head and was silent. I told her I only wanted to stay with our family and wait for Telehemet. She sighed. "I'm blind, Catrine, and you must see for me, sunflower girl."

I think of these things as I bathe my feet in the stream and try to find peace in the wind weaving sunlight through the trees. I remember how close I felt to the Great Spirit as I watched golden sunlight caress the green leaves of trees. I was ever so happy and content when I was in the forest and woods as a young girl. Now we're advised not to go far away from our village and homes, for the French have been making incursions into this valley to persuade the Indians, by any means, to trade with them. There have been many skirmishes and deaths.

I hear a sound behind me and turn quickly to see Esther rushing toward me. I jump up to meet her and note she's out of breath and crying.

"Roland is missing! He didn't return with the other boys from playing. I told them not to go beyond the fields, but they didn't listen and drifted near the woods. The older boys were frightened and left, but Roland refused to leave. My sister, your son doesn't listen to the older boys and is disobedient."

I hurry with Esther toward our home and tell her that Roland knows the woods well and is brave like his father.

Esther stops and faces me. "You're always in a dreamy world and don't face the truths of life. Our mother is worried for you. And now this has happened!"

Esther married a young warrior a few years ago and has had three children already. Her husband and our father are close and hunt much together. Neither he nor my father are that friendly to Telehemet. They haven't had time to get to know one another because Telehemet is gone most of the time and when he's here, my father and Esther's husband are usually on a hunt.

"What truths should I face, Esther?"

"That Telehemet has another wife far from here and isn't a good husband and father as he should be."

I turn from Esther and rush ahead. I yell back at her, "You speak lies, Esther, and don't know the great warrior and good man he is to me and our children."

We return and my mother and the children are waiting for us. My father and men in the village assess what is happening and agree to go on a search party for Roland. There are five strapping young warriors and two white men. I tell them I want to go with them, but they advise I stay with the women and wait.

The men leave and I sit with the other children and ask them about the last time they saw Roland. My mother and Esther leave and continue working on harvesting the corn and other crops. They said there is nothing they can do but wring their hands and they'd rather work with their hands.

Esther's son, Jacob, a wiry four year old who wishes to be older, tells me, "We chased a turkey and wanted a bow and arrow. We chased the ugly thing into the forest and sat down laughing. Roland wasn't sitting with us and we called for him."

"We didn't dare go into the forest, but when we called for him, he yelled he didn't want to come back yet," Jacob's brother, Eli, says.

"He was deep inside the forest," Jacob says.

"No, he wasn't . . . he was on the edge of the forest. I saw him," Eli says and the two brothers argue, reminding me of Esther and myself when we were children.

My son, John, is four years and sits wide-eyed and quiet.

"John, did you see your brother go into the forest?" I ask. It was the first time the older boys had allowed Roland to bring his younger brother.

John cries and rushes to sit on my lap. I hold him and cuddle him, this boy whose features remind me so much of his father's.

"Roland was talking in the forest. He was invisible. I saw him and then I didn't see him."

"Was your brother talking to an Indian or was he talking to a white man?"

John cries harder and shakes his head. "I don't know. He was invisible."

ALTHOUGH THE SUN has ripened the fields and the essence of bounty is everywhere, I stay inside our cabin with the children. I feel the need to be secluded with them. If only my friend, Anna, was here visiting now. As much as the prayers of the missionaries irritate me, Anna's prayers are genuine and strong. I give the children tasks in husking corn and making food for the next day. Soon my mother and sisters come in looking weary and distressed. I suggest they sit down to eat and serve them to keep my mind from thinking too much. John clings to me so I ask him to help serve our mothers with me. He helps and then we serve the children their succotash and other food I've prepared. I dish out food for both of us and we sit together to eat. He looks away in the distance and hardly eats. We're all quiet and the hopeful light of day dims. After we eat, we become sleepy and although Roland's name isn't spoken, we only think of him. I help put the children to sleep and then rush back and forth to the door to see if the men are returning with Roland. When I see the bright orange sun lowering itself to sleep behind the earth, I panic. It will soon be dark and my son is not home and the conjuring spirits will be creating havoc. I retrieve my blanket and go to my mother and Esther sitting in the corner of the cabin.

"I'm going to the field before night settles in with blackness. I'll be careful. I can no longer wait here for Roland, but must look for him."

Little John gets up from his mat and rushes to me, cries, and clings to my leg. Esther picks him up and soothes him.

"You're foolish to go where there is danger, Catrine. Please stay here with all of us."

"We have to be patient and pray to Jesus," my mother says.

I turn to leave before I change my mind.

I stand at the edge of the woods and listen to the late summer crickets and owls crying out their messages. I think of the ritual of cleansing my people do after someone has been deep into the woods on travels. There are dangers in the forest and one can return with many changes. I have never been afraid of being changed by the woods. Maybe if I go now into the deep woods, I'll be able to find Roland. As I ponder my son and his fearlessness, I consider plunging myself into these woods and trust that the spirits I've loved will guide me to him. But it's dusk and getting too dark and it's a foolish thought, a desperate one that only a mother would consider.

"Great Spirit, where are you and where's my son?" I cry aloud.

"The Great Spirit is everywhere, Catharine Montour," a voice behind me responds.

Surprised, I turn to see an old grandmother of our people. I hadn't noticed the moon, half of its face hidden from us. It's illuminating the old woman's face now.

"Your son will be found. I've seen that he's with friends of the Montours."

"What friends and why do they not bring him to me?" I ask.

"I don't know, but he's safe."

"Are you a medicine woman?"

"Your grandmother and I were friends years ago and I've come to visit her. I am Queen Alliquippa and live not far from you."

"I've heard of you. You're a sovereign of your people. It's George Croghan who has spoken well of you."

My face reddens as I say his name and sense this old woman sees this, even in the dark. She moves close to me and places her hand on my shoulder and shuts her eyes. I want to rush back to my home. Medicine women and Christian missionary women often think they know everything. I sigh and stand awkwardly until she opens her eyes and smiles.

"Yes, it's George Croghan, my good friend. And your son is with him and he'll be safe . . ."

"George Croghan has no right to keep him from me! How did Roland end up with him?"

Queen Alliquippa steps back and ponders my face. I want to shake her, to shake someone.

"Roland doesn't know where George Croghan's trading posts are. And why would he want to go to him? My uncle is George's friend and they work together . . . why would George Croghan steal my child?"

"He hasn't stolen your child. He has saved your child."

"How do you know this?"

"I don't know how Roland ended up with George Croghan. But I have visions and when I came to the door of your cabin, I immediately saw a light-skinned boy with George at his large trading post a few miles from here. Your son has been saved from something or someone with evil intent. I know George Croghan and know that your son will be safe. How he came to him, I don't know."

"How can I believe you?"

"You have lost your vision, but it will return in time. For now, trust me. There's nothing to be done this dark night. Come, let's return to the cabin and drink some tea. We'll go to your son tomorrow."

This queen of her people, like my grandmother, places her authoritative hand on my shoulder again and I wonder why someone is always trying to guide my life.

We return to the cabin and much tension disappears being next to this very strong and impressive woman who has visions. Maybe it's the Great Spirit who has brought this medicine woman to me, and if so, maybe I'll be able to return to a place of peace once Roland is found.

Chapter Thirteen

QUEEN ALLIQUIPPA LIVES on an island not far from Logstown. She is the sovereign of the Mingo people who are independent Ho-De'-No-Sau-Nee, mostly mixed Seneca and Cayuga hunters. Three miles from her home, just upstream from where the Allegheny joins the Monongahela, is the Delaware village of Shannopin. Nearby trails and waterways are travelled by both French and English traders. It's a place of lush beauty, as well as fierce loyalties and upheavals. This is why Queen Alliquippa plays an important role in these times. And it's why Sattelihu was originally sent to observe the French, their trading, and incursions into Pennsylvania. George Croghan, the charmer and excellent gamesman, has a post three miles upstream from Shannopin. This post is close to his friends, Queen Alliquippa and the Montours. From this location, George Croghan and my uncle can easily travel the waterways together to gather information.

Queen Alliquippa receives goods and necessities from George Croghan and likes his good humor and generosity. She's a woman who possesses wisdom and vision, but is blind to some of the ways of this man. Perhaps this is because she and he are of the same spirit, each believing in their absolute power.

No one can ignore this queen. Colonial agents, military officers, and her own people don't want to incur her wrath. Conrad Weiser recently traveled near her village on his way to a council meeting. When Queen Alliquippa learned that he had passed by without stopping, she sent word demanding he come and pay tribute. He quickly acquiesced and brought her gunpowder and match coats. She's fiercely committed to the British and for this, she demands loyalty and gifts. She and my grandmother, Madame Montour, are friends. Grandmother likewise expects respect, but Queen Alliquippa demands it. And so it's been given to both of them for their loyalty and work to bring together the various peoples of the regions. Queen Alliquippa exchanges information for the goods that George Croghan stores at his trading post and this gives her continued respect from the Mingos and others. She can then have her people's ear and thus oversee their lives. As a child, she was a seer, and it plummeted her into one travail after another until she gained wisdom as an adult. The seer in her remains, but its path has taken a different course, one that includes acquisition of earthly goods. When Queen Alliquippa traveled to visit Madame Montour, her friend from many years before, the seer in her was awakened when she found me distraught by the edge of the woods.

THE NEXT MORNING just after sunrise, Sattelihu and Grandmother return from the trip to Venango and we tell them what has happened to Roland. My uncle says he will take Queen Aliquippa and myself to George Croghan's post.

"Roland will be well and George will help us."

Sattelihu turns away from everyone, overcome with emotion. His wife has left him again and is living in Shamokin. He's preparing to move away from this tumultuous place in Ohio and back to the familiarity of Pennsylvania. Grandmother is nearly blind now and he wants her to be at peace and also hopes his wife will join him there.

Grandmother feels her way around the cabin and hugs her friend, Queen Alliquippa. She is tired, but vigorously welcomes her friend from long ago.

"I've lost my vision, Alliquippa. My outer vision is no longer, but my inner vision is stronger. I'm at peace about our Roland being with George Croghan if you have seen this in your mind. You and I both trust this man."

My mother, father, Esther, her children, my brothers, and my son, John, have risen from their beds and the scent of corn bread and sweetness is strong in our cabin. Queen Alliquippa helps Grandmother to the cook fire and they ask me to sit with them. They pull me down between them and the three of us are quiet as Esther places food in our hands. Sattelihu leaves the cabin to gather his thoughts and strength for another journey so soon after traveling with Grandmother. My mother reaches for the kettle over the fire and pours from it. She places a steaming mug of dried strawberries infused with maple syrup in my hand. Our dried berries are usually saved for the winter months when we need to ward off the sicknesses that winter brings. It's a luxury to have it in the summer and my mother is offering me comfort.

"Mother, thank you. I'm grateful for you and Grandmother." My mother places her hands on my shoulders and prays to Jesus in the French language and steps away to feed the children. Queen Alliquippa and Grandmother each place a hand on my shoulder and I listen to prayers in the Indian language. I close my eyes to these soothing sounds and find some peace.

BY THE TIME we arrive at George Croghan's trading post three miles up the Cuyahoga River by canoe, the little peace I had dissipates. I'm overcome with fear for my son and vow to never let him or my son, John, out of my sight until they become warriors.

There's commotion in front of the trading post when we arrive. A few Indians argue as they surround a barrel of rum. One of the Indians strikes another with a cup and they struggle and fall to the ground. George Croghan rushes out the door of the two story log house and shouts in their language at them. They immediately get up and stagger off into a field. George greets us with a big smile and, looking at me, grasps my hands with much emotion.

"Where's my son?"

"He's here, Catrine . . . here safe with me."

I pull my hands away and rush up the steps and into the trading post.

I smell men's over wrought sweat and the musky odor of animal pelts. I like the scent that is earthy, but the men's sweat is greedy and not like the odor on Telehemet's skin after the hunt. A rancid and pungent smell of animal fat that hasn't been scraped well emanates in the stale air. I'm familiar with all these aromas of animals and don't mind, but it's the men's scent that sticks in my throat and makes me cough. It's much worse than the rotten smell of un-scraped fat on skins.

My eyes adjust to the darkness of the trading house. There's a long table in front of the door and a white man is packing beaver furs in a large wooden box. A leather bound book for logging information sits next to the box. I look around and see shelves with furs on one side and shelves with European goods on the other. A few men are working, but there are no children to be seen. The door slams behind me and George Croghan, Queen Alliquippa, and my uncle stand next to me.

"Where's my son?"

George takes my hand and leads me to a stairway at the back of the room and Queen Alliquippa and my uncle follow behind us. Halfway up the stairs, George turns to us.

"Roland is playing with another child and the child's mother is looking after both of them. Your son, Catharine, was brought to me by Orontony who found him in the woods. He assumed Roland was French because your boy would only speak French, not English. As you know, the French persuade the Indians to trade with them, but then cheat them after they've been given furs. Chief Orontony has been unsure of who to be loyal to and when he thought he found a French boy in the woods, he wanted to use him as ransom to get the goods owed to him for furs given to the stinking French traders. When Roland started crying on the boat that his uncle Satttelihu Montour would kill Orontony for stealing him, Orontony came to his senses. He brought Roland here, fearing to face Andrew, and, of course, the mother of the boy."

George looks at my uncle and then smiles at me before continuing up the stairs. My heart is pounding over how close my dear Roland had come to being given to the French. Anger rises against my mother, for she has insisted my children learn French and use it in our everyday lives, just as we had to as children.

Roland comes to me and we embrace and sit on the floor, weeping and clinging to one another. Eventually, Roland and I gain control of our emotions and George invites us to have something to eat. The Indian woman, a Delaware, with her son, leads us outside to the cook fire. I look around for Queen Alliquippa, but she has disappeared. A few fur traders and George's friends come to sit with us. The Delaware woman serving us is older than me and beautiful. She is especially attentive to George and, looking at her son, I wonder if he's George Croghan's child. He isn't married and maybe this woman is his for comfort when he isn't traveling. He's always on the go with pack horses loaded with goods and he doesn't stay long at any of his trading posts and houses. This is the way of men, I think. I look over by the trading post and George and my uncle are engrossed in a serious conversation. George glances at me and I look away. The men around the fire talk among themselves and one asks where we live, but other than this, I'm quiet and the woman serving us doesn't speak to me. Roland and I finish eating, give our thanks to the woman, and say goodbye to the men at the cook fire. We go to Sattelihu and George and wait for them to end their conversation. I'm suddenly anxious and wish to be home safe with John, Roland, and my family.

"Sattelihu, we should leave. If we leave soon, we'll be able to be at home before dusk."

"We'll leave now, Catrine. I was waiting for you and Roland to have refreshment."

George touches my uncle's arm and turns to me. "Before you leave, Catharine, I've gifts for you and your mothers. Come with me into the post and I'll show you."

"Roland and I'll wait for you here. Hurry, Catrine," Sattelihu says.

I reach for Roland.

"He can come, too."

Roland squirms away from me and smiles at Sattelihu. "I'll go with my uncle to prepare the canoe."

"Good lad, Roland. Go on ahead to the river with Andrew. I'll bring your mother there in a few minutes." George tussles Roland's hair.

George presses his palm on my lower back and guides me into the building. His touch is gentle and relieves tension in my body. Inside the trading post, we stand before the shelves of European goods received from merchants in Philadelphia.

"These will be given to the Indians for their furs, of course. All the way from London! Sometimes goods get a little worn by sea travel and sitting in Philly too long, but I won't accept anything inferior to be traded at my posts."

George pulls out a pair of red stockings and hands them to me.

"For you, Catrine . . . I would say that your loveliness needs no further adornment but when I saw these fine things, I bought them for you. You're a jewel in the crown of the Iroquois and as natural in your beauty as a wildflower."

I hold the stockings feeling shyness overtake me. I love the color and the feel of the stockings and I want them.

"A sunflower. Yes, I could name many flowers, but your brightness is a sunflower."

I'm surprised and embarrassed. Has he heard Grandmother call me her sunflower girl? He retrieves another item from the shelf.

"This is lace for your sewing," he says, placing a bolt of lace in my hands.

He turns to the shelves, looking for something else and I note his strong back and wavy hair that is brown with streaks of sunlight. I imagine running my hands through his hair and my face reddens. I don't know where this thought has come from. It's indeed George Croghan's strong medicine. He turns back to me and he must know I'm in the grip of his medicine, for he smiles and I return a smile.

"And here, please share these ribbons for all the women in your family."

My arms are full of his gifts. He turns yet again to the shelves. I shouldn't receive so many gifts from a man who isn't my husband or family member.

"Give this to your grandmother, for she's old and needs more warmth."

He places a beautiful blue blanket on top of the other gifts. He leads me to the long table and others stare, including the woman with her child I spy in the corner of the room.

"Thomas, secure all these items in a tight box for my friend and her family. She'll take them in the boat back to her home today. Bring them to us outside the post when you're done."

Thomas looks at George curiously, but mutters, "Yes, sir." I follow George out of the building and we stand at the bottom of the steps. He takes my hands in his.

"I admire you, Catrine, but not just your beauty. You possess mystery . . . and presence. There's strength in you and I feel there's much more you'll do in your life. I don't know what it is . . ."

I slowly pull my hands out of his, overcome with emotion.

"I'm sorry if I've said something inappropriate, Catrine."

I look sharply at him after wiping tears from my eyes. "Only those in my family call me Catrine. You have no right to do so."

I've hurt his feelings and his smile dims. We're silent for a few moments, but continue to read one another's faces. I read much and I think he does, too.

The door opens and the box of gifts is given to George. We walk to the river where Sattelihu and Roland are waiting. He nervously chatters non-stop about his trading posts and his travels.

"Andrew is moving with your grandmother to settle on Penn lands again. They'll be at Lowther Manor on the Conodoguinet Creek. I'm assuming you and the rest of the family will move there, too. This is good news, for Andrew will keep the land from squatters and safe for Indian use only. My farm at Pennsboro will provide you with food and whatever else you need."

"Yes, and my husband, Telehemet, will return and live with us there."

"I see . . ."

We come to the river's edge and Sattelihu and Roland are in the canoe ready to go. Sattelihu stands up and George hands the box to him.

"Special gifts for Catri . . . Catharine and the others."

Sattelihu grimaces and takes the box.

George helps me into the canoe and our eyes meet before he turns to Sattelihu.

"I'll be visiting soon, Andrew. Weiser and the chiefs are meeting in Logstown to discuss the Ohio Valley. This conference will happen before your move back to Pennsylvania."

I sit next to Roland and hold him close to me, smelling his special scent. Yes, George Croghan has kept my son safe and although he's a man who talks big, he does big things, and he also has a heart larger than many. I smile and wave goodbye as we float away. Sattelihu looks at me with curiosity and my face reddens.

Chapter Fourteen

IN OCTOBER 1750, we move again to Penn lands at Lowther Manor on the little Conodoguinet Creek across the Susquehanna from Harris Ferry. It's fairly safe here and easy to get to Philadelphia and Shamokin. It's a perfect location for Sattelihu, George Croghan, and others for their travels. We have plenty to live on and some of our food is provided by George Croghan's farm at Pennsboro and the goods that come from Harris Ferry. Our house is full of people all the time, including our Moravian friends living nearby. My friend, Anna, is not here for she married the Count and they're traveling to convert the Indians to Jesus.

We have peaceful Indians living among us, although when the rum flows they lose that peace and start railing against the Montours, complaining we've become the white men's slaves. Yes, they're jealous, for we have cattle and horses and live abundantly. My mother, Margaret, and my father, are going to move again closer to Shamokin and Mother said she'll call her land, Margaret's Town. I don't want to go with her, but my children and I require the protection of her care, for I've not seen Telehemet in nearly two years. Esther and her children will move with her, too, for her husband is always away on warring and hunting parties. When Esther's husband returns to her, he gives her more babies. I'm worried that if my children and I go with my mother, I'll miss living with Grandmother. Her burdens placed on me are less now, but even if I disliked them at times, they've always come with keen insight. She's a happy, worn-out old moccasin, her eyes are blind, but there are times her soul still envisions the future. In Margaret's Town, I'll have the endless teachings of my mother's Jesus and Esther's boasting of her husband's strength and thighs. I'm still young and listening to their grunting and groaning when her husband returns creates longing for Telehemet.

When we move back to Penn's lands, we grieve to learn that malaria has ravaged the Indian people here. Allumpapes died and Sattelihu is sorrowful because Allumpapes had been as a father to him. And now Sattelihu's wife refuses to live with him and has left him for good. Our dear, clear-sighted Shikellamy suffered the most and greatly, for his wife and his son-in-law, daughter-in-law, and ten grandchildren died from malaria. There has been too much loss at once.

During this time, our new home is filled with the burning of herbs for mourning. The Moravians come to comfort Shikellamy and he's so distraught he's convinced he must travel to Bethlehem to learn more of Jesus. My mother is all for this and wants to go with him, but stays at home. Shikellamy leaves with the Moravians, taking off his necklace of the Manitou, our symbol of the Great Spirit. When he returns from Bethlehem, he collapses and dies. Our dear Shikellamy was grieving and vulnerable when he was asked to give up his Indian beliefs.

I feel the heavy spirit of death and mourning in our community and this is natural for a time, but it shouldn't linger. When I was younger, I wasn't fearful of death because I had seen the Great Spirit cloak the dead trees in winter with the snows of comfort that brought renewal in spring. They slept only for a time. How foolish I was. Some flowers don't return in spring and some trees die forever. There are a great many endings without beginnings, for Telehemet has not come home to me and his children. And our Shikellamy cast aside his Great Manitou necklace and has left us. My tears flow for many reasons, right along with the other mourners in our village and home.

Time passes and peace comes again for us. I think of all that has happened and how I've changed from being a sunflower girl to a rose with thorns. For a rose is a woman's flower, whereas a sunflower is frivolous and more suitable for a young girl.

George Croghan is a loyal friend to my uncle. He often reminds Sattelihu that the oak tree in Ireland is most revered because of its strength and he and Sattelihu are like oak trees and kings of the forest. I'm unsure if there can be more than one king in a kingdom, but for now these two men are glad for their influence in negotiations and acquisitions.

When George learns that our village and his friend and brother are in sorrow, he comes bearing gifts and his charm. Everyone is comforted, and especially me.

Grandmother pleaded with Shikellamy to keep his necklace of the Great Manitou, but he wanted nothing more to do with it. He said God punished him for not believing in Jesus and this was why so many of his family died from malaria. When Grandmother said the Manitou and God were the same and not to lose hope, he thrust the necklace into her hands and whispered to her to bury it. Grandmother didn't bury the necklace and as she has always done with certain burdens, she placed the Manitou around my neck. And when Shikellamy died, I didn't want to wear the Manitou and was ready to do what Shikellamy wanted Grandmother to do and that was to bury this necklace.

WEEKS LATER, I'M alone and it's so rare! My mother is busy in Shamokin and has taken Esther, my children, and her children with her. My father has gone on a hunt and I feel free, although Grandmother is here and always resting. Sattelihu has also gone to Shamokin to be with Allumpapes' family to help with their grieving and his own. And although he does not say, he's hoping his wife will return with him.

It's a warm late April evening, the time of the gloaming when any hardness of a day melts away. The tree limbs wear a crown of newborn green that reach up to the sky. A singular large maple has flowered and bloomed red, showing off before its leaves turn green. I sit on the ground to bury the Manitou necklace near the trunk of this tree. It's been a long time since I've felt love from nature and the Great Spirit, as I haven't had time to be alone without the noisome clan we've become. Tears fall onto the Manitou necklace I hold in my hands and then lay upon the earth.

A few minutes later, there's a gentle touch upon my shoulder and I slowly turn to see the face of George Croghan. Above his head, the sky has turned midnight blue and is filled with stars that wrap around us as a necklace, like a great Manitou necklace. He sits beside me and we embrace and come together as natural and real as the maple that witnesses our love.

We speak no words as we love one another as pure as the sky has loved the earth. I have no remorse. The earth beneath the tree is wet with dew and my tears and it becomes our bed. The wind breathing in the leaves matches our own while our limbs entwine. A barred owl calls out a lonely cry as our longings are met.

Our lovemaking is like a summer storm that comes and leaves, one that is full of thrill and refreshment. After, I speak to him of the stories in the stars and play my flute for him. Later, I wonder why I feel it was the first time I opened my womanhood to someone. Some questions cannot be answered in the present and only time will give meaning.

TELEHEMET RETURNS TO me a month after George Croghan left for Pickawillany. Grandmother's eyes, although unseeing, have followed me curiously ever since the night George and I loved one another beneath the maple tree. I say nothing to her and don't feel shame, for I have experienced passion of a different color than what I've had with my husband. These long times without Telehemet have also shown me we both are our own people and not two trees rooted from one trunk. I've always admired a circle of trees bound together, but not all can live so closely. I love my Telehemet and he loves me. I'm also not unwise about his need for another and just as my sister, Esther, said, he has another wife. I don't ask if he has other children, for I don't want to know. I'm not surprised by this news, nor am I saddened. This is why I must have become a rose and am no longer a sunflower.

Telehemet is as vigorous in lovemaking as ever and although I enjoy our physical closeness, I'm not as eager with him as I once was. I had longed for him whenever he quickly left me after our unions. Now I'm as accepting of his leave taking as I am of the changing seasons. He's attentive and playful with his two boys, but seems to caress John more than Roland. It has occurred to me it's because Roland is more European in appearance and character than our John.

I tuck away my thoughts of George Croghan and place them beneath the old maple tree. He is in Pickawillany and curiously doesn't visit Sattelihu at our home as he once did, but my uncle spends the winter of 1751 with him at his trading post with the Miamis. French incursions have become more common in the area and Sattelihu, George, and others are vigilant. Telehemet left in autumn and I don't expect to see him again until summer of next year. By this time, I'll have birthed another child. The baby I carry is George Croghan's and not Telehemet's, as I counted the days since being with George.

Chapter Fifteen

George Croghan

GEORGE IS WORRIED about Old Briton. He is one of his favorite Indian friends and the old chief's superstitions are getting the best of him.

"What's got into your head, Old Briton, to worry so much? The French have pomp and fury in their threats, but we're fairly safe here. Yes, old man, some French-allied tribes are settling into the Ohio region and are all around us, but you and the Miamis left the French. And more Indians will, too! The English care more for your creature comforts than the French. You . . . we outnumber the French bastards."

Old Briton, or Memeskia, a Miami, was once aligned with the French and lived with his tribe near the Maumee River. At one time he liked the French except they smelled worse than the English. He was pleased at first that they had established an outpost called Fort Miamis to do business with him and his people. But when the Pennsylvania traders, including the friendly George Croghan, traveled further into the Ohio Valley bearing greater goods than the French, it was a new story for Memeskia. There were few shipments arriving from France because they were occupied with a war with the Austrians. Eventually, it was Memeskia who led a faction of his people to move sixty miles to form the town of Pickawillany and trade with George Croghan and other Pennsylvania traders.

"I see a blood-filled sky in my dreams, my brother, and it is not good. You and Sattelihu have spent two winters here to rally the Illinois Nation to the English, but it will be in vain in the end. You will suffer, too, and I fear you will leave all of us."

George throws a blanket over the old Indian's shoulder as they sit around a fire outside the log house. "I hope my ancestors won't be calling me for a long time."

"No, George, not leaving the earth, but leaving the Ohio Valley . . . Pennsylvania . . ."

"No worries, my friend . . . no worries. I have too much at stake in these parts and I won't be leaving them."

Old Briton drops his head, puffs on his pipe, and stares into the fire. George looks up into the sky at the stars and sighs. He remembers the stars the night he and Catharine were together at Lowther Manor. She told him stories about the stars and played her flute for him. His head falls heavy to his chest and he does what he has been doing ever since that night with Catharine—reliving it vividly in his mind.

Catharine

TWO WINTERS PASS and my mother and father have not moved. Belle, my sweet daughter, is pale skinned as her father, George Croghan, but no one makes comment. I'm sure they see she favors me, not Telehemet. When Sattelihu comes home from Pickawillany, he gives me trinkets and cloth from George and I hide them away for Belle. I'll give them to her when she's grown and I tell her about her father. My uncle doesn't say anything, but smiles as he places George's gifts in my hands. George always sends blankets or beads to my grandmother and mother, so my gifts are not singular. How I wish George would send me a message, but maybe he doesn't know I can read some words. I consider sending him one, but what can I say to him with poor writing? Should I tell him about Belle and will he want to see her? And could we ever come together again under the maple tree? I try to put away the longing for George and in its place, I have Belle and carry the warmth of the love we had that one night. These days I feel a certain contentment. I have my three children and a rambunctious and lively family. And eventually I come to not mind the many days without Telehemet and when he does come home to me, it is merely pleasant.

One day, Grandmother catches me alone by the cook fire. The men, young and old, are out on a hunt and the younger children are playing by the field their mothers are working in. My Belle sits near me playing with a corn husk doll as I stir a stew in a pot over the fire.

"My mind is not as dimmed as my eyes, Catrine. I touch Belle and know she is not Telehemet's child. And in the sunlight, I have seen her eyes sparkle the blue of a cloudless sky."

I turn to her, surprised she knows my secret. It's been over two years and she hasn't said anything to me until now. I quit stirring the pot and sit across from her, knowing I cannot escape.

"Yes, Grandmother, Belle is George Croghan's daughter. And Telehemet doesn't know this. Am I to be tarred and feathered like the white women who are unfaithful to their husbands? I've not been unfaithful to Telehemet anymore than he has been to me."

"I wish you no shame, daughter. I had children from many men I loved. Shame over love and passion is the burden of the missionaries and white men and women."

"Why have you not spoken to me about Belle before this time, Grandmother? Why not speak to me of your other children and grandchildren?"

"Your love for George Croghan was for you to share with me, Catrine, but you never confided in me. Your mother doesn't have eyes to see. My inner seeing eyes are better than your mother's. But I'm glad Margaret doesn't see, for she is a follower of the missionaries' ways more than any of us. I don't know what she would say to you. She declares no drink be allowed and next, I fear, she'll tell us we must not spread our legs like we're made to do. But me, an old moccasin, need not worry. But you, Catrine, are made for love and it sorrows me to see you with so little of it in your life. And about my French children . . . they are in my past and in my heart. We send many messages to one another."

I'm flustered, for as is typical with Grandmother, she reveals the very heart of a matter. I don't feel my life unloved, but now Grandmother's words make me feel I'm an empty vessel without real love from a man. George has given me the love of Belle and I don't miss Telehemet as I once did. Maybe I see myself as an old cow that doesn't milk as much anymore. I might be happy to be left alone grazing and chewing the cud, for I'm pleased with my children and memories.

"You are still a young woman and George Croghan is a lusty man. How can you not wish for more of one another?"

"He doesn't visit with Sattelihu as he once did and I have a husband."

"Telehemet doesn't come often and when he does, are you satisfied?"

"I am content, Grandmother."

"Is that all you want from your life and not to be a vessel of passion and purpose as your grandmother was before she became an old moccasin?"

"What is my purpose?"

I stand up and walk around the room nervously.

"Am I to wish for more than this? I have warmth and love of family, as well as a husband, even if he doesn't come to me often. I have the seasons of the Great Spirit, I have food and . . ."

"And a spirit that has not yet become vibrant with vision for her people and hope for peace with the Europeans who take our lands and belittle us."

"We, the Montours, are not belittled! We're respected and given gifts. You and Sattelihu have worked hard for what we have. The horses and cattle are the envy of other Indians. Who are my people? I'm Indian and French! And Sattelihu is an interpreter and respected by the Iroquois Council and in Philadelphia. Now the Virginia Company is asking him to help them . . . how much more . . ."

"Catharine, I see you in my visions going to Philadelphia and helping to bring peace and understanding . . ."

"No, Grandmother! I'm not like you or my uncle. And I'm not like my mother who likes to speak up at meetings. I'm most happy to be in the fields and woods, to be right here in a home cooking and sewing . . ."

"You are still too young to know yourself, Catrine. I hope you'll remember my words."

"I'll always remember your words, Grandmother, but I'm a woman and mother now and know my heart. I cannot be as you were and I'm sorry for disappointing you, but you're right about one thing . . . I am in need of more love than I receive from Telehemet, but I don't know what I can do."

I would like to hide my feelings from Grandmother, but it's impossible. I decided years ago I could live with the love given to me whenever it came. I'm more of a solitary person that the other women in my family, anyway. But now Grandmother's words dig deep into my heart and bring up the truth that I do want more. I don't want to always wait for Telehemet and become an old moccasin before my time.

"Catharine, come back to the fire and sit by me. For now, I will accept that you don't want to go to Philadelphia and be fawned over by the wealthy ladies as I was, but you could accompany your uncle. I cannot accept your life being full of loneliness when you're a special, smart young woman."

"I cannot accept it, either, Grandmother."

"Then go to George Croghan and tell him about Belle."

I sit down next to Grandmother and she wraps the blue shawl that George gave her over my shoulders. Little Belle crawls over to us and Grandmother places the shawl over her. The three of us sitting together feels just right for now.

"If you desire his love and he desires you, and I know he does, then be discreet, but give yourself. I've watched George adore you for many years, ever since you were a young girl. You were once frightened by his attention, but as you have matured into a woman, let go of the fear in love."

My tears flow quietly as I think up a plan to visit George Croghan.

Chapter Sixteen

"PLEASE, SATTELIHU, SIT with me by the fire. I have something important to tell you."

He has just returned from the Iroquois Council in Onondaga. Sattelihu is fair and even tempered in his diplomatic life, although there are times he drinks to excess and is solemn. I gaze at his face and feel compassion for him, for he's tired and his mind is elsewhere. His spirit has not yet settled back into his beautiful home with all of us. The important rituals Indians perform after travel through the woods my uncle doesn't have time for. Like my mother, he believes in Jesus, but he's mostly happy with Jesus when the missionaries are here. I place a cup of elderberry tea in his hands after he sits down and stares into the fire without drinking.

"My Belle is George's daughter. She's not Telehemet's."

Sattelihu doesn't take his gaze from the fire, but drinks his tea all at once and sets his cup down before he speaks.

"I've watched George's eyes follow you over the years. I've keenly watched to see if he was disrespectful in any way and didn't find him to be. He's a man who enjoys women, but never have I seen him mistreat a woman, nor an Indian, for that matter. Although he and I have never spoken about you, I believe he has admired you all these years."

Sattelihu turns his serious gaze on me and I look into his face seeking his thoughts . . . and hope for understanding.

"I thought that after you and Telehemet married, George would be careful to stay away from you and you from him."

"I want to visit George and tell him that we have a daughter. I'd like to bring Belle with me. Will you take us to him, Sattelihu? I don't want to travel alone and you're planning to meet with him in Pickawillany."

Sattelihu stands up and walks around the room as he talks. I'm glad Grandmother had convinced everyone to leave the house on this crisp late autumn day. We have privacy and I don't want my mother and Esther to know about Belle and my plans.

"You'll have to wait a few months and then the snows will come. It'll be difficult travel. George and I'll spend another winter at Pickawillany to keep trade honest and the Miamis and George's employees protected from the French. There's a large stockade that keeps the storehouses and people safe, but it will still be dangerous for you and for all of us. There's talk the French are going to strike. And George . . . Catrine, I don't want you to be disappointed . . ."

"He has a woman?" I ask.

"She's been a friend. Indian, yes. He's tentative about her, but talks of marriage and asks me my opinion, but I stay quiet and so he waits . . ."

"Then I won't disturb him . . . them . . . their plans for union . . ."

I get up and busy myself at the cook fire, preparing for our next meal. Grandmother's right, I'm becoming discontent being here so much. Later, this home will be filled with little ones and family members and never do I have the quiet I need. I must let George Croghan leave my thoughts, just as I have tried to let Telehemet come and go in my life. But what do I do with my longings? I'm not a mere animal who wishes to satisfy natural hungers. Where is a man like him?

Sattelihu stops pacing and comes near me.

"But she . . . George's friend, is in Pickawillany. And right now, he's not there, but at Croghan's Gap, five miles from Harris Ferry. There'll be much going on there, as usual. Traders, emissaries, and missionaries stopping there. Ha! George can't get enough land, it seems. The Seneca nation just gave George 200,000 acres, but this 300 acre tract at the Gap is where he likes to call home. Home with lots of people coming and going. I'll send a message to him that we're coming . . ."

"No. Let me surprise him and see his honesty. I don't want him to prepare for me."

"But I must contact him, for George is always on the go. I'll tell him I'm coming to talk about strategy for the winter at Pickawillany."

"Can we tell our family that I go to assist you?

"I'd like to believe, as would your grandmother, you mean to assist me."

My face flushes and agitation creeps into my belly. So Sattelihu and Grandmother have spoken about me taking up their work. My uncle's face is so earnest that I can't contradict him. I smile and bow my head in respect before returning to the cook fire.

UNCLE, BELLE, AND I arrive a week later at Croghan's Gap, George's home situated between the Blue Mountains in the Cumberland Gap. The sun is near setting and vivid orange and red colors splash over the trees and his impressive stockade and buildings. There are many log warehouses that provide storage for skins, furs, and Indian goods. A large tract of land is used for a tanyard. Belle rides in front of me on my horse and when we ride through the gate, I see many people, mostly men, Indian and white, bustling with urgency. The air is thick with smoke and the scent of animals being tanned. I suddenly feel nervous and out of place.

A few Indians recognize Sattelihu and rush to greet him and take his horse. One of the Indians, a young man my age with beautiful dark skin and a gentle face, smiles at me. He helps Belle down and as I climb off my horse, he wraps his hands around my waist and lifts me easily and sets me down. Belle rushes to hide in my skirts. She sees many people coming and going at our home, but this place is three times larger than ours.

"Is George Croghan about?" Sattelihu asks.

"He's in his house by the river. I can take you to him," the young man says, still smiling at me.

Another Indian takes my horse and the young man who tells us his name is George because he honors George Croghan, leads us through a field between buildings to a large log home by the river. Flowers grow outside his door and blue morning glories climb up the posts of his porch. George appreciates beauty and isn't only about business. We stand before the house while Indian George knocks on the door and lets himself inside. Belle fidgets with the bells attached to my skirt and the ribbons George gave me long ago. I've braided my hair the Indian way and have put beads throughout them. I'm wearing my most colorful clothing. My mother and Esther were surprised in the care I took in my traveling clothes. I don't usually take so much care, except for our festivals, and my mother and sister thought it strange, but I told them I wanted Sattelihu to be proud of me.

The door opens and George comes bursting through it with a broad smile as cheerful as his flowers. I'm relieved, for he must be glad to see me! It's been over two years and he hasn't changed at all. His demeanor is still handsome and rugged. I see he continues to be a swaggering man full of optimism and confidence. He doesn't take his eyes off me and hardly notices my uncle, his friend, standing next to me. His eyes look at Belle and then at me and then at Belle and back at me again.

"Catharine, it's been so long. And you have a young child."

George squats down before Belle. "I'm Mr. George and what is your name?"

"Belle," our daughter says timidly.

"An apt name for a lovely girl."

George walks over to my uncle and they do their traditional handshakes and pats on the back greetings.

"Come in . . . I apologize for the mess in my home. I've got papers everywhere and Regina hasn't come to clean for weeks."

He takes my hand and Belle's hand and leads us inside.

GEORGE ASKS INDIAN George to prepare us tea.

"George, don't stand there gawking at Catharine. Don't I know she's a beauty! Go make us some tea and then ask one of your aunts to make us supper. Tell them to serve some of the bear meat from yesterday."

I'm not known for being beautiful and feel self-conscious and awkward. Indian George smiles nervously at me and then rushes across the room to prepare tea. This home is twice the size of our home and it doesn't feel warm and comfortable. A few chairs are placed about the room and I wonder where he sleeps. George walks to a large table scattered with papers and pipes and tobacco. He quickly gathers the papers to one side and clears away the tobacco and pipes. He invites us to sit down and pulls a chair out for me. He picks up Belle and places her on my lap. Belle smiles at him and I solemnly wonder what is next in all of this, me being here with his daughter. Me who is married with two other children and George an important trader and about to be married. He looks from me to my uncle and then they become engrossed in a conversation about the traders and the threat of the French. I have nothing to contribute to this conversation, but George eventually turns to me to ask what I think as Indian George serves us tea. I hesitate. He'll not be pleased with what I have to say.

"Go ahead, Catrine . . . Catharine, please tell me how we can get rid of the French."

I look into his blue eyes, the same eyes my Belle has, and hesitate before speaking. "You have many lands, homes, pack horses, and traders who work for you. But you're restless and not pleased with what you have. You often travel right over the Allegheny and into the Detroit, which is dangerous. You like to go beyond the limits of life. My uncle tells me that you persuaded the Miamis to leave the French and now Pickawillany could easily come under French attack."

George looks from me to my uncle and laughs before turning back to me. "You've been interested in my travels. And you seem to know much about me. I'm flattered, even if you consider me restless and an unhappy man. Should I settle down and not seek profit? Do you know that making friends with as many Indians as possible can only bring them into peace with us all?"

"I'm not here to tell you how to live, George Croghan. What I said is only my opinion."

My face is hot and my heart is pounding. George looks again at my uncle and asks him if he thinks the same. My uncle appears irritated with this conversation.

"George, you and I have known one another a long time. And during this time, you've increased your trade and lands, most of which have been given to you by the Iroquois for protecting the lands from squatters. But I think like Catrine in this matter. You're pushing too far into territory the French claim for their trading. It'll put us all in danger."

"But I'm not merely a greedy man, Sattelihu. I'm curious and love an adventure. And peace is possible if there's respect for the Indian, Iroquois, Delaware, Shawnee, Miami, and even the Ottowa and those Indians loyal to the French. Ha! Maybe there's hope for the French and British to live in peace with one another."

Sattelihu and I remain silent. We're not big talkers like George Croghan. George turns to me with those eyes full of optimism as a summer sky without clouds.

"What would help me settle down would be an Indian woman I admired, but they're already nestled into marriages."

I kiss the top of Belle's head and she bounces happily, reaching for George.

"Can I hold her?"

I nod yes and he gently takes Belle and sets her on his lap and circles his strong arm around her. He gives her a brief hug and she looks up into his face.

"Belle. Beautiful is your name, Belle. And a beautiful girl like your mother."

Belle reaches up and strokes George's beard and then pulls her hand back, laughing. She doesn't remember Telehemet, for she was merely a few months old when they met. Indian men don't wear beards, but Belle is somewhat used to the beards of the missionary men and traders who stop at our home. She giggles and George strokes her hair. I notice a rose color rises up his neck and onto his face.

"So you've not fathered any children before Belle?" I ask outright.

George nervously looks at Sattelihu and then back to me.

"So Belle is my own. I thought so as soon as I set eyes on her." George turns again to my uncle. "Did you know this, Sattelihu? Why would you not tell me I had a daughter?"

"I didn't know until a few days ago when Catrine told me she wanted to visit you."

I could see creases of worry beneath George's eyes. "Does Telehemet know Belle is mine?"

"No, Telehemet doesn't know. And, George . . . you fathered Belle, but she is not yours."

George stands up with Belle in his arms and walks around the table.

"If I could marry you and . . ."

I stand up and Sattelihu looks at me wearily.

"I'm already married . . ."

"Yes, of course . . . I'd never take an Indian man's wife, Catrine."

George is using my family name and calling my uncle Sattelihu. He has always called him Andrew. He is too bold. But then George has been close to both Sattelihu and me and perhaps closer to both of us than our marriage partners. I'm suddenly very tired and wish not to think about George Croghan, Telehemet, Grandmother's words, and the problem with the French.

Sattelihu stands up and George sets Belle down. She comes to me, clings to my skirts, but looks up at George.

"Man . . . sad . . . Mama . . ." she says, pointing at George.

Indian George walks in with an older, stout, Indian woman whose face is wreathed in smiles. She carries one pot and Indian George carries another. They set them down on the table and there is a delicious aroma. The woman goes into another room and comes back with pottery and eating utensils.

"Let's only speak of good times and future peace and bounty as we eat," George said.

AFTER OUR MEAL of bear stew and succotash, we sit around an outside fire with Sattelihu, George, Indian George, and a couple of other Indian men. George sent a few Indians away, for they had begun their rum drinking. He reprimanded them and took the rum away, hiding it under lock and key. He states proudly he only allows the Indians a meager portion of rum once a week after their work is done. I wonder if this can be true, for the demon rum in Indians isn't happy with only embers, but requires bursts of flame that consume.

Indian George and I take Belle to a log cabin to be with the other children. She will sleep and later, I'll curl up with her on a bear skin rug for our bed. After we return to the fire, Indian George places a steaming cup of sassafras root tea in my hands. It soothes me and warms my belly. I sip this satisfying tea and stare quietly into the fire and wonder if our journey to George Croghan has been wasteful. I listen to him converse with Sattelihu about speculating, the French, and war. It's all that is on their minds, these men, but what is on women's minds? Our children, of course, and sowing, harvesting, and trying to steer our men in and out of wars. So it is enough, I tell myself. I've learned how to read many English words, but I have no books, so I try not to desire these words that might break open their secrets to me. I try not to crave words and love. Little attention is given to love's play upon hearts in our Indian way of life. It just happens without thinking and isn't sweet like the sticky sap we make maple syrup with. Sometimes it can be bitter and we either endure or leave. I've tasted sweetness with Telehemet and with George Croghan, but I don't know if they have tasted it with me. I've been giving much thought about love between men and women since Belle was born. Why shouldn't men's minds think more about their children and love, rather than the hunt and war?

I go over George's words about marrying and my heart beats with excitement. He's a proud and good man and wouldn't take me from Telehemet, although Telehemet has already taken himself away from me and I live as an unmarried woman. Would I go with George and leave Telehemet if George asked me to? I could tell Telehemet that he has already left me and so I'll go to George Croghan. I've already accepted that Telehemet has a second wife. Why can't I have another husband? Can I have two husbands? I'm not like Grandmother, but I'm also not an imprisoned wife. As far away from my life Telehemet is most of the time, I love him and he's the father of my two children. My eyes fill with tears thinking about my losses and yet how strange I feel being at ease without my husband. I'm a different woman from the young woman I was when Telehemet and I married.

Sattelihu and George stop talking and Sattelihu looks over at me. "I want to leave tomorrow before the sun rises, Catrine, so we must sleep now. I'll sleep in George's cabin and you can go now to your daughter."

Indian George jumps up quickly and stands next to me. I sit and stare into the fire. My uncle doesn't have the right to command me to go to bed.

"I will not sleep yet," I say, still staring into the fire.

"You and Belle be ready at five a.m. I'll have the horses ready."

Sattelihu nods to George Croghan, as if suggesting George accompany him to the cabin, but George sits down across from me.

"Catharine and I need to talk about Belle and my responsibilities."

Uncle grunts and I hear him mutter, "Talk is not all you'll be doing," as he walks off angrily toward the cabin.

The other Indian men stand up and leave and Indian George sits back down next to me.

"What are you, my watch dog, George? I'll walk Catharine to the cabin later. You can go to sleep yourself, man, for we're headed out early tomorrow with a few packhorses and men."

Indian George mutters a disappointed goodnight and hurries off. George and I are alone and I continue to stare into the fire and wish I had never come to introduce George to his daughter. We are quiet for some time and then he awkwardly speaks about sending me money through Sattelihu for Belle's care. He tells me he'll stay away from seeing her if this is what I desire. I'm silent as he stumbles in his speech trying to figure out how to be a father and not a husband.

"I don't need your money, George Croghan."

"Do you need me?"

I look at him and know my answer, but I won't say it.

George gets up and sits close to me. I turn to him and he kisses me gently, over and over. Telehemet's kisses have never been like this, but only hungry and aggressive.

George stops kissing me and laughs. "Sattelihu is probably looking at us from a window of the cabin and I feel like a schoolboy sneaking a kiss from a girl."

"Is that what you did in Ireland when you were a boy?"

George laughs again and stands up. "Give me your hand, Catrine, and I'll walk you to the cabin. It's getting late."

We walk towards the cabin, but before we get there, George changes direction and walks me to the edge of the field where a small barn stands. I don't resist, but follow him into the barn where a few goats are sleeping in a stall. He picks up a lantern by the door, lights it, and leads me to another stall where there is bedding already laid out. Sunflowers and wildflowers are scattered all about the stall.

"For a sunflower girl," George says, as we lay down together.

Much later, I try to sleep nestling in close to Belle's sweet scented body, smelling her and smelling him, but my thoughts return again and again to the passion that recently coursed through my body.

Chapter Seventeen

A YEAR PASSES slowly as I wait for Telehemet and yes, for George Croghan. My family and I are busy preparing for another move. The Montour home will always be boisterous and my quiet times will be when I go to the forest. My mother desires more land for our livestock and her growing family. My father agrees with her decisions and Esther and her husband go wherever my mother goes. Telehemet can find me anywhere, if he wants to. George Croghan can always find me through Sattelihu, if he wants to. My mother and I have become peaceful companions, especially as Grandmother grows increasingly frail and silent.

I receive many treasured gifts from George Croghan through my uncle, but he doesn't visit. After out last time together, I waited to become round and happy with new life from our union, but George's seed did not take root within me. My sister, however, had another baby and our home is now even more crowded. In spring of 1752, my large family and I move to the west bank of the Susquehanna, not far from Sherman's Creek in the Juanita Valley where Grandmother and Uncle have moved. Sherman's Creek is a stopover point where tired and hungry travelers can recover on their way west toward Ohio or east towards Philadelphia. There are many of us, although some members of our family have moved elsewhere. My eldest brother, Karontase, lives near Shamokin, is unmarried and always fighting the Catawbas. He visits just enough to keep my mother at ease. My sister, Molly, and brother, Nicolas, both married into the Mohawk tribe a few years ago and live in New York. We don't see them often, but hear from them through messages from Indians passing through.

I visit Grandmother and her eyesight is worse, but she whispers that she can still see visions for my life. The seasons fill me with hope as I watch the changes the earth receives and accepts and know that I can do the same.

Telehemet visited once in winter, coming in for warmth from our home and from my body before venturing out again with his pack of Indian brothers. I was surprised by my anger when he left. Anger that he and his friends come and go as they please and he can drop his seed whenever he pleases! I don't become round with his child, either, so maybe I'm drying up as the corn fields in late autumn.

I find some peace being on the mighty banks of the Susquehanna. Before our move, I had a dream of the thunderous Eagle Cliff Falls and I considered going there by way of a trip to my husband's family in New York. During Telehemet's visit this past winter, I asked him if we could take our children to introduce them to his family. Telehemet grunted a response. "I'm away so often on the hunt and keeping our enemies at bay. I think not, Catrine." After he left, I lay in bed each night for a week imagining the waterfalls. I schemed how I could someday return to this place that had left its imprint on my heart as the eagle had left its imprint on the cliffs near the waterfalls.

Time passes and Grandmother revives in her new stone house in Juaniata Valley on 140 acres of land. My uncle, whose wife left him long ago, married again this past year. This wife is kind to Grandmother and has given her another grandchild. He has become more respected and is now an interpreter-diplomat for the Ohio Company. It pleased Grandmother when Conrad Weiser told her that her son was indispensable to the colonial governments. Sattelihu remains humble even with his position with the Ohio Company and being on the Great Council of the Six Nations. He has acquired a lot of money and land, but not as much land as George Croghan. This place, Sattelihu promised Grandmother, will be their final home. He assured her she was safe and only by her request would travelers visit. No more missionaries and travelers, white and Indian, stopping anytime they pleased. Grandmother needs quiet and he has forbidden her to be disturbed. My uncle cannot control his mother! The hospitality of my grandmother and the Montours is legendary and continues to be offered to everyone. She never turns anyone away and because Sattelihu travels, he doesn't know she isn't as quiet as he intended for her to be. In fact, Grandmother has gathered strength, although her vision continues to diminish.

Our home and town, a modest one compared to Uncle's, is known as French Margaret's Town. My father is away as much as Telehemet, and as everyone knows and respects, it's the Indian woman who becomes the queen of her domain. My mother reigns and commands her family and although she's still in love with Jesus, she's less demanding for others to believe the same. I hear her praying each evening for all of us and it warms my heart. A few weeks ago, Esther and her husband with five children moved down the river a few miles and now there's my mother, my father who is mostly away, and my children. It's still busy in our household because the missionaries, fur traders, and Indians come to visit. I'm always cooking and when the missionaries come, there's much prayer and talk about Jesus. My mother thrives on these times, but I often whither inside, longing for quiet.

When the fur traders and others visit, there's much heated and fearful talk of the French and a war looming over us all in Pennsylvania and Ohio. My spirit is vexed and I determine to seek the still spirits of the forest. I'm warned it's too dangerous to go deeply into the woods, but how can we live with so much fear? Tribes of Indians have always fought, but there was an order to their warring, unlike now when no one seems to know who is an enemy or friend. During this chaotic time, my mind and heart continue to return to Eagle Cliff Falls in the colony of New York.

WE HAVEN'T BEEN celebrating the seasonal festivals, but we plant and harvest and give thanks at our meals. I miss the dancing, singing, and feasts of the community that were held during celebrations. Here, we are a strange brew of different beliefs and although I learn new words and ideas that interest me, there is hollowness to the thanksgiving we give now. We should be giving our thanksgivings more thought and return to our celebratory festivals. When time is given for creating form and shape to our thanksgivings in a community, we become one with the Great Spirit and one with another. It's sadly missing as the white man's ways intrude upon our lives more and more.

After our move in early spring, summer became so busy I hardly took it in, and then we leaned into the brittle winter ways until late May. I'm pleased to be at home, tending to planting and caring for our gardens. My Belle is always at my side and my boys are growing and being introduced to the ways of men in the hunt. I don't like to think they'll someday be introduced to the ways of war. They rarely ask about their father and there are enough Indian men here who let them trail along with them who listen to their inquisitive chatter. In the evenings with Grandmother, I'm quiet and listen to talk around the fire about the Ohio Company and their ongoing interest in establishing settlements in the west. The French are interested, as well, and feel this land belongs to them. I wonder how long this pot of Indian, French, and British stew is going to simmer before it boils over. This has been going on for years. Grandmother says there's to be a conference in Logstown and I should go with Sattelihu to assist him. I'm not knowledgeable about the treaties and rituals exercised at these conferences. She never gives up on trying to convince me I have a mission.

"Sattelihu said he wishes I was young again to go with him to bring the wisdom of the mothers to these treaties and meetings. There's too much strutting and display by the male peacocks and the soft, wise, but stern, corn mothers are sorely needed. Go Catharine. Go for your grandmother. You won't have to be a voice now, but you can gather the intentions of all these men by listening and watching. And you, my sunflower granddaughter, have always been closer to the Great Spirit than any of my other grandchildren, will know the wisdom that is the best medicine for our lands and people."

Logstown Conference, 1752

I SIT IN the first row of benches in the Council House at Logstown with a few old Delaware chiefs. They wear headdresses made of one large eagle feather set in the crown with a cluster of small white feathers below. They also wear the traditional leggings and the braided belts over their shoulders. There is much ornamentation, including necklaces in the shape of crosses. I love their regal dress and comportment. It reminds me of festival times and celebrations that are displays of pride and beauty. There is low grunting and I smell bear grease and their body smells that are unique to them. A few Indian grandmothers sit in the back. Sattelihu insisted I stay in the front to watch and learn and believes my presence will be helpful.

When we first arrived in Logstown, I washed and changed into the special clothing I wore to meet George Croghan when I brought Belle to him. George sits in this Council House with Christopher Gist, Sattelihu, and the commissioners. I don't know if he recognizes I'm wearing the same skirt, for men are mostly occupied with other things more important. I'm at once embarrassed to be wearing it again, as if I'm weak and under his spell, what once I called the strong medicine of George Croghan.

We traveled in four large canoes lashed together carrying many goods for the Indian chiefs. We stopped twice to greet Delaware Indian chiefs and exchange formalities and wampum strings. When we arrived with the English colors flying onto Queen Alliquippa's town shore, we were saluted by the discharge of fire arms. And there standing next to the queen was George smiling and welcoming all of us. The queen whispered in my ear, "Granddaughter of Isabelle, I'm pleased you are here, for you are deeply loved." I didn't know if she meant loved by her or by George, for she smiled secretly as she came close. We went to her home and the queen presented a string of wampum to us to clear our way to Logstown. She gave a delicious dish of fish to carry with us and fed us with hearty food. I sat between George and Uncle while we ate. George and I didn't speak to one another, but our arms brushed and familiar embers burned within me. After dinner, the colonial commissioners presented a brass kettle, tobacco, and other trifles to the queen. If I could have her stature and position among both the Indians and Europeans, it might be more rewarding than being an interpreter as my uncle or grandmother. Later, we stay nearby at a trader's house and I try to sleep on the floor next to Sattelihu, but it's impossible because George is nearby. In the morning when I leave the house for water, he comes to me and cups my chin in his hands and lightly kisses my lips and hurries on. No one, I believe, saw this gesture and I'm relieved, but pleased with his kisses. He later joins us to travel on to Logstown.

When we began this journey, my uncle introduced me as Madame Montour's granddaughter to Christopher Gist, an agent for the Ohio Company. I don't think this man remembered my grandmother. Sattelihu is nervous. Obsequious . . . a word Anna had taught me long ago.

"Catharine's quiet, but when she speaks in many languages, it's with eloquence and wisdom."

Mr. Gist looks at me with disinterest, a fake crack of a smile.

"A pleasure to meet you, Catharine. Andrew is our interpreter . . . and what will you do?"

I glance at Sattelihu and down at my feet, but recover quickly. "I will watch with keen eyes and ears and interpret with my heart."

Mr. Gist only nods with his false face and turns away. I stay quiet and don't say much to Sattelihu or anyone else on our journey to Logstown.

As I sit in the front row in the Council House, my mind wanders over the past two days as everyone settles into further formalities and wampum string exchanges. My eyes skip over George Croghan's face and I focus instead on the commissioners, chiefs, and Sattelihu. I'm uncomfortable at this conference and disgusted with white men's double tongued words. It will sadden me to see the Indians eventually bow down to these men in the end. Maybe not this time, I hope, but what can I possibly do to make a difference?

Chapter Eighteen

GEORGE CROGHAN SPEAKS on behalf of the Ohio Company with a face I haven't seen before. It is half-closed down, unlike his open, gentle face I had caressed with my eyes and hands.

"Brethren, you sent a string of wampum when we met on the road, by which you acquainted us that you heard of our coming to visit. You welcomed us so far on our journey yesterday and when we arrived here this morning, you gave us another string of wampum to bid us welcome and to open our eyes that we may see the sun clearly and look upon you as brothers who are willing to receive us. This we take kindly and assure you of our hearty inclinations to live in friendship, and to confirm this, we present you with a string of wampum."

George presents the string to the chief sitting next to me. The old dignified chief stands to receive the string and George glances at me and his other face appears for a brief moment. My uncle stoically interprets all of George's words to the Delaware chiefs. The chiefs somberly nod and Joshua Fry, a commissioner, stands to speak.

"Brethren, you delivered to us two strings of wampum to clear our hearts from any flying reports of ill news and that we might speak our minds freely. Brethren, we assure you of our willingness to remove all misunderstanding out of our hearts and breasts which might impede or hinder the friendship subsisting between us."

My uncle interprets and I stifle a yawn and wonder how long this conference is going to take to persuade the chiefs to give up more land. This commissioner also has a false face. He tries to convince the Indians they're brothers by addressing them brethren before each sentence. The thin, unpleasant man continues to speak and my uncle interprets.

"Now Brethren (Mr. Fry hesitates, puts his head down a moment and then speaks again) Brethren, we are here to acquaint you, or rather, we have been sent hither by the Great King . . . by the King of Great Britain, our Father, your Father, too, Brethren . . . who, not forgetting his children on this side of the great waters, has ordered us to deliver to you, our brethren a large parcel of goods in his name, which we have brought with us. We understand we must wait for some of the chiefs of the Onondaga Council, whom you shortly expect. We will wait with patience, Brethren, and then faithfully deliver you the goods and open our hearts to you. In assurance, we present you with this string of wampum."

Mr. Fry gives the string of wampum to the same chief who stands to receive it and then replies, "I am glad that you have the consideration to wait for the coming of our chiefs."

The commissioners, George, and others stand up to dismiss the gathering. The chiefs and I stand and they surround me and smile. One chief pats my arm affectionately.

"You are your grandmother's image. Strong and dignified as she is. And you are here with Sattelihu, our respected brother. He is a true brother and we honor all the Montour family and their peacekeeping spirit."

These elders have spoken their heart and I'm warmed. I bow my head slightly at each one and at once words flow out of me unconstrained.

"Will there be peace for the Delaware, Shawnee, Mingo, and those living in Ohio and on the great river? My uncle has said you request a strong house on the banks of the river to supply you with powder and lead to defend yourselves and the traders from the French. So what does this father of ours across the sea say about this? My uncle hasn't told me what it is these men from Virginia want. He tells me that he is a go-between and will only give his opinion if asked, but he won't be asked. I'm curious now that I am here, for I never intended to be here."

The smiles of the chiefs fade. We women are respected for our quick tongues, especially in matters of treaties, and each of these chiefs will be leaving here and confiding in the women who have come with them. But these chiefs are my elders and maybe I've offended them.

The chief who received the wampum strings and given them in return tells the others he'll speak to me in private.

"If indeed you carry your grandmother and Sattelihu's gift for speaking truth and bringing peace, be warned that although governors and other white men in these colonies of long ago respected your grandmother, they will only tolerate you at this time. Our lives have changed in our relationship with them and even with our Ho-De'-No-Sau-Nee brothers. The peace we had is ending and none of us, but the Great Spirit know what is before us. You, daughter, must be wise and it's true that we request a strong house for our protection and our brother, George Croghan, knows this, but he sometimes follows his white blood and not the red blood he loves so well. He is torn between us and them, but we understand. He, too, is a go-between and it's easy to become a puppet. They want him to make us believe we are indeed brethren and that they care for our lives. But we know that at this conference, there will be a request for us to give them something we don't want to give. And it is usually land. But we must wait for the wise council of the Ho-De'-No-Sau-Nee and Tanaghrisson, the Half King, to come and help us in this conference. Tomorrow, daughter, it will take place. Please come sit next to me again, for I need your young strength for the days ahead, as you will need our wisdom."

Early that evening, George sought me out and we walked in a field near the woods. We sat upon a log until the moon rose and dew shimmered on the grass. We became lovers again, but he was too preoccupied with the Ohio Company and their sudden esteem of him to be fully mine for the evening. I tried to tell him that he was merely a tool in their hands to get what they wanted and that was land in the Ohio Valley. But he didn't hear what I had to say and pressed his lips to my neck and breathed heavily. I knew his breath was not of his heart, but of his mind and his pride. I felt a separation from him then, a sudden understanding that we could never be in union, for I didn't have his ambitions and a man's hunger for land and power. And I had also heard from my uncle that George had married the Mohawk woman.

THE NEXT DAY, many chiefs of the Onondaga Council arrive and the conference continues with stiff formal declarations and exchanges of wampum. It's the end of May and the strawberries are almost ripe. During a break in meetings, I walk alone in a field of wild flowers, pick a few early ripened berries, and feel sustained by the sweet melodies of birds and sunshine. The forest, fields, and rivers are where my woman's spirit dwells and not inside meeting houses where men preside with pomp and greed.

George and Sattelihu walk together next to the field and keep an eye on me as they meander and talk. I watch them and realize my uncle and George are indeed brothers, brothers in ambition for the praise of others and for land. Before I came to this conference, I considered my uncle a true Indian who put his people above the desire for personal triumph. Although he has not done wrong in deed, his spirit has altered. He values the white and Indian men in power more than the truth. Were my eyes blind all along to his true nature or am I being too harsh and my vision dimmed?

Back inside the Council House, I sit next to the Delaware, Shawnee, and Mingo chiefs once again, but this time they ask me to sit in the midst of them and not to the side. I have known many Delaware chiefs growing up and I've watched their demeanors change from peaceful hunters to somber, even angry men. They lost their land in what became known as Ye Running Purchase, a ploy the Pennsylvania government used to trick the Delaware out of their land. The Delaware misunderstood the purchase, but the Pennsylvania government understood their misunderstanding and was glad for it. It was long ago, but the humiliation continues. The Ho-De'-No-Sau-Nee, the powerful Six Nations, who reign over many tribes, have deemed the Delaware as women who cannot go to war. The Delaware and most other tribes will acquiesce to these powerful, bold Iroquois, as the French call them. This is why many Delaware have left for the Ohio region! They want to resist the Ho-De'-No-Sau-Nee influence and gain back some honor and pride. My uncle and George Croghan have always respected them, but now I see with my inner eyes the state of my brothers, the Delaware, as well as the Mingo, and Shawnee. These tribes and others are struggling to live and they only ask for a strong house, a fort, to be built by the British, to protect their lives and work from the French. But other schemes are in place and they have been set in place long before today's conference.

The Seneca Chief, Tanaghrisson, known as the Half King, sits rigid on a bench opposite us, next to my uncle and the chiefs of the Ho-De'-No-Sau-Nee Council. These chiefs have reasserted their influence over the Delaware and the Ohio Indians through this Half King. The Ohio Indians have mostly accepted him into their lives for the last five years. He is here at the Council to help them secure the strong house they need and to speak for their necessities.

A commissioner representing Virginia, Maryland, and Pennsylvania stands, gray-faced and slight, but strong in voice. "Brethren, the Delaware, the Shawnee, the Windot, and others who come from the Ohio region, we thank you for the kind reception you have given us. We advise and exhort you to beware of French Councils and ask that you adhere to a strict friendship with us, the Six Nations, and your brethren who live toward the sun setting. We present you with these belts of wampum for each tribe."

The chief next to me stands proudly to receive the belts of wampum and carefully puts them on my lap. The belts feel heavy. I shut my eyes for I'm tired and weary, but the chiefs on both sides of me tap my arms to keep me awake.

Next is the presentation of goods to the Half King and the chiefs next to me. The goods are divided equally among the tribes represented at the conference. It's impressive the amount given to them and it's all done in an orderly way. Soon the chiefs are back sitting next to me. I have deliberately not looked at George, but now he, who has assisted the chiefs with the goods, walks near me before sitting back down. I catch his eyes and smell his scent and feel weakness.

The Half King stands with a ten rowed belt of wampum in his hand, directing his speech to my uncle. "Child, remember that you are one of our own people and have transacted a great deal of business among us before. You were employed by our brethren of Pennsylvania and Virginia. You are an interpreter between us and our brethren. But you are not interpreter only, for you are one of our Council, have an equal right with us to all these lands, and may transact any public business on behalf of us, the Six Nations, as well as any of us, for we look upon you as much as we do upon any of the chief counsellors. And to confirm what we have said, we present you with this belt of wampum."

Sattelihu stands tall and handsome and receives the belt of wampum. I note his back is straight and his chest puffed out beyond his usual comportment. Yes, he is a son of both, the Ho-De'-No-Sau-Nee and the white men. I think curiously that his white blood is serving him well. If I do the same, what might I obtain?

I'm surprised when the Half King addresses himself to the commissioners of Virginia and all the Indians present, holding a string of wampum in his hand, as he speaks about George Croghan, who they refer to as the Buck.

"Brother, it is a great while since you, our brother, the Buck, have been doing business between us and our brothers of Pennsylvania, but we understand you do not intend to do any more, so I now inform you that you, George Croghan, are approved of by our Council at Onondaga, for we let them know you have helped us in our councils here and to let you know that you are one of our people and shall help us still and be one of our Council. I deliver you this string of wampum."

George stands and receives the belt of wampum and his demeanor is also like my uncle's. Both men I love are puffed up peacocks who spread their wings so far out, no one can get very close to their hearts. On one hand, I'm proud of both of them, but on the other, I feel they've become less than themselves.

There are more formalities and strings of wampum given. I'm becoming irritable sitting so long with the belts that are heavy. How will this end? I want to be outside to walk in the setting sun and to sleep.

And then the Half King stands again and faces the Governor of Virginia.

"Brother, Governor of Virginia, yesterday you presented us with the copy of the deed made by the Onondaga Council at the Treaty of Lancaster and asked that the brethren of Ohio might likewise confirm this deed. This deed confirms we have given you a quantity of land in Virginia, which you have a right to. We never understood before that the lands then sold were to extend further to the sun setting than the hill on the other side of the Alleghany Hill, so we can't give you a further answer now. We have desired a strong house, at the fork of the Mohongalio, to keep goods, powder, lead, and necessaries, but did not know you desired a settlement of your people on the Ohio lands. You have declared the Virginia lands we deeded to you contain these Ohio lands, as there was no clear line between the two. Brethren, after consultation with my brethren of the Onondaga Council, I will answer if the Ohio brethren will sign."

There is sudden uneasiness, squirming, and grunting among the chiefs next to me. The conference is dismissed for a meal and will continue in an hour. The chiefs sitting with me stand and talk quietly to one another. I wonder what to do with the wampum and sit quietly and impatiently. I hear them complain that the Half King hadn't told them there would be white settlements on the Forks of the Ohio. They're aggrieved, as they wanted a fort to protect them, but it's clear they will not get it unless they sign this deed.

The chiefs finally remember I'm there and remove the belts. I stand and the Delaware chief who spoke to me the day before takes my hands in his. "Now you know, granddaughter of Madame Montour, what white tongues are greased with to make smooth talk to the poor Indians who have become too happy with their rum, presents, and protection. But we have no choice but to honor Tanaghrisson, the Half King of the Six Nations, and if he tells us to sign the deed confirming the Treaty of Lancaster's intention to stretch the Virginia land into Ohio land, there is nothing we can do."

There's nothing left for me to say. I can only nod in sadness. I remember the Lancaster Treaty and the vision I had of what's to come. Should I tell them? Should I tell them that the Indians' bountiful harvest of corn, beans, and squash will be slashed and burned? I'm angry, but before I can speak, George and Sattelihu come for me. I smile at these wonderful chiefs and leave, having said nothing. Later, the meeting resumes and the deed is signed. It's over and it's too late. Now there will be feasting, bon fires, and dancing, but I ask to be undisturbed and sleep until late in the evening when my uncle comes to tell me we'll be leaving early in the morning, I ask him if I can see the Delaware chiefs, for I've decided to speak to them about my vision.

"They have torn down their tents and left, Catrine. And none of them are too pleased by the Half-King's quiet signing of the treaty. No doubt that in time they'll accept the settlers into the Ohio Valley."

"George once told me the rich landowners of Virginia had given money to own this land, the land of the Indians who don't claim to own land, for it'd be like trying to own the Great Spirit. Sattelihu, are you putting the Indian first?"

Sattelihu looks displeased. "George talks too much and spends too much time with you. He has a wife now, Catrine, and you need to let him go."

"I'd like to speak to him before we leave tomorrow."

"It's too late. He left with the Half-King and some other Indians. He's returning to Pickawillany, for there's talk of a raid by the French."

My heart is sore. I rub my chest gently, for it truly feels bruised. My friends, the Delaware chiefs, have departed and so has my lover, George Croghan. I also think of Telehemet. I'm betrayed and alone. My uncle leaves and I walk in the field next to the woods and hear the call of the crows and in their conversation with one another, I hear my own voice strong within me.

I, Catharine, will receive my grandmother's mantle that I have thrown off again and again. I'll wear it my own way and may it nurture and wrap me in strength and wisdom for the people the Great Spirit will bring into my life. And if my children will come beneath this mantle with me, will I be able to live as good and proud as Madame Montour and Queen Alliquippa?

Chapter Nineteen

George Croghan

GEORGE PULLS A bandana from his pocket and ties it around his forehead to keep the sweat from pouring into his eyes. It's unseasonably warm for the early June morning and everyone at Pickawillany is feeling the heat. Many of the men are hunting, the women are in the fields, and he and some of the older Indians have been in the stockade assessing supplies and ammunition. Their overall necessities are diminishing and he's preparing to leave with a couple of men to go for replenishments. He wants his Miami friend, Old Briton, to travel with him, but the old man is moody and tells George he wants to stay and watch over the village and fort. George thinks he's unusually anxious, but he says goodbye and quickly gets his things together and leaves without his friend.

After seeing to the supplies, George plans to visit Andrew. It's important to assess the mood of the Ohio Indians since the Logstown Conference and Andrew will have been in contact with them. And he secretly hopes to see Catharine and Belle. He's disappointed Andrew told Catharine he had married. George would have eventually told Catharine his marriage had been strongly encouraged by Sir William Johnson, the Superintendent of Indian Affairs. George cares for the Mohawk woman enough, but it's a marriage of convenience, not for love. Ha! Who marries for love! Johnson has a Mohawk wife and is fond of this tribe and he wants George to be, too. George already was proud of the Mohawks before marrying a Mohawk woman.

His brain is tired from thinking about Catharine, but he figures if he tries to reason it all out there, his heart won't ache. It's too late to marry her, even though Catharine's husband isn't much in the picture. He might have convinced her to leave Telehemet, but he couldn't foul his relationship with the Montours. If he had persuaded Catharine to leave her husband and marry him, it would have caused friction, even damage to these relations. And he's now a welcome member of the Iroquois Council and would cut off his right arm before destroying that relationship.

George Croghan never cheated an Indian, nor his fellow trader. He is honest and fair, but doesn't take kindly to anyone getting in his way or telling him what he can't do. His bold business endeavors have prevailed and the Indians honor and respect him. They call him, *our brother, the Buck*. He treats Indians like human beings, not like dogs as many whites do. He knows their customs, their languages, and he's a real friend. No such fondness for George Croghan exists in the hearts of the governors and his chief competitors. One of the reasons for the formation of the Ohio Company in 1749 was to secure a profitable trade which was then monopolized by Croghan and the Pennsylvania traders. It was clear that Gist and the Ohio Company were jealous of Croghan's success, but George hadn't noticed. He was too immersed in adventure, profit, and his friendships to have paid much attention to anyone's envy. From 1749 until the present, he has lost fifteen employees and fifty packhorses due to French attacks. His losses are now piling up. And so he said yes to the Ohio Company to help at Logstown and now he has said yes to Johnson. He hopes to play all fields and believes optimistically in William Penn's peaceable kingdom. Confidence is his, except with Catharine and how she can strip him of all his bravado and render him naked before himself. He sees in her eyes that he isn't of the stature he thinks himself.

George and two other Indians ride their horses along the Great Miami River. It is sweltering and they've only been traveling an hour. He wipes the sweat from his forehead again and again, more times than necessary. He is trying to wipe away his thoughts of Catharine and the worrisome feeling he has about his friend, Old Briton. The man has visions and he's usually right, but this morning he wasn't going on about any dream he had. He'd been like a nervous hen over her brood, rushing back and forth from the fort to the field, trying to ensure everyone was safe and doing what they were supposed to be doing.

George takes off his hat and lays it over the reins. He needs the flow of air around his head. He looks back at the two Indians riding along with him. They gesture in acknowledgement and look to be unaffected by the heat. How he loves their ways. George breathes in the hot air, squints in the sun, and pus his hat back on. His horse clip clops along the narrow, worn path and he becomes resolute, exchanging his thoughts for engagement with the vision of the river. The overheated wind touches the river's dark waters and creates ripples of glimmering silver. Starlight sparks hypnotize him as he rides and he cares not that he is blinded by beauty. His horse knows the path and isn't this why he left Ireland, to be led into unknown radiance?

A few minutes later, George hears a cry, an alarming call only an Indian makes to other Indians. He comes out of his trance and jumps off his horse. His two friends do the same. They wait, as they know they must, and it's another ten minutes before their friend, Seeing Fox, rides to where they are.

"The French have attacked Pickawillany and many are dead."

OLD BRITON, THE Miami, who had led his people sixty miles south of the French outpost, Fort Miamis, on the Maumee River, to found the new town of Pickawillany, is dead. George Croghan's grief turns to anger at the slaughter of his friend and the villagers at Pickawillany. When he is shown the remains of his friend who has been dismembered, boiled, and eaten by his enemies, George's guts heave and he falls onto his own puke. He lays there unable to fathom the atrocity and then stands and grabs a bloody thigh bone of Old Briton's and puts it in his knapsack. He gets on his horse and leaves with his two Indian friends and a few survivors who escaped into the woods nearby. He vows never to return to this village. His losses are great, but the loss of his friend is greater. He rides away and leaves more than his dead friend. His shoulders slope, tears run down his face, and he'll never again raise his glass in hope for better days without skepticism. From here on out, he'll be trying to recover his losses and his soul.

Behind George and his sorrowing entourage, Pickawillany sits plundered and smoldering with bodies lying everywhere. The French have conquered this village and will be back. Charles Langlade, the son of a French father and Ottawa woman, led the ferocious raid, along with Indian allies.

When Old Briton led his people away from the French to this village, it had been for survival. Four hundred families had not been pleased with less and less French merchandise and had become loyal to the British, for their goods, but also to what they believed was their goodness, especially shown to them in George Croghan. For several years, other tribes will leave French outposts, as well—the Piankashaw and Ouiatanon are only a few. British trade draws French-allied Indians like a magnet to the Illinois country.

Opportunity has been more alluring than worry over danger for the Ohio Indians and their Pennsylvania trading partners. In 1749 the governor of New France began to assert French control and then Virginia's House of Burgesses, unbeknownst to the traders or Indians, granted a huge tract of land on the upper Ohio to a group of wealthy planters who wanted to establish new settlements in the west. A storehouse had been built and Christopher Gist was sent out to search for more Ohio lands. Alas, the Logstown Conference then made it legal and the Iroquois helped. Ohio was the grand prize and was now being torn asunder by the French. After George saw his beloved friend, Old Briton and others he cared for, dead, the brilliance of the vast unknown he had loved was now dulling into a dark pool of blood-red hate.

Chapter Twenty

Catharine

I PLACE THE scarlet blanket gently over Grandmother as she sleeps. "It's time," her grandmother said to her yesterday, "time to go to the ancestors and to slide out of my old, weathered skin. Like a snake, Catrine, squirming and struggling to be free of its skin."

Grandmother's death is nearing and a sensation of being lost in a dark forest comes over me when I think of her dying. She has helped me see myself more clearly, and when she is gone?

My desires are being re-arranged after being with the magnificent Delaware chiefs and sitting in conference between the colonists and Indians. It has stirred my mixed blood.

In my visions, the blood on the destroyed fields was one color—the color of the European and the Indian. It flowed into the earth and into the streams and rivers and mixed together. Water is life and there's thanksgiving for water and its strength and cleansing. Water speaks to me and my fellow Indians, but what does water speak when human blood spills into it?

I lay down on the rug by Grandmother's bed. Everyone in the cabin is sleeping and I agreed to watch over her through the night. I close my eyes and fall into a dream and see myself standing behind a waterfall saturated by sunlight. Streams of colors flow through the droplets of the waterfall into a pool. And then men and women emerge from the pool naked, one after another. Pale, dark, small, large, and people of every age swim to the rocks to sit. I go to them and try to speak, but they look through me or past me. They don't see or hear me. I yell at them, but they don't hear me. I wake and sit up startled and disturbed by this dream.

"Come, Catrine, and lie beside me. I want to tell you about my dream."

I lay beside her on her bed with my heart beating loudly in my ears. "I had a dream, too . . . can I tell you of it?"

Grandmother's raspy voice is strong. "Let me first tell you of my dream. My dream is for you to bring understanding between people who don't know the language of the Great Spirit's love."

"They won't listen to me. I dreamed people rose from the water and sat on rocks around a waterfall. I walked among them and spoke, but they didn't see or hear me."

"It's your spirit you saw and it will dwell in that place long after you have left this earth. Many people of different colors and ways will visit this place, but they'll have difficulty seeing or hearing the ways of the Great Spirit and the ways of the ancient ones who dwelled in this place and on this earth."

"I don't understand."

"We don't have to understand. The sun gives light at the beginning of the day, but doesn't instruct how to live that day. The light is enough to see where to walk and you'll walk where the light is the strongest."

Grandmother pulls on the blankets covering her and grasps the scarlet blanket. She has little vision, but can see the red of the blanket.

"What's this? This must not cover me now. I gave it to you long ago and it's to cover you only, not me. Don't bury me with this blanket, for you'll bury my dreams for you."

Grandmother struggles to get out from under the blanket and I remove it and place it over myself. The blue blanket George gave Grandmother was beneath the scarlet blanket and I tuck it beneath Grandmother's chin and lay my hand on her forehead.

"Be still, Grandmother. I'll not bury your dreams."

I SLEEP AGAIN and when I wake in the morning, I know. Madame Montour, Isabelle Montour, daughter of Pierre Couc, eighty-five years of age, wife of Joachin Germano, Outoutagan, Pierre Tichenet, and Carondowana; an "Interpretess," advisor, go-between, and a woman who crossed the chasm between European and Native, is dead. We believe the spirits of the dead hover for a long time before departing to heaven. I've never doubted this, but no other spirit of the departed has been this palpable as Grandmother's spirit is right now.

Sometime later during the mourning rituals of honor and tribute with many Europeans and Indians coming to pay respect to my grandmother, Madame Montour, I place the mantle of my grandmother over me with a full heart. In spite of my loss, there is calm resolution and hope.

EVERYONE LEAVES THE grave of Madame Montour and I stay until dusk wraps me in its mystery. A midnight blue sky with a half-moon casts a peaceful mien over the mound of earth covered in flowers, corn husk dolls, trinkets, and plates of food. I sit cross-legged in front of the grave with Grandmother's red blanket around my shoulders. A light breeze caresses my face and I'm filled with sorrowing peace. This evening my grandmother and the Great Spirit are present as I close my eyes and feel lifted out of my human form and merged into one with the sky and stars. No fear plagues me and as my soul soars, my body still feels grounded to the earth. And then I open my eyes and return to the reality she is gone.

How Grandmother? How can I carry your dreams for me? Minutes pass and a hand gently touches my shoulder. I look up into George Croghan's face. I would know his face in light or darkness. He sits beside me and places a bird cage next to the grave. I hear the desperate fluttering of bird wings.

"I wanted to give you time alone, Catrine. I know you'll want to return here many times, but you know she'll always be with you and all of us."

"You've brought a bird!"

"Andrew told me about the Iroquois belief that the spirit of the deceased hovers around the body for a time before it takes final departure. And about the custom in capturing a bird and freeing it over the grave on the evening of the burial."

I peer inside and see a cardinal beating its wings in desperation to be free.

"How did you catch a cardinal? They're timid and fly away at the smallest movement."

"It's a female . . . they like to be caught, don't they? No . . . no . . . I'm teasing . . . yes, it was damn hard to catch her, but I had help. There are steely hunters in your family and their footsteps are lighter than my heavy booted ones. It was your son, Roland, who helped me."

George stands to his feet and reaches for my hand. I stand next to him and he wraps his arms around me and cradles my head to his chest. I cry silently and feel Grandmother's arms reaching around us both. My grandmother had seen the strong thread of love that bound us together before I had known it myself.

After a few moments, we release the cardinal over the grave of Madame Montour. The moonlight appears brighter after we open the cage and the cardinal is freed. As the bird flies out, its wing flaps against my cheek. I touch my cheek, feeling heat and take in a startled breath.

"My grandmother's last word to me."

George laughs and hugs me. "And what was that word?"

I hesitate and wait, listening within, before answering. "She called me her sunflower girl. I believe she wants me to live boldly and to shine."

"Oh yes, I believe this, too, but I would call you a sunflower woman now."

Chapter Twenty-One

I CARRY MY grief for Grandmother as I carried each of my babies, with love and tenderness. I tend the fields and gardens and allow my tears to fall into the soil. My mind is quiet and empty, so my feelings flow easily and there are times I hear Grandmother's words come back to me.

Our town, French Margaret's Town, is the first little town on the side of Quenischachachque, ten miles from Otsonwakin, where I was born. Although I estimate I'm only thirty-three years, I possess the gravity and melancholy of an old woman. I'm not without simple happiness and how I love my Belle, Roland, and John. I grow accustomed to life as it is and listen and wait to know how I can wear Grandmother's mantle of peacemaking. I'm content to have returned to this land, although Otsonwakin has altered. Before Chief Shikellamy died, he agreed to allow the Moravian Brothers to build a gunsmith shop in Shamokin, which isn't far from us. The Moravian Brothers intended to spread their good news of Christianity to the Indians. Chief Shikellamy insisted the Brothers plant our Three Sisters (corn, beans, and squash) and potatoes. At the time, he was fearful any other European plantings would create a European plantation and a loss of an Indian community. The Moravians obliged him and have lived simple, single lives dedicated to their mission of replacing the Manitou, our Great Spirit, with Jesus Christ. They're a gentle, hardworking group of people, much like our old friends, the Macks, and my friend, Anna. They're disappointed there aren't more Indians living near them to proselytize, for most of the Indians left after Shikellamy died. Shikellamy's son lives nearby, as well as John Logan and his wife, and a few others we knew before. Conrad Weiser lives in Tulpehocken, a hundred miles from here, and has a grist mill where many buy their flour. My mother and I visited the smithy one day and heard Brother Grube say to Brother David.

"The only Indians left, except Shikellamy's family and the Montours, are a few Tutelos, Conoys, Cayugas, and Mohicans. And they're mostly ruined by whites . . . they drink and steal, but we'll trust our Lord to help us with them."

By now, most of the Indian nations know and trust the Moravian missionaries. I, however, sense superiority in them, something I saw in Count Zinzendorf many years ago. The Montours have always puzzled them, but now with Grandmother having left this earth, my mother's faith is big enough for them to believe their religious work is satisfactory in our regard. They haven't asked me what I believe and I don't offer any of my thoughts about my life with the Great Spirit. When we visit the Brothers for smithy work and supplies, my mother often insists we stay for one of their love feasts and singing hours they conduct once a week. I sing and eat little, for my heart is not compatible with their ways. I appreciate that they help the local Indians and the many Indians traveling through, feeding them and taking care of their smithy orders. And they don't involve themselves in taking sides in the many warring factions.

Mother and I were at the mission one day when a group of Wyoming Christian Indians came for smithy orders at the same time a few Seneca warriors stopped with fresh war scalps. The Christian Indians were preaching to the other Indians and I waited to question the Seneca warriors about Telehemet. After a long wait, they answered they had not seen him and I had to shake away fears he had been killed. Although Shamokin is not inhabited by many now, there's a constant flow of travelers, both Indian and white. Shamokin is also an established station for the Six Nations when they're at war against the Catawbas, which seems to be always, and this is why Telehemet has been gone for many months.

YESTERDAY, SATTELIHU RETURNED from Bethlehem after meeting with the Moravian missionary, David Zeisberger, to receive a letter to take to the Onondaga Council. Many Indians want to know the way to blessedness and to hear about the Savior and sometimes Sattelihu is a go-between not only between the colonial governments and Indians, but between the missionaries and Indians. He is almost never home and this means our home expands with the many visits from his wife and children when he is gone.

"I'm going to Onondaga for a month or more, Margaret. When does Katarioniecha come home?" He turns to me. "And when does Telehemet ever come home to you, Catrine?"

I'm weaving corn dolls with Belle and Mary, Sattelihu's five year old daughter. I don't look up or answer, for tears well up in my eyes.

"The stable Indians we know aren't near enough and there's too many drunken Indians and strange white people passing through. The Brothers wouldn't shoot a dog, let alone a drunken Indian up to no good. I don't like it that you haven't your husbands here to protect you."

"Sattelihu, what kind of thinking is this?" my mother asks. "We're protected by Jesus and we've lived alone as women for most of our lives. Wherever we've lived, our men have been away to hunt or fight more than they've been home."

"Old Chief Shikellamy is dead and his home welcoming everyone and our friends is of the past. I never had worries being gone when he was alive. Now this place has become a place of turmoil and confusion with travelers bringing messages of a coming war with France."

"John Logan is the light bringer and he's assumed his father's leadership," my mother replies. "He, his wife, and others from Shikellamy's family are nearby. And don't I know how to use a gun, Sattelihu?"

My mother is not a woman to be crossed and although I can take up a gun, it would be the last resort. My mother carries it around town as if she's going to need to use it at any moment. She's a very rich woman, my mother, French Margaret. Through Grandmother's and Sattelihu's many years of being hired by the colonial governments of New York, Pennsylvania, and Ohio, she has thirty horses, several cows, and forty pigs. We have planted eight acres of Indian corn and our home is large and comfortable, although my mother still calls it a hut.

"Roland is old enough to travel with me. Where is the boy, Catrine? I'd like him to go with me to Onondaga."

"He's too young . . . I don't want him to . . ."

"He's too much with women. You've fussed over him and he only wants to fish and float around the forest as you do. His father has no influence on him or John. And where is John, but probably sitting at the smithy waiting for some drunken Indians to come and tell him stories."

Sattelihu's words sting. My boys have free range and they've learned how to use a gun and a knife to protect themselves, but they forget to carry any protection when they're around the town and mission. I've trusted the Brothers to protect them and my boys are of a peaceful nature, although Roland can become easily angered, but he'd resort to his tongue before a weapon.

"And you, Catrine, what has become of the woman who sat in the front seat at the Council with the chiefs? Since my mother died, you've become gloomy and weak. Where is your spirit?"

I stand up slowly to face Sattelihu. Belle gets up, too, and clings to my skirts.

"You've not asked me to travel with you. I've not asked because there's much work here to help my mother and care for the children. The Indians hired to help us with our animals are not to be depended on, for their rum drinking becomes worse by the day. Some of the Indian women also come under the influence of the demon rum and cannot help us with our planting, which is food for their families, too. The Brothers have helped us with the planting and yes, we're a house of strong women holding down the fort while our men go about their important lives of council meetings, war parties, and hunting . . . with wives and families elsewhere."

"Catharine!" my mother says. "Your father and Sattelihu don't have other wives and families."

"Catrine is thinking of her husband, Telehemet, who is more with his other family than with her and his sons."

I take Belle's hand and walk past Sattelihu and out the door. The air is cool on a late summer afternoon and it soothes my temper and nerves. I lead Belle away from our home for a walk to the mighty river that will speak loudly over my tumultuous mind and heart. Perhaps I'll hear a new message, one from Grandmother, for the sad peace I had found in my grief over her death is being replaced with anger.

SATTELIHU LEAVES AND takes Roland with him to Onondaga without my consent. If Grandmother was here, she would not have allowed it if Roland didn't want to go. Grandmother would have been empathetic to Roland and myself, but now that she is no longer the matriarch, Sattelihu is becoming oppressive in directing our family. My mother and father don't interfere with his decisions, except my mother does put up a good argument. Concerning Roland, she feels it's best because he's becoming too much like a girl hiding in my skirts. I resent her for saying this, for he's merely twelve years. The gap between my mother and me is widening again. Since Grandmother's death and other family members moving away, our home, although quieter, is missing Grandmother's bright presence and wisdom. I resign myself to Roland being gone and convince myself he'll be safe with Sattelihu. At least he isn't going to fight the Catawbas like his father.

MANY DAYS LATER while harvesting our corn, my father arrives home with others from our village. They've been on an early hunt near the Seneca camp not far from here. While there, a messenger came from the Seneca camp to deliver news to my father. This news would catapult me into more melancholy.

We look up from the field to see my father, Katarioniecha, and the others arrive. My son, John, is fishing with the older boys from the village and Belle, five, is by my side helping me pull the corn from the stalks and placing them into a large basket I carry over my shoulder. My mother and a few other Indian women from the village are working in the field. It's a late summer day and Sky Mother has welcomed autumn in to dance with summer. There are enlivening winds and the sunlight spreads across the landscape in sheets of gold. It's not a day for bad news and when I will look back to this day, I'll remember feeling mocked by the sunny weather. If it had been rainy, I would have believed the Great Spirit was crying with me. But this day, I'll cry alone as my mother will have tears she cannot share.

We leave the field and hurry to my father and even from afar, I note his stiff and somber countenance. As we get close to him, the other Indians move back to ready for the storm they know is coming. My father's eyes are red as he turns to my mother and places his hands on her shoulders. He looks deep into her eyes and is silent for a few moments. And then he speaks clear and without emotion.

"Our son, Karontase, is dead, killed by the Catawbas. He will be with his grandmother and many of our people in the heavens."

My mother crumples to her knees and sobs into the grass.

"Oh Lord! Oh Lord! Not my son! My son, Karontase!"

My father turns to me and places his hands on my shoulders. I know at once what he will tell me, so I turn from him and help my mother to her feet. *Telehemet is also dead.* My mother and I walk into our home with the children and our women friends trailing us. Our men stay outside unable to enter into the sorrow that fills the house of women. My father will stay with the men of the village for comfort this day. It'll take time for himself and my mother to console one another. As I enter our home, I look over to where Grandmother used to sit on her visits and see her ghost look at me with tears in her eyes.

MY MOTHER AND I dress in somber dark mourning clothing so soon after Grandmother's death. Many years ago, we learned from the Moravians that wearing black after a death is respectful to the dead and for those who mourn. As a young girl, I didn't understand why the Moravians, especially the women, appeared to be in mourning all the time. Anna instructed us that in wearing mourning clothing, others in the community will remember that the grieving are tender and in need of compassion. I never saw Grandmother wear this clothing when Chief Shikellamy and others died. It was my mother who insisted we begin this custom after our Moravian friends encouraged us it is what Christians do. It's what the white people do and although it makes sense, I feel restricted in my grief, wearing this black, ugly dress with no color.

The Ho-De'-No-Sau-Nee believe that after death the soul will eventually travel into warm, living light. There, one is met by spiritual guardians and taken on a journey into the sky and a walk along the path of the Milky Way Galaxy. And then a meeting with beloved family and friends before entering into a celestial home. I imagine my Telehemet playing his flute dancing through the stars and wonder if he'll have two homes in the heavens as he had here on earth. My mother is heartbroken over my brother, as I am. Two deaths so close to grandmother's death is hard for me to bear. Over the next few months, I leave our home with my flute and Grandmother's scarlet blanket and go to the edge of the forest to grieve alone.

Chapter Twenty-Two

July 1755

SEASONS GO BY, a year or longer? I think it's the year 1755. My mother and I still wear crow colors and I'm becoming accustomed to this drab clothing. Others are not as likely to speak to me when we're in the fields or visiting in the village. They're uncomfortable with this display of loss that never ends. Although I miss the colors of my beaded clothing, I don't mind taking on the demeanor of a crow or raven for this time. They're the most intelligent of birds and are considered good luck. Crows and ravens share the same distinct characteristics and there are many stories about them, including how they bring fire to people. I tell my children some crow stories and decide to wear the crow's slick midnight color until there's fire in my heart again.

My mother and I are on our way to visit the smithy in Shamokin. She insists we get the flints and locks on our guns fixed and cleaned. My father has taken Roland with some of the other men in the village to hunt near the Seneca camp. John and Belle are staying with Sattelihu's wife and children while we are gone. Grief has been a long visitor with my father. On this hunt, he will meet with some of the warriors at the camp to speak about Karontase and he'll drink rum with them in his son's and Telehemet's memory. My mother cannot forbid him this ritual rum drinking in her son's name.

Strawberry season comes and goes without a festival with dancing and games again this year. Many of our friends have moved away and the few Indians left in our town are busy and show disinterest. I thought of asking the Moravian Brothers to assist us in a thanksgiving festival because they have thanksgiving feasts and cups of thanksgiving rituals in their Christian practices, but decided they're too strict in their rituals and celebrations. My mother insists the Brothers' religious celebrations are much better than our old customs. I'm disappointed, as I wish for my children to participate in the seasonal festivals of the Ho-De'-No-Sau-Nee as I did as a child.

On our way to the Brothers in Shamokin, we come to Otsonwakin where I was born and have many memories. Autumn and winter passed since stopping here and we're dismayed to find the town abandoned. We walk around the village whose lonely, tattered vision is in stark contrast to the burgeoning flowering trees and wildflowers encompassing it. The many low structured tree-barked huts scattered amongst a few log cabins have basts missing and a stench of rancid meat bones and ashes assaults us when we look inside open doors. Old worn brass kettles and a few clay pots lay about in front of some of the cabins. The cabins have been cleaned out and the wooden window shutters torn off. No one is here, except a couple of threatening looking skinny dogs meandering about. The switchgrass, golden rod, milkweed and purple and blue asters have grown profusely, pleased their verdant life isn't being trampled on. I'd like to stay here longer because there's a familiar song in the wind. While my mother collects utensils and plates left behind at some of the huts, I make my way over to the edge of the village where we once lived.

Our cabin has been inhabited by at least two or three families since we left, Christian Indians, who desired to live in homes resembling the homes of the colonists. These were Indians who did well in trade. Although our cabin was simple, it was highly regarded by other Indians. My belly tightens as I enter my first home again. My eyes adjust to the dark as I squat down before the cook fire that has ashes and memories of gathering around it for sustenance and love. I see Grandmother in the corner wrapped in the scarlet blanket telling me about her days as an interpreter in New York. I look to my right and there is Telehemet next to me with a sober and proud countenance, his tattooed arm muscles making my young girl's heart flutter. And I look to the left and there is George Croghan, the heat of him making me angry. I stand up and walk around the cabin. I can see and feel Grandmother and Telehemet, even my brother, Karontase, here, but George? I turn to leave and see a dirty corn husk doll lying near the door. I pick it up and clutch it to my bosom, wishing we didn't have to go to the smithy and spend the night. I suddenly want to go home to Belle and hold her closely.

Mother and I make our way to the Brothers, talking about the abandoned Otsonwakin.

"The Delaware and Mingo have left to move closer to the French, Catrine. The French are offering more of what they will never give these Indians. The poor Indians think the French are stronger than the British."

"They're confused. And they're weary of the settlements being built around them without permission of the Council. Sattelihu has been back and forth from Philadelphia to Onondaga, but there hasn't been a solution. There's little peace now. There's strange war between the British and French and we are caught in the middle. The French have built forts all over the Ohio region and there seems to be no end to this conflict."

"Sattelihu will help the governors make peace soon. We have to trust our Lord Jesus. I'll go to Bethlehem soon and you and the children come, too. It's been a long time and it'll be good to be with people who believe in God."

I end the conversation with my mother. She's frightened, still grieving over Karontase and worried about the fighting and the confusion of the

Indians around us. Bethlehem, Pennsylvania is the headquarters of the Moravian Brothers and my mother and other Christian Indians like to visit there. Anytime she is especially worried, she talks of traveling there. I've shut out any fear and have been sheltering in my own grief and finding peace with my family and the seasons. But today seeing Otsonwakin abandoned, I'm concerned about war and safety. I shudder and clutch Grandmother's scarlet blanket tightly around my shoulders. *Please, Great Spirit, I ask you to hold my children in your love and care.*

Arriving in Shamokin, my mother declares we'll stay two nights, maybe longer. She wishes to partake in some of the services conducted in the Indians' huts who live here. There are Christian Indians who preach and, of course, the Brothers, encourage this. I suddenly feel a child again, not a grown woman who has been married and has children. I try to persuade my mother we need to go home.

"We should return as soon as we can to our home, for there's danger in the air and there are too many people here we don't know."

"We're staying. Of course there are strangers here we don't know. This is a place of travelers coming and going to buy goods and food, Catrine. We'll sleep in our hut and be safe. And our family is where we left them and they're safe. We must trust the Lord Jesus and it'll be good for you and your unhappiness to trust him, too."

Grandmother's hut is here from when she and my grandfather first lived before building the cabin in Otsonwakin where I was born. Chief Shikellamy and his family watched over it and now his sons and their families do. My mother allows the Brothers to use it for travelers when their home is too full. She is proud that she has a place the Lord can use.

I agree to stay here more than a night, feeling powerless, but gentle toward my mother who lights up with new life at the prospect of being in the middle of the Moravian Brothers' mission.

Brother Grube and Brother Wesa greet us as if we're family members they haven't seen in a long time. This is the way of the Moravian Brothers and I'm uncomfortable with such displays of affection.

"Our sister, Margaret, we're please you've come for a visit. And you've brought your daughter, Catharine, as well," Brother Grube exclaims, his face honey colored from working in the fields.

Leonhardt, an Indian who is staying with the Brothers to learn their ways, eagerly takes our horses to feed and water. As we follow the Brothers to their large cabin, we see a family camped in front, their horses laden with maize and food. We stop to greet them and recognize they are Delawares from Otsonwakin from long ago.

"We passed Otsonwakin and everyone has left it empty. It's very sorrowful to see it without life," my mother says. "Why are you here and why did everyone leave?"

The father whose name I cannot remember has a face etched in deep lines and wears none of the bright clothing he used to wear. His somber wife, who is also in tattered clothing, stands next to him. The Brothers, anxious to get back to work, invite us to come inside when we're ready.

"We miss the Montours and Madame Montour," the father exclaims. "We had to leave Otsonwakin because many of our brothers are going to the French. Some go and when they return to Otsonwakin, they try to take us to the French and if we don't go, they threaten us. We will move near Bethlehem now and the Brothers have given us corn and food for our journey."

We say goodbye to the sad looking Delaware family and leave our guns with Brother Wesa, the smithy, and have sapas and warm milk with the Brothers. We exchange news, mostly about the Indians who come for services, for the Brothers don't get involved in war talk or engage in fighting. After, we settle into our hut and as I'm preparing to rest, we hear a loud commotion. I try to ignore it because there are always drunken Indians about. My mother, however, leaves the hut to find out what is happening and will probably try to pray with the drunken Indians. I cover my ears with my blanket and fall into sleep.

"Wake up, Catrine! Wake now! We're having a prayer meeting."

My mother pulls my blanket off as Brother Grube and a number of Indians follow her into our hut. I'm groggy, unsure where I am at first, and when I realize I'm in our hut in Shamokin with a bunch of praying Indians, I turn my back to the wall.

"Are you ill, Sister Catharine?" Brother Grube asks.

I don't reply. I want to return to sleep, but I slowly stand to my feet, wrapping my blanket around my shoulders. There's still daylight, but the sun is preparing to take its leave and I'd like to give my farewells to its rays and be alone.

"I'm well, but tired, and I'm still mourning my husband's death," I reply, hoping for understanding of my reluctance to participate in the evening's ceremony.

My mother begins wailing, "Oh Lord! Oh Lord, help us in our grief."

I put my arm around her and encourage her to sit down on one of the bear rugs near the fire. I sit next to her and wonder if I'll be able to escape to the sunset. Brother Grube places a gentle hand on my mother's shoulder and she cries harder. He motions to one of the Indians to light a fire and quickly two Indians create a fire that brings some warmth to the chill in the early night air. The Indians and Brother Grube sit around the fire and bow their heads for silent prayer. My mother stops crying and holds my hand so tightly I'm surprised at her emotion. I didn't know she was still this bereft with grief over our loss.

In a sing song, comforting, way, Brother Grube reads from his big black Bible.

You have turned my mourning into dancing for me: You have taken off my sackcloth and clothed me with joy, that my soul may sing praise to You and not be silent. O Lord my God, I will give thanks to You forever.

"Oh Lord! Oh Lord!" my mother whispers quietly in French and English over and over after Brother Grube finishes reading.

There's stillness and a sense of peace in our hut, although we can hear a drum beating in the village and the sounds of song and dancing. Out there is where I desire to be, but I must stay with my mother and not embarrass her by leaving. The words of the Bible the Brother has spoken are comforting, but should we not be doing what it says to do . . . removing our mourning clothes, our sackcloth, and dance and sing praise now? As the Indians murmur and fidget while Brother Grube sings a solemn song, I think how strange life is with Indians dancing before the Great Spirit outside and Indians trying to pray to God like white men inside.

After Brother Grube leaves with the Indians and my mother to visit Indian huts who want the gospel, I meander around the village, catching glimpses of the colors the sun painted for the end of this day. These vivid colors are a gift for the soul and I'm happy for these moments. I walk toward the music and find a few men and women dancing a rabbit dance in a circle around a fire and a handful of women dancing outside of the circle. There are women sitting on the ground watching and talking. They stop talking and look at me as I come near and I sense anxiety, not joy. The dance the men are doing is like our strawberry festival dance and it's a social dance that invites all into it. I begin to dance with the other women, closing my eyes so as not to feel conspicuous. I'm in the thrall of remembering how good it feels to dance to our music and song. After a few minutes, the music changes, the drums beat faster, and the dancing resembles a war dance. I stop dancing, as do the other women in the circle and outside of it, and we sit down to watch. I wonder why it suddenly changed to a war dance, for there is no treaty meeting or guests to impress. There are no speeches by the performers. Our war dances are intricate performances and not to be entered into at random. There is whispering among the women near me, but I can't hear what they're saying. Suddenly, a group of Indians and white men dressed as Indians enter into the circle and throw down scalps. The scalps are fresh and the color of blood with its vitality, not brown when life has left it.

"The French and their Indians were here! We killed many, but there are more surrounding us. We have to protect Shamokin!" a white man shouts, his booming voice bringing terror into the faces around me.

"We must leave!" an Indian cries, standing in front of the man. I recognize the Mohican, Samuel.

Indian and white, these men wear the same blood on their clothing from this recent battle. Everyone, including the plantations of whites who settled here, have been in danger of being attacked by the French and their Indian allies. I wait, unsure whether to return to our hut or stay to learn more. The air is thick with fear among the Indians who are mostly Macqua, Cayuga, Tutelo, Conoy, and Mohican.

The bloody men wander through the crowd of dancers and Indians who have ended their evening of entertainment and joy. I stand outside the crowd not knowing what to do, what my mother and I must do, to get home safely to our family. My children. Oh Lord, Great Spirit, is there mercy? Will the Montours be spared because we have French blood? I know this question is foolish, for Grandmother let out most of our French blood long ago and stitched our Indian blood up with British threads. We are forever bound to the British and certainly, the French already know the Montours well, for Sattelihu has met in counsel with the French agent Joncaire and others. Joncaire, the assassin who murdered Grandmother's brother, Louis Montour. I hurry toward our hut to find my mother and think of Grandmother. *My father was a well-known French general from Canada.* Always this same statement to important white visitors who were fascinated with my grandmother's many languages and reputation. Maybe I could also use Grandmother's tactic to protect us from the French and their allies who want to slaughter the Montours. *Please, spare our lives, for remember that my grandmother was the daughter of General Frontenauc in New France. And I am the great granddaughter of a famous general.* I laugh out loud, for I'm not Grandmother and this is not true.

My mother and I hardly sleep through the night, talking and planning how we'll get home safely. Before we tried to sleep, the Moravian Brothers preached comfort from the pages of the Bible and said God would deliver us and promises protection. They assured us they'll continue to ask for counsel from the Lord as to when they should flee from Shamokin, but for now they will stay. John Logan and John Petty, an Indian friend from Otsonwakin, offer to accompany us back to French Margaret's Town. I'm certain my father and Roland will have heard of these French attacks and will have come home.

As we prepare to leave in the morning, Sattelihu rides into Shamokin with a group of white men and Indians. He and his entourage, along with John Logan and John Petty, will now ride with us home. There's fierce and dark talk regarding the attacks by our brothers, the Delaware, Mingo, and Shawnee who have sided with the French. No, not all are going this way of war and rage, for there are Delawares with us now. But even the warring Delawares are my brothers who are attacking defenseless farmsteads all over Pennsylvania and intimidating the Indians who won't rampage with them. These massacres are shaking the very foundation of Pennsylvania. Everyone is fleeing in terror and confusion. My uncle is serious and speaks strongly.

"General Braddock failed in his march on Fort Duquesne and is dead. He was an arrogant general who called the Ohio Indians savages and told them that once the British took back their land the French had taken, it would be the British Empire's. This is why there is outrage among the Delaware, for they feel abandoned by their British brothers. General Washington has been unable to bring them back to our side. But we must still follow our British generals and try to bring order and peace."

There are dark shadows under Sattelihu's eyes and his usual confidence is wavering.

"Sattelihu, I believe you and others can bring peace again," my mother says, nervously.

"These problems have been building for a long time and now they've exploded. There'll be further marches to destroy the French forts, but George Croghan, myself, and others will seek to bring the Indians to counsel once again."

So George Croghan is still alive.

"I remember the treaties," I say to Sattelihu, "the hunger for land by the Ohio Company started long ago. It will always be that the Europeans will want to devour our land like the locust. And you know our friends, the Delawares, have lost much more land than most. Our family, too, is affected, for we're surrounded by new settlers and the Connecticut settlers are the most bold and arrogant, even to the Montours."

Sattelihu doesn't respond, but I hear the Indians behind us mutter and grunt in agreement. He has come from Onondaga and the Six Nations Council carrying the black belt of wampum to deliver to Philadelphia. This belt is the declaration of the Six Nations to enter into this war alongside the British to fight the French. The Ho-De'-No-Sau-Nee claimed neutrality during these long years of discord between the French and British. Many years ago, they signed a treaty of peace with the French and at the same time signed a covenant of friendship with the British. The Ho-De'-No-Sau-Nee had been wise Indians to maintain peace with the French and the British so they could keep their power. And the Europeans have always known they need to have the fierce and powerful Iroquois on their side. Over the years, a few have strayed, and in these past years, I've seen the mighty fabric of the Council beginning to fray. I'm surprised by this dark wampum. What does it really mean? I feel a whirlwind of chaos and darkness sweeping over my beloved land and people I love. We travel quietly, steadfast, and alert, and I can only think of escaping to one place. And now that Telehemet and Grandmother are with the ancestors, George Croghan married, and Pennsylvania unsafe and vulnerable, I'll take my children and journey to where there is peace in a waterfall.

Chapter Twenty-Three

November 1755
George Croghan

"I HAD OVER a hundred pack animals and a dozen men working for me. I ran a circuit from Alleghany to the southwest of the Scioto River. Even French Indians came to trade when we traveled all the way to the Detroit. I had larger quantities, better goods, and prices than the French could provide. They were too busy warring in Europe. And now what? It's over for me, for all of us traders. A year ago, there were seven of us not far from Shawnee Town near the Kentucky River. Yes, I tell you. Kentucky. I was there, me, George Croghan. But two years back, we were attacked by over seventy French and Indians and everything was lost. We've lost everything and owe more to our creditors than we can repay."

George Croghan, his sometimes partner, William Trent, a number of traders, creditors, the traders' eastern merchants, have come together in Philadelphia to seek restitution from French aggression. George wipes the sweat off his brow with an old handkerchief. His partner, Trent, and the others spoke before him and they sit nervously expecting him to make a difference. Governor Morris and the council members are silent and shuffle papers. Virginia and Maryland governors were supposed to be here, too, but didn't think it important enough. George has little hope that their large, motley bunch gathered to sign affidavits and seek to collect losses will impress the Governor. They all agreed to ask the Ohio Company for reimbursement for losses incurred from George Washington's failed march. They also want compensation from Braddock's battle and failure and much more.

Governor Morris sighs before speaking. He wonders if half of what George Croghan claims is true. The man's a braggart, but perhaps he has a right to be. He's been more successful than any other trader in the region.

"Governor Dinwiddie, a shareholder in the Ohio Company, mind you, asked the colonial governors in '53 to mount a military challenge to the French. He sent George Washington, a high ranking officer from the militia. We all know the story now, Mr. Croghan, don't we? Do I have to repeat it again to show you its importance?"

Morris is mad and George knows he's in for a lecture.

"Washington meets the Ohio Indians, who want a fort built to protect their trading interests, but finds these Indians unwilling to support him. And the French have no more respect for our claims to the region than the Ohio Indians. He and his rag tag army slog back to Williamsburg, all the while the French are advancing. Dinwiddie gives Washington more men to march back to the Ohio with. And your partner, Trent, here, is initiated to build a fort. You, Crogan, interpret for Washington when he tries to give gifts to the Indians, but they've entirely given up on us. And with good reason, I conjecture. Mr. Croghan, it's well known that you know these Indians personally. You speak their language . . ."

"Yes, I've known them well, sir, very well, but I've nothing to win back trust now that everything's gone. I already have destitute Indians at Aughwick who seek protection. I've lost buildings, boats, horses, and even worse, men I knew for years. Years of building up trust with the Indians, increasing my trade, and having a successful business is ruined. I've traveled the country and known freedom in western wilderness. The sky has been my roof more than the roofs of my homes and buildings. Now I can't travel anywhere east because I'll be imprisoned for debt. Some of my creditors have come here to ask for help, but there are many who'll haul my ass to prison."

"Okay, Mr. Croghan, for you to understand the seriousness, let me re-tell this story."

Morris shakes his head and pounds his fist on the table. "Why do I need to repeat this, for Christ's sake?" He's silent for a few moments. "The French built Fort Duquesne and Washington couldn't force them to abandon it. He had been carrying orders to make prisoner, kill, or destroy anyone who interfered with the Ohio Company's own fort-building project. But then Washington finally makes some Indian friends and then he, some Senecas and the Half King, Tanacharison, lose control. He learns a French detachment is coming and before he knows what the hell is happening, his very few Indian friends attack and kill General Jumonville. And then a damn massacre occurs. More troops are sent to help, Fort Necessity is built, and again Washington and men set out for Fort Duquesne. And again, none of the Delaware, Shawnee, and Mingo leaders will assist him. And again, Washington retreats. I'll add here, Croghan, that many horses and wagons were lost in Washington's sorry army. So the colonial governments have had loss, as well, so how shall we pay for your own losses? We've all lost and we're still losing. We are now really at war with the French and at war with our Indians who once were on our side, and you expect to have all restored? Are you mad?"

George shuffles, leans back against the table, and waits before saying anything. *Our Indians . . . the British consider the Indians their subjects and he knows damn well they aren't.* This governor has somewhat of a heart, but he's damn long winded. *They were there, by God.*

"Back to Fort Necessity they go and then the French come. They fight, but are trapped, and General Villiers offers Washington a way out if he surrenders. So Washington and men retreat and now the French have control of the Ohio Valley. We're all back to the drawing board to figure out what to do. Our King has warned us about this back country and has had grave concerns that ambitious colonists will alienate our Indian allies and trigger further confrontation with the French. And isn't this what is happening, Croghan?"

Governor Morris takes a long breath before continuing.

"We know how well Braddock faired, don't we? The Delaware, Shawnee, Mingo . . . how many other tribes are on a rampage against us and even some of the Seneca tribe, who are easily seduced by the French? How many, Mr. Croghan? You had opportunity, along with the others who trade and live with the Indians day and night, to persuade them from turning against us. You, George Croghan, who have curried favor with the Indians and have had their world at your feet. You were even given a captain's commission to command the Indian contingent during Braddock's campaign. You are now in Pennsylvania service, might I remind you. This is your bread and butter now, not trading."

Governor Morris pounds the table again with his fist, staring at George.

George stares back and decides he doesn't give a rat's ass about being respectful. "That's god damn unfair, Governor. I've been an honest businessman and it isn't me they're warring against. It's you and the governor of Virginia and the Ohio Company. Dinwiddie, as you said, had stakes in the Ohio, as do most of the House of Burgess. All opportunists ready to take Indian land that the French want, too. And then you don't even give them a fort to protect them on their own land. Even Washington has family interests in the Ohio. What about the Susquehanna Company and the Connecticut settlers claiming charter in Wyoming and the Shamokin area? The Delaware and Shawnee have been pushed off this land."

Governor Morris puts up his hands. "And you have not been an opportunist yourself? How much land have the Senecas given you for keeping squatters away? In regards to the Connecticut contingent, it's believed the Iroquois sold that land to the Susquehanna Company. The Indians want the money and gifts, so isn't this the way of commerce with Indians?"

"No . . . no . . . the Iroquois didn't sell that land. I'm an honored member of their council and they've informed me there were renegade Iroquois who acted on behalf of the Iroquois to sell, but they never sanctioned the sale."

"That is a matter of opinion, Croghan. You know the Iroquois have reigned over the Delaware and other tribes for years and are aware they're rapidly going to the French side. They want these brothers to return and you're the man for this. Let's stick to the subject."

"Why would the Delawares want to return to be under foot of the Iroquois and the British? They're being driven into French arms and it's damn understandable. The French are telling them if we win the war, we'll take all of their land. Isn't this true?"

"It's not up to you to understand, Croghan, and as governor of this colony, I'm asking you to prevail upon them to return to us. And it's not just the Delaware. There are what . . . how many? Ten tribes under this Chief Teedyuscung? They'll be glad for the many gifts and rum they'll get, I'm certain of it."

"I've never stopped prevailing upon these Indians to be aligned with us, their so-called compassionate brothers, the British. My God, all I want is to go home to Aughwick Creek and have some peace. And now I ask for restitution for myself and my fellow traders. Today, right now, Indians loyal to us are here in Philadelphia staying in my home to be protected by our government. They need food and a fort to protect them. They're caught in the cross fire and I fear they'll head to the French. I've been caring for them from my meager income. And to bring back the point of why we're all here—if it wasn't for traders, where would this colony be? And if Washington can command me to take my pack horses and equipment into battle, as an order of the government, and they're killed and everything destroyed, then I need reimbursement from this government."

"Here! Here!" the traders and merchants cry out.

Governor Morris demands silence. "If indeed the Ohio Indians don't see you as an enemy and aren't warring against you, George Croghan, then I'll ask you to go to them again, along with our loyal Indians, who will be compensated well, and not only with rum. Please persuade them to meet with us and you can promise them we'll take care of their needs and concerns. And bring Teedyuscung here, that wily chief, when the Iroquois come to talk about Wyoming Valley and the settlers. He's been riling up the Indians even more. We'll try to get his demands and this Connecticut problem taken care of once and for all. And Mr. Croghan, I'll increase your commission."

George is surprised and glances back at his fellow traders.

Governor Morris continues. "I'll sign the documents now and Trent will draw up a memorial on your behalf and the others to be presented to the Crown. Let's hope you will all get some reimbursement, but I can't promise anything. Your creditors have asked for a ten year extension on the loans and we'll pursue this immediately. Take some time off, Croghan, and then make a trip to the Indians and get back to me."

George's face suddenly appears younger. "How much time, Governor? How much time can I take off?"

"A fortnight . . . and then go to the Indians, George . . . we need to address the acceleration of the attacks on our colonists. We'll win this war with the French, but it'll be difficult with the Delaware and Ohio Indians deserting us."

GEORGE CROGHAN AND a few of his Indian friends set out for Aughwick Creek. While traveling, George ponders Andrew Montour's whereabouts. He and Montour had been together with Chief Shingas at Logstown to give gifts and convince this leader of the Delaware Indians on the Ohio to be loyal to the British. A lot of good that did, for after this meeting, Shingas deserted to the French and his braves started massacring the border settlers. It had been another failed trip and then the two friends parted, as Andrew was called to Onondaga and George went to Philadelphia.

George and his companions stop for a rest and he makes a decision to go to Shamokin, in hopes Andrew will be home by then. He needs this Indian brother and wants to see Catharine and Belle again. Andrew promised George he'd keep Catharine and Belle safe. He plans on being at Aughwick Creek to seek some peace and quiet and then he'll have to follow the governor's orders. He's well aware that William Johnson is eyeing him to become his assistant and has been for some time. Things are rapidly changing and George is uncomfortable.

ON THE WAY to Shamokin, George encounters Chief Teedyuscung and his band of warriors, including the Mohican leader, Abraham. It's as if he had just listened in on the meeting in Philadelphia. A chief of ten Delaware tribes, he's respected by many Indians and settlers and looks to be his usual dignified pompous self. Dressed in a match coat with many brass buttons and earrings, he stops, gets off his horse, and asks George to dismount.

"Big talk. All big talk and no action for the Delaware, George Croghan."

George has empathy for this high spirited and cunning chief. Ever since the Walking Purchase forced Teedyuscung and his followers from their land across the Delaware River, he and his people have felt abandoned. The Iroquois gave away land to the Moravians and the chief, under duress, found a home with the Moravians at their mission, New Gnadenhuetten, also called Huts of Grace. Exchanging land for huts was a slap in the face for the Delaware and George didn't see the grace in it at all. It wasn't long before Teedyuscung, along with five hundred Indians, began accepting their religion and lifestyle. Teedyuscung had been baptized and given the Christian name, Gideon. Many Indians take Christian names and want to be under the safe tutelage of the missionaries. The chief wanted this Christianity if he could have a place to live and eat and have respect as an Indian, but Teedyuscung is his own man and honors his Indian heritage. Ultimately, he couldn't abide by the life of the Moravians and left them.

George gets off his horse and bows in respect to Teedyuscung and Abraham. Teedyuscung has the good sense in making friends with enemies and still keep his dignity, and George feels kindred to this. He likes the man, but he perceives in his countenance a dark root of discontent has risen and Teedyuscung is not to be crossed. George is certain his ire and machismo has become the stealth behind some of the recent Indian attacks.

"Chief Teedyuscung . . . Gideon, I'm pleased we've encountered one another in these woods that are becoming darker by the hour. I understand the Connecticut settlers in Wyoming are becoming more of a nuisance. You and your people have moved back to stand your ground in peace. I've just left Governor Morris and he tells me there's going to be a meeting with the Iroquois Council to discuss the sale of land to these settlers. He'd like you to be present. Will I be able to find you in Wyoming or at your cabin at Gnadenhuetten?"

"We're living in Wyoming to defend this land, our land, against these Connecticut settlers. I will not go to Gnadenhuetten again. I've asked our people to leave there to return to Wyoming to reclaim their land, but many of them refuse. They're under the magic spell of the Christians and no longer care for our ways and land."

"Perhaps they feel it's futile. You can understand this. You yourself settled in with the Moravians and lived with them and broke bread with them."

"What choice did I have, but to make sure my people, all of them, had a home and didn't starve?"

"Chief, I respect you and the governor honors your leadership among your people and values your friendship with the British, but you need to accept the Iroquois Council's wisdom on these matters."

"My Iroquois uncles will always have my respect, but I'm chief over these tribes and need to make decisions. In 1736, these Iroquois uncles promised only to sell to Pennsylvanians. They gave away too much once, but now they don't want any further land given to white settlers. And do you remember what Chief Hendrick said to the commissioners in Philadelphia? I was there and you were, also."

"I do remember. It was a threat and now it's being carried out. I understand, but we need to take council and seek peace . . ."

"Don't tell me to seek peace. You were not born here. You're not an Indian, no matter how many languages you learn and how much land the Senecas give you."

George says nothing and allows Teedyuscung to expound as he is wont to do.

"My Mohawk uncle said that we will never part with the land at Shamokin and Wyoming. Our bones are scattered there and on this land there has always been a great council fire. We will not part with it, for we reserve it to settle such of our nations upon it as shall come from the Ohio, or any other Indians coming to us. We shall invite all Indians to come and live here and so we may strengthen ourselves."

Teedyuscung shakes his kingly head and his earrings shimmer in the sunlight. He continues to speak and George patiently listens.

"And these uncles promised the Delaware the Wyoming Valley long ago and why should we have it taken from us by settlers? To speak truthfully, I don't think the governors value friendship with us, George Croghan. If they valued me and my people, we wouldn't have to defend ourselves alone. If the British were true brothers, we would have our land back and not have to turn to the French."

"Have you turned your friendship away from us when we have not done so with you? We're asking for your council and are seeking to bring everyone together to settle this matter in Wyoming. Will you promise to participate in this council?"

"My time is valuable, George Croghan, even if I'm not valued . . ."

"Governor Morris will reward you and your people with gifts and . . ."

"My people and I want more than rum and shrouds."

"You'll receive more than those things . . . and with respect," George answers, bowing to the chief. As he and his band take leave, he hears grunts and murmurs and knows there's murder in the air.

GEORGE TRAVELS INTO Shamokin the next day and goes to Andrew's home to find no one there. He rides to French Margaret's Town and it's eerily quiet. Margaret's home is closed up and a few stray dogs linger around the door. Surrounding the village and Margaret's fields, he sees new buildings and homes, but there's no one about. He knows these structures were built by the Susquehanna Company from Connecticut. George walks around the cabin calling for Margaret and Catharine, but there's no answer. As he and his friends leave and slowly ride through town, a couple of Indians come riding down the main street.

"Gnadenhuetten is being attacked," Isaac Still, a Moravian Christian Indian, cries out as he approaches George and his friends. George knows this messenger and interpreter. He's no lying man and was baptized and trained by the missionaries at Huts of Grace.

"What happened Isacc?"

"Chief Shingas and his band of warriors are killing and burning."

"Is Teedyuscung with him?"

"No! Teedyuscung and five hundred braves from Wyoming came to the huts a while back to get the Indians to return to the valley to help defend the land against white settlers, but most of them refused to leave."

"I know this, Isaac, and he was back there again asking them to leave a few months ago. He's wavering all the time, like Shingas, between the French and us. Could he be with Shingas now? George knows that Isaac respects Teedyuscung."

"Teddyuscung, my brother, would not do this."

"Did you just come from Gnadenhuetten?"

"No . . . I was on my way there and a few Indians who escaped met me and gave me this news. I've come for Sattelihu to get his help."

George looks back at his friends who sit on their horses quietly, listening and observing. Thus far, they're still aligned with him and the British. He speaks in Lenape and asks if they want to go to Gnadenhuetten, warning them they might encounter their own brothers committing this rampage. These braves are used to battle, but confusion is rampant now and he wonders what is best. They agree to go with him.

The Moravian missionaries are gentle peace-keeping pacifists and take care of the Indians when they're sick and hungry. George wonders how the Indians have become so bitter to attack the Moravians, but as soon as he thinks this, he knows why. It's been gradual, a god damn, and slow take over. His Irish roots rise in him as he remembers the dire oppression of the British in his country. He, a Protestant, and part of the problem. This was why he had left for a new land. To start over with a clean slate and to do honest work and learn about these fascinating people he has grown to respect. And yes, to make some god damn money. As they ride toward Gnadenhuetten, a bitter taste fills his mouth as he realizes he is once again a part of the problem.

WHEN GEORGE AND the warriors arrive, it's too late for them to do anything. The house, buildings, and huts have been burned to the ground. It's quiet and there's no sound of human voices, only a robust robin singing loudly nearby. His Indian friends know this rampage was done by some of their people and remain on their horses waiting for George to tell them what's to be done. George doesn't know what to do. There's terror in this land and he wants to find Catharine and Belle and take them to safety. He wants to go to Aughwick and make sure his Mohawk wife, Suzanne, is safe. He wants this horror to cease and peace to come, but he knows it won't for a long time, if ever. The attackers have left and those who might have escaped are gone. He gets off his horse to look at a body lying on the ground. It's Martin Nitschmann he met at the Montour home years ago. He's been scalped and lies dead, an eerie half smile frozen on his gentle face. George wonders if the man's wife is alive. He can do nothing now, but count the dead and look in the nearby woods for any survivors. But he doesn't hear any moans of the injured and except for that one ridiculous bird, it's hauntingly quiet, church quiet. He looks over at where the church would have been, but it's smoldering, burnt to the ground. He tells his friends to look around the mission.

As George walks through the destruction of the house, he doesn't notice that his boot has caught fire from cinders until it reaches the hem of his pants. He cries out, stomps, and puts out the flames, moving quickly around the mission.

He eventually finds eleven bodies, some scalped outside the house as they tried to flee and the others caught in the house fire who now lay among debris. They're barely distinguishable as human. The barns and stables are burned and all the corn, hay, and cattle destroyed. He's never smelled the stench of human and animal flesh together and he clutches his stomach and covers his mouth and nose with the sleeve of his jacket. He walks slowly to a hut that is still standing, wondering if someone is inside. Next to the hut is a cook fire and there's a left-over meal of bread and milk just eaten by the marauding murderers. George kicks over the bowls and mugs and turns to the sky to scream at that damn bird who sings cheerfully in a peaceful blue sky with billowing soft clouds.

Chapter Twenty-Four

Catharine

I DON'T KNOW for certain what caused me to *really* see the despair of my Indian brothers and sisters. Their despair gradually whittled away at my happiness, this knife of oppression against my fellow Indians. Stories happened nearby or far away and to some in our village, but they were not mine. I only half listened to these stories, preferring to escape to the woods. And then I sat in treaty and heard and saw greed taking its toll on whites and Indians. I had been sheltered in love and mostly abundance. There was scarcity at times as a child, but it didn't last and there was always a forest, festivals, and then a marriage to find joy in. Even with the disdain of some of the whites who visited our home, it paled compared to the love of my family. I grew up with my fellow Indians and although I was Catrine with the light skin who had special privileges as a Montour, we played together as children and I listened to their stories. When I was dizzy molting from girlhood to womanhood, I preferred the forest and Great Spirit over playing our Indian games and being with the village Indian children. And because there were always many people crowding our cabin, I didn't have time to see and listen to my friends as I once did as a child. John Logan had been one of my closest friends, but since the silly dancing we did at the Lancaster Conference, we have hardly seen one another. He married and I married and I see him and other childhood friends only at ceremonies and festivals. And then with all our moves and the recent worries over war with the French, festivals and village life are being neglected in our village.

It has been a series of events that pulled the scales off my eyes to see the dire plight of my Indian brothers and sisters . . . and the difficulty for myself and family. We returned from our visit to the smithy and the mission and there were more white families from Connecticut building a settlement surrounding our village. The Pennsylvania government is opposed to this and the Iroquois stated they never sold them land and so we must leave it to the Iroquois Council to intervene. My Indian people are being forced to live with missionaries and to go to the Ohio and now where will we, the Montours, end up in all of this? We'll be sending our children to their schools, praying to their God in their churches, and will always be inferior in their eyes. When I saw Roland's face bruised from a fight with one of the children from this new settlement, my blood rose and boiled over and Grandmother's voice was no longer heard. Grandmother's and Sattelihu's allegiance to the British isn't mine. I have never felt great loyalty to the British and don't understand the obedience required in this long time covenant chain of friendship. The Montours are identified more as Ho-De'-No-Sau-Nee and I have always assumed we had the power over the British governors and not the other way around. I have been quite blind. I have lived my life like a canoe made of strong oak that floats down the Susquehanna River. I have been carried sometimes gently and sometimes roughly along, having no say or will in my journey. I am of my strong oak family and Indian blood, living on this mother river, Susquehanna, which in Algonquian, means people of the muddy river. My great grandmother was an Algonquian woman from Quebec and it's fitting that I was born near this river that has carried me well. And then one day in 1755, Chief Teedyuscung met me by the Susquehanna and told me the history of the Susquehannocks.

I was sitting with Belle who is now six years old. I was teaching her how to fish and had taken some time away from the noise and discussion in our home. Because of so much violence in our land, Sattelihu is going to send his family to Philadelphia for protection under Governor Morris. His daughter, Madelina, Kayadaghscroony, however, refuses to go. She's in love with a Delaware brave and wants to stay with his family. My uncle objects, but she is strong and will get her way. Sattelihu, commissioned by the British, to bring our Delaware brothers, the Ohio Indians and others who are feeding out of French hands, back to the British, is anxious. He wants us all to go to Philadelphia. My mother wants to go to Bethlehem with the Moravians and insists I go, too. My father, dignified as ever, is silent. There was too much argument and confusion in our home and I took Belle and went to this river that always calms me.

I placed an eel in a basket between Belle and me. Belle is surprised to see it move, for she has only seen it cooked over a fire and eaten its tasty flesh. I don't wish to bring my daughter unease, but it's time she learn that death can bring us life.

"Put it back in the water. I don't want to eat it. It wants to go back to the river, Mama!"

Belle touches it and pulls her hand away. The eel squirms less and I take Belle's hands in mine.

"We will give thanks to the Great Spirit for this eel's life and how it will nourish us later."

Belle pulls her hands away at the same time I hear someone behind me. I turn to look at the well-known Chief Teedyuscung who is with a band of Indians. I stand to greet him and Belle throws the eel back into the river.

"Belle! Now we'll not have anything good for tonight's meal."

Belle rushes to hide in my skirts as Teedyuscung and the Indians chuckle over my child's behavior.

"Belle has her own mind and this is good for someday she'll serve her clan well," Teedyuscung says.

I wonder about my clan. We Montours with our European blood. French, Algonquin, Oneida, my mother is all three and my father is Mohawk. And I married a Seneca and Belle's father is Irish. Who will Belle become? I shake off my fearful thoughts for the future. I want to live by this river and be at peace, but of late, there is no peace.

"Chief Teedyuscung, it's been a long time since I've seen you. There are rumors you are fighting for all of us to stay in Wyoming Valley, but need you go to the French for help?"

There I go again . . . it seems every time I'm in the presence of chiefs, I speak without thinking. It's not like me. I should have more experience so it wouldn't become so awkward, but it's been a long time since I've been with Sattelihu at a treaty.

Chief Teedyuscung motions to his men to water the horses and after he dismounts, he sits by the river, beckoning me to sit next to him. I do so reluctantly, as I know Sattelihu has spoken of his ire toward him now as he stirs up the Indians against the colonists.

"Granddaughter of Madame Montour, do you know the history of this river? Do you know that the Susquehannocks, the people of the muddy river of long ago were killed by the smallpox epidemic given to them from the white men? Then it was the Ho-De'-No-Sau-Nee who fought and defeated them. The few who remained were driven from here and the rest disappeared when they settled with the Mohawk and Oneida . . . which is your blood, as well. It's good you honor this river and take her fish."

I'm uncomfortable. I didn't know this story of the river and wish I had known. I had heard little of the Susquehannocks and sometimes I was perplexed by so many tribes, many of the smaller ones this chief is now courting to the French.

"I'm pleased to hear this truth, for I didn't know these facts and isn't it the story of tribes to be driven away by disease or others."

"The Ho-De'-No-Sau-Nee are powerful uncles in our lives and it was you, wasn't it, at the treaty in Lancaster, who saw that more land was given to the whites because of them? I give respect to my uncles, but the Delaware needs to make new homes far from them, and the Ohio has been drawing many of my people there for years. And in Wyoming where I settled long ago, there are more white settlers coming to take our land. They're already building houses and buildings and refusing to give us a school or cabins to live in. My people are being pushed out. And if our British brothers destroy the French, they will destroy us next."

Belle rushes from me to sit closer to the river. She is humming to herself, trying to ignore this grown up talk.

"I've felt the Delaware's loss, but I'm not one to make decisions about war and peace. And Sattelihu . . ."

"Your uncle is a good man, Catharine, and he cares for all tribes, but he is fearful of losing British coins."

"He's only trying to bring you and your people and the other tribes back to our British brothers for peace and protection."

"Oh daughter . . . you are a mockingbird now? Do you have the spirit of a mockingbird? Are the British your brothers? The lesson I leave you with, granddaughter of a wise woman, is for you, too, to become wise. We all will become like the Susquehannocks and be no more. We'll become the brooms we sell to the whites and they will use us to sweep up our land and ways. Was it not your grandmother's wish for you to become a word maker as she was?"

IT WAS AFTER this time on the banks of the Susquehanna with Teedyuscung, in the midst of the stormy winds of change in our land, that my life capsized. I could no longer drift on this river. It was time to separate from this mother and perhaps my powerful mother, Margaret. As our family fled from the violence and chaos of this ongoing war between the French and British and their allies, my mother and father went to Tioga Point and I went to Kah-ni-sti-oh, New York. We are not far from one another, for the Kah-ni-sti-oh River is a tributary of the Tioga River, but my mother's birth waters from now on will not drown out my own voice. It was the Susquehanna who carried me on her waters to this new river, Kah-ni-sti-oh. Kah-ni-sti-oh is a Seneca name meaning *putting in of canoe* and so I'm still like a canoe, but I control my course now. There are many creeks and hidden waterfalls, high ridges and deep valleys. This village is only twenty miles long and the river courses through it. People here tell me I'm not far from Eagle Cliff Falls, the waterfall that captured my affection many years ago. This is Seneca territory and I'm welcomed because I was married to the Seneca Telehemet, but also because Teedyuscung helped me come here. There are many Delawares here, for the Seneca and Delaware are acting as one during these turbulent times.

Kah-ni-sti-oh is a refuge from Shamokin and the Wyoming Valley and there are many log houses, a council house, forts, orchards, and fields of corn. There are a couple of renegade British soldiers living here quietly, as well as some Indians and former slaves who have left behind the past and seek to be hidden. Besides the Delawares and Senecas, there are members of other tribes. Kah-ni-sti-oh is a secret hideaway and there is more solitude for me here than in Wyoming Valley. I live in a log home with my three children and on occasion, travelers like

Teedyuscung and his friends stay with me. I have bought horses and cattle, even a few hogs and chickens, and have a field for planting. The women here help one another with the planting of corn and vegetables. Kah-ni-sti-oh is also a place for schemes to be made to bring justice to our people. And yes, there's some French alliance, although no one proclaims this outright. We live as if we are just another Indian village, planting, harvesting, hunting, and there's been time for some of the festivals. I respect and love Sattelihu and the people I've known all my life, including George Croghan, but it's important for me to leave everyone. My uncle is displeased and whether he knows my sentiments and some of the lives of the people here, I don't know. As for George Croghan, I dream of him and, of course, see his face in Belle's. My sister, Esther, and her family are still in the Wyoming Valley, safely away from the turmoil, she says. She'll take care of our mother's land and livestock. She'll, no doubt, help Teedyuscung as I'm willing to do. No one would want to cross Esther and she'll have her way no matter who is ruling the land. My sister, Molly, and her family live in the Mohawk Valley. My mother insists that when this craziness is over, we'll return to Shamokin and the Wyoming Valley and Molly will return, too. I, however, have become like a turtle and I'm comfortable making my own shell wherever I move to. I want to make a home with love for my children. I've been pursued by an old chief, a couple of young warriors, and one of the white soldiers, but my heart is not inclined to marriage. My passion is for my children, solitude, and justice for the Indian. My dreams satisfy my longing for what I once had with Telehemet and George Croghan. I'm much too busy, I tell myself, for another marriage.

The French esteem the Indian more than the British do and don't treat us as an inferior people with double talk. For once, I'm at ease speaking French and acknowledging that my great grandfather was a French fur trader, although sometimes like Grandmother, I like to say general. I don't feel compelled to be anyone but Catrine here and my voice is taking on its own timbre. My face has changed, too, and the face I wear is sometimes painted black for strength. I go to this new Kah-ni-sti-oh River for courage and to paint my face and let this new mother river instruct me. I'm ready, but I've not worn red, the color of war, although I've sat in my home and by the fires with Teedyuscung and given approval for this war paint that also symbolizes strength and success. Today my children are playing with some of the Indian children near our home and I've come to the river to paint my face blue and green. Blue for wisdom and green for endurance, for although I wash all of these paints off before I return to my cabin, their power is given to me from this time at the river. And it is today, Teedyuscung is traveling from Fort Niagara to Bethlehem, but is stopping at my home first. I've caught fish from this river and we'll have a feast with others from the village. A messenger sent by Teedyuscung said he is in need of a horse, for the French disappointed him, and he wants to exchange a white prisoner for a horse.

This is why I've come to the river and painted my face the colors of wisdom and endurance. I'd rather have my horses than white captives who will interfere with the rhythm of this new life.

Chapter Twenty-Five

PALEFACE. NO ONE in my family ever called a white person a paleface and neither had I. The term had little to do with the color of skin, but what that color, or lack of color, symbolized. *Oppression. Arrogance. Lies.* Certainly, the top soil of my life as a Montour had given me some protection, but when I dug further into living as an Indian, I struck the similar rock of intolerance and hate as my people had. *We who are of the barbarous nature and live savage, ignorant lives.*

But here before me now is a woman who looks to be about my years and the first word that comes to me is paleface. Her dark wool cloak is torn and dirty, but still loosely tied around her neck. Long red hair has fallen out of her cap, telling the truth of her fire. She wears a simple, dark green woolen dress with sleeve ruffles that attempt to defy her dull clothing. Her cotton apron, once white, is brown from grease, ale, and spots of blood. Her fists are clenched by her sides, she shakes and hisses incoherent prayers, and refuses to look at me.

Earlier, Chief Teedyuscung and his warriors, including the Beaver King, feasted on corn with shredded fish and ground-up nuts, roasted venison, and stewed pumpkins. Belle was my helper over the cook fire and Roland and John had hunted with a few village men the day before for today's feast. My children were all abed at the end of the cabin, but I knew they listened and watched. All the while my friend, Teedyuscung, and his warriors ate and drank my rum, I didn't know whether the messenger had been right about a captive, for no prisoner had entered my home. I hardly ate as Teedyuscung boasted about his exploits and adventures back and forth from Wyoming Valley to Fort Niagara to meet with the French. He did, however, echo my own feelings about the relationship with the British and the French. The French were triumphing in war at present and we were playing with fire with both.

"The Indians can make peace and the Indians can also break peace when made," Teedyuscung says confidently as he guzzled more rum. Looking over at me, he smiles. "Don't ever believe you are without power, Catharine. God has made the Indian and white man equal and we Indians will remind them of this."

Teedyuscung struggles with yearning to go back to the Moravians' beliefs, but stays this course to seek justice for his people. He enjoys his own strength and speech among the Indians and Europeans and hopes history will include his name. Maybe they will, I ponder, and if my name is next to his, will I be proud?

Teedyuscung and his party finish eating and decide to travel at night to Bethlehem. I'm relieved that I'm not going to be tested by my river face painting and hold captive an English prisoner, for there had been no prisoner whoop when Teedyuscung and his men came into town. As soon as I think this, one of the warriors leaves the cabin and returns with this frightened and defiant woman. *Paleface.*

Teedyuscung smiles at me and speaks in the Lenape language. "Let me choose a horse from the barn, Catharine, and I'll promise to see you before the snows arrive. This woman is called Elsa. She's a strange white woman who can act like a bobcat, but she'll do what you wish and you are now her mistress. Listen to your grandmother, Madame Montour, for she'll guide you with her wisdom. She's very much alive in you."

Teedyuscung and his warriors leave and I stand trembling almost as much as this sad creature before me. I think of my beautiful missionary friend, Anna, and all I want to do is drink a cup of sassafras tea with this woman, for she's in need of comfort. Yes, Grandmother, I need your wisdom. But as I see Grandmother's face in my mind, I can't be as hospitable as she had been. I pull out a chair from the table that is laden with the dirty dishes from the feast.

"Sit down and be still. If you are praying, stop. Your prayers I don't wish to hear. They make no sense. I need quiet in this home and I don't want to hear you make any sounds unless I speak to you first."

Elsa defiantly locks eyes with mine. We stand this way for a few moments and then I gently put my hands on her shoulders and push her into the chair. She doesn't resist, but sits and drops her head and weeps so loudly I fear Belle will come running. I don't know what to do with this outburst. I have hardly ever cried in front of my family or husband and never before a stranger or visitor. My mother's tears are for Jesus and I'm used to them, but this woman's outburst is akin to an animal stuck in a hunter's trap.

I let her weep as I clear the table and bring in the dogs to give them the bones left over on the plates. Eventually, her crying turns to whimpering, and then she is silent, but her head remains down. The dogs chew on the bones and then bring them to Elsa's feet and drop them. They nuzzle her knee caps as if asking her what is wrong. They are gentle mutts, but fierce enough to protect me. They don't sense this woman is a threat or they would be growling. I pull a chair out and sit across from Elsa and fold my arms. I have to make certain both the dogs and this woman know I am the matron of this home.

"Look at me, Elsa. We must talk."

Elsa looks up and her face has softened. Her eyes are red rimmed and I can smell her odors. *This woman hasn't bathed in a long time.* Her cheeks are wet with tears that smear over the tiny brown spots on her face. I have never seen a white woman with so many of these marks which make her ghost-like and strange.

These sun spots make the paleness of her skin stand out all the more. A moon of a face, she has, round and full, and as interesting as one of our Indian false faces in ceremonies for healing.

"You speak very good English, Indian woman. Better than me. I don't know many Indians speak so good as you."

"I speak many languages, but probably not your language."

"I am from Sweden two years ago."

Elsa utters in her mother tongue while staring into my face like a wild woman.

"Stop! You will not speak your faraway words while you are living with me and my family. Speak only English and maybe you'll learn to speak it better and when you return to your people, you can tell them you learned good English from an Indian woman."

I laugh at this irony and Elsa quiets, but doesn't laugh.

"So Chief Teedyuscung took you to the French, but they didn't want you?"

Elsa looks away from me.

"You were taken in an attack and your sorrows are real. I'm sorry for your grief. Many Indians suffer from years of sorrow at the hands of white men and now is our time to negotiate with war paint. You will become a part of this family and village. You'll work in the fields and make food and help keep this home clean, for we aren't dirty savages. Indian women laugh at the cook fires and tables of the white people, for they see that you bake your bread in dirty ashes and are careless about cleanliness when you cook your meat. We are delicate in our eating and are particular about cooking. We have many recipes and you will learn them."

Elsa looks at me, wiping her eyes. "I'll not become your servant or part of this family."

Elsa and I stand at the same time. Roland and John come from the other side of the cabin and stand behind Elsa, ready to assist if she tries to strike me or attempt to leave. She turns to see the two boys and then moves toward the door of the cabin. The dogs growl and stay by me, ready. Roland and John quickly grasp Elsa's arms before she escapes and as my boys hold her arms back, I tie her hands with a rope Roland hands to me.

"I don't want to hurt you or make you uncomfortable, but you'll not defy me and for this night, you'll sleep next to me without the use of your arms. And if you cry and scream, I'll cover your mouth."

I nod to the boys to return to their beds and take Elsa's arm and guide her to the corner of the house where my bed is. I let go of her and place a few blankets on the floor.

"Sleep now and tomorrow morning we'll go to the river and wash, for you stink like a possum long dead."

Elsa slumps to the floor, turns her back to my bed, and closes her eyes. I watch her for a few moments and then leave the house and stand outside beneath the crooked smile of a moon. It's quiet, except for the screech of an owl. I look up at the thin lipped moon and smile back. My trembling has ceased and the moon and I are now sisters in this death of one season and the beginning of another, for I now have my first captive.

THE DAYS WALK on into autumn and then there is much work to be done for the harvest. Elsa has difficulty settling in, but whatever I ask her to do, she does it well. She is strong and especially likes to care for the horses and livestock more than gardening and cooking over the fire. The only time I see her smile is when she's caring for the animals and whispering to them in her language. When she's inside my home, she is stoic and rigid, but follows orders. One day, I notice her staring at Belle with tears in her eyes. I've not asked Elsa about her children and we never speak of anything but garden work, cooking, and cleaning. I fear Elsa's children might have been killed or taken captive and I don't want to know if they died.

Teedyuscung and his warriors, and none of the Indians in the village, discuss the attacks upon white settlements when he is here. Teedyuscung met with the Pennsylvania governor and commissioners in negotiations, but denies involvement in these attacks. When I heard of the massacre at Gnadenhuetten, I sorrowed for the missionaries, but was relieved to know Teedyuscung wasn't responsible. The Shawnee Chief, Shingas, was. Teedyuscung is not one to cross, but he's not a brutal man and his wife told me all he wants is their ancestral land for his people and to live in peace. And if it can only come through warfare, it has to be so. Sattelihu and Grandmother always said the Delawares are less ruthless than other Indians. Teedyuscung claims his war parties are small and that he's a diplomat first and foremost and he doesn't like to take up the hatchet. Teedyuscung has lost two of his children to smallpox in the last year and this makes him especially tender toward all children. I hope he is merciful in these raids. These matters of warfare and death are everyday occurrences in our Indian lives now. I once welcomed home my husband who had blood on his clothing from warring with the Catawbas. I have welcomed my father, uncle, and Indians in my village home from warring and hunting and for most of my life, these two kinds of deaths merged together. I did not see human blood from warring, except on the scalps brought home. The bloody animals from the hunt are as natural to me as the corn taken from its stalks. Thanks is always given for the animals whose flesh give us life, but are there thanks for the lives taken in war? Here I am now a participant not in treaty and peace talks, but in taking prisoners during this strange war the Delaware and other Indians are having with the British.

I STAND AT the entrance of the barn and see Elsa sitting on a bale of hay near Roger as he grooms one of my horses. Roger is mysterious and I want to talk with him, but his English words swing so far up into the air and then down, I can hardly understand him. He's a fair haired man with strong shoulders and a kind face. He, his wife, and son came from Scotland years ago to homestead in the New York colony. Some time ago, his wife and son died from a Huron Indian raid. He had been out in a neighbor's field and didn't know what happened until he returned home. Roger then sold his farm and walked to nowhere, not caring where he would end up. He walked right here into Kah-ni-sti-oh and when he saw the Indians, he welcomed them to kill him. Instead, they invited him to live with them and he built a small cabin and works his own garden, keeps to himself, but helps care for the buildings and goes on the hunts with the other men. He doesn't participate in the festivals or sit around the fire at night and drink with the village men and women who live here. A few months ago, he asked if he could help care for my horses, for the barn is my own. Some of the other villagers keep their livestock in my barn for the winter. My children and I are able to care for our animals and at first I refused Roger, but then I said yes because it frees me to go to the river and gives me time to make moccasins and add ornamentation to clothing. My boys love to help Roger in the barn and I have had no complaints.

Once this past winter, I brought soup and cornbread to the men working in the barn. As I served them, their talk turned to anger over the settlers moving into Wyoming Valley. Roger never participated and only nodded in agreement. He'd glance at me as if trying to read my mind, but I was quiet. And now seeing Elsa and Roger near one another engaged in quiet conversation stirs a fire within me. I listen, but can't understand what they're saying. Memories of times with my Telehemet and George Croghan come back to me and I realize how much I miss conversations with a man. I rustle my skirt and walk into the barn.

"Are you finished with the horses, Elsa? If there's no other work to be done here, begin the meal for tonight. There will be ten or twelve of us."

Elsa blushes and tries to hide her anger. She immediately stands and swishes past me. I can smell her sweat, the sweat of longing and arousal. I look at Roger as he puts his hat on, preparing to leave. His eyes always appear sorrowful, but there's a slight shimmer in them now.

"We meant no harm. Elsa is missing her family and I'm missing mine. Penn's Creek Massacre, fourteen killed. You must know of it."

"Yes, but here in this village, we don't talk about the attacks. Some men here plan for raids, but this place has many, like you, who do not. When you accepted to live here, you understood you were in an Indian village that sometimes goes to war, even with white men."

Roger's face darkens with anger and his usual sorrowful countenance disappears. "Her husband was killed in that attack and her daughter was taken captive. She would like to know what you are going to do with her and where her daughter is."

Suddenly, I know Roger doesn't see me as a friend, but an enemy. The same as the Indians who killed his family and Elsa's husband.

"My husband was killed in war against an enemy tribe. Elsa and you are not the only ones who sorrow. She and her family and you and your family came to this land with dreams of making it your own. But this land had others who dwelled here since ancient times. And these people, my people, had been dreamed by the Great Creator. All this land you desire to possess will become like the Indian who will not be seized. The land and the Indian will harden against you, for they are of the same spirit. The feet of the Indian has roots going deep into this land, but your feet are rootless. The Europeans speak silky words about sharing this land of the Great Spirit, but they're slippery words and soon the Indian finds he's living on a small parcel of his own land and the white man has a bigger piece of his land. Land that has the Indians' roots in it and you want to dig up these roots and plant other roots that don't belong here. Bigger buildings, houses, and schools that are not for our children unless we dress and speak like you. I've watched it all my life and now I want my children to live free with the roots of their feet planted in their own land."

"You are also French, Catharine?" Roger asks.

"My great grandfather was a French fur trader who came to this land to take from it, yes. And while he tried to plant his feet in our land, he planted his seed in an Algonquin woman."

Roger takes off his hat and moves closer to Catharine. "Forgive me if what I say angers you, Catharine, but you are Iroquois, yes?"

"Ho-De'-No-Sau-Ne. I am Oneida and Mohawk . . ."

"And these Indians, the Ho-De'-No-Sau-Ne, have fought other tribes and dug up the roots of their brother and sister Indians to cast them out. Indians have always fought one another and still fight one another and don't always live a peaceful existence together. They tore other tribes' roots up so their feet had nowhere to rest. My country, too, has had root problems, as you say. There were once clans who fought one another and then Great Britain came to rule all of us. All over the world, this happens. People are uprooted and the usurpers plant their own roots."

"But here we were all Indian . . . Indian feet have the same roots and when we're uprooted by tribal warring, our feet transplant in soil we know well. If we fight, it is a family fight and we become one another's family."

"It's gone too far now, Catharine. People from other lands have heard the siren call of this land's wilderness and freedom and no matter the danger, they have been allured and enticed to its hope."

"I don't understand siren call . . ."

"It comes from Greece of long ago . . . a land . . . a story . . . myths . . . you have many stories here, too. And in this one, a creature, half bird and half woman, lures sailors to destruction by the sweetness of her song. Across the seas, we have been lured by the stories of fecund and beautiful land and yes, the stories of people, like you, so different from us who we want to know."

"You want to know? You want to possess, control, and destroy."

Catharine stomps her foot and turns away from Roger. Her thoughts are in turmoil and she knows much of what Roger says is true. She feels a gentle touch upon her shoulder and it reminds her of George Croghan's touch. It softens her and she faces Roger.

"No, Catharine. I don't want to possess, control, and destroy. I've been allured by the sweetness of this land and then destroyed by its people. I'll never be the same man and will never listen to the siren call again."

Catharine feels tears pooling in her eyes and wonders if she will suddenly weep loudly like Elsa. She lets them fall as Roger lets his tears fall, both silently. *Tears, not roots, are what matters.*

Chapter Twenty-Six

George Croghan and Andrew Montour

GEORGE LAUGHS HEARTILY as he, his brother, and a couple of Indian friends travel on the Great Shamokin Path on the way to Fort Augusta.

"I'm finally going to get relief. The Pennsylvania Assembly saw fit to pass the bill. And now to the mighty Fort Augusta that has kept hundreds of the French and their Indians away. There's been a turning favor in my life and a turning favor in this god damn war with the French. I'll pay my creditors eventually or be damned, but I won't pay interest."

"You gave away land to pay your creditors, George. Will you obtain legal titles to what is left?" asks his half-brother, Edward, who came from Ireland a year ago and was more than eager to follow in his brother's footsteps, although constantly challenging him.

"No worries, little brother. I've traveled the wilderness and know Indian customs well enough and these skills keep me from being imprisoned for my debts. The British government sorely needs my expertise to negotiate with the tribes in the Susquehanna and Ohio valleys."

"You're ever so humble, George," Edward says, laughing. "I've come too late to see these vast lands you've told me about, the wild animals, and the pelts you've traded, and now there's war. War against the French by god, is one thing, but for the Governor to declare war on the Delaware and other Indians will only push them further into French arms."

"Don't ruin my mood. It was a rash decision and made over the heads of the Iroquois who should be the only ones to deal with the Delaware. I'm meeting Andrew at the fort and then, little brother, we'll go home to Aughwick. I still have this slice of paradise to lay my head down on in peace before I vow to leave it, the trading, and all it stands for."

"No time for Aughwick, really, George, and you won't leave it. The Delawares are brutal in their attacks and they've been taking captives. You, Johnson, and Montour will have a hard time bringing them back."

"My God, Edward, you are indeed destroying my good feelings about the future. Now will ye shut your trap and let us ride in peace?"

"SO YOU'RE JOHNSON'S deputy now, George Croghan. Will you move to New York?" Sattelihu asks George when they meet privately after feasting on venison and bear with the soldiers stationed at Fort Augusta. The morale is high since the fort was built that is holding back the French.

"I'll be resigning from serving the Governor . . . who by the way, is foolish declaring war on the Indians before meeting with the Iroquois."

"I'm on my way to meet with the Council about this matter. Will you be traveling with me? They respect your opinions . . ."

George shakes his head while poking a stick at the fire he and Sattelihu sit by. The night is clear and George looks up into the sky with a myriad of stars. He thinks of Catharine and wants to ask Sattelihu about her. He heard that Margaret, Catharine, and the children had left this valley. George, bewitched by the blanket of stars, wonders if he should wish upon one.

"George . . . My sister, Margaret, and her family . . . and Catharine are no longer in Shamokin. Hardly anyone is left but a few Indians and soldiers. Our once friendly Indians have abandoned the area and destroyed everything since war was declared. My family was threatened, but are safe now. Esther stays nearby with her family and although I'm concerned for her, she's strong and has her husband. And she's keeping watch over our homes."

George is relieved Catharine is safe, but he wants more information. He'll ask for further information later, after Sattelihu warms up to him.

"I can't go to the Council with you now," George says, "but Johnson and others would like the two of us, and maybe Weiser, to meet at Fort Johnson with a few Mohican and Seneca chiefs. But first, I need to go to Aughwick and then try to find Teedyuscung, that crazy chief. The man is all over the place, back and forth with the governor, asking for this and that. And he gets what he wants, too. He's damn eloquent, speaks good English, claims he's a Christian and you can't blame him still being angry over the Walking Purchase. He's the spokesperson for the displaced Indian tribes and by God, what Indian has that kind of charisma charm to stand up like he has . . ."

"And do you wish I had this charm, as you call it, to stand up for the Indians? Or do you wish to be Indian yourself, George, and lead the Delaware?"

"Oh hell, Andrew, don't misinterpret me, you the grand interpreter. You act more white than Indian, except scaring the hell out of the colonists when you dress in your fine Indian regalia . . . I don't think even Teedyuscung can look as kingly as you."

Sattelihu is quiet, keeping his tongue. He is ever so good at this, keeping his tongue, but what tongue is it that he is keeping, he wonders, white or Indian? He doesn't know whether to feel honored or angry by what his friend just said, so he changes the subject.

"You know Teedyuscung assembled a Delaware, Mohican, and Shawnee war party and has launched raids against the settlers and those who stake claim to the Wyoming Valley.

"You know well they were thrown off much of the land way back with the Walking Purchase and then wasn't it promised that the Delaware would always have a right to live on the rest of this Iroquois land in perpetuity?"

Sattelihu shook his head, irritated that George Croghan thinks he knows everything.

"He pretends to be a man of peace treaties and is eloquent and a Christian. But I think Teedyuscung . . . Gideon . . . left his God back at Gnadenhueten . . ."

"It was Chief Shingas who committed that heinous attack, not Teedyuscung. Please come with me when I go to Teedyuscung. He's insisted he's the only one who can convince the western Indians to cease their war against us and I believe he can. Johnson thinks we can have another final peace treaty with him at Easton, but we have to convince him. You and I can do this together."

SATTELIHU GRUNTS, STANDS up, and walks around the fire. A few soldiers linger nearby and he wonders if they're listening. With most of these soldiers and especially before the governors and George Washington, he has to remember proper protocol and deference to them . . . to be submissive. But not with George Croghan. He has always felt an equal with him, even if George often misses the mark in understanding him as an Indian. He sits back down next to his friend. He has to tell him what has happened and maybe George will understand why he is angry with Teedyuscung.

"Well, we could smoke the peace pipe if we had one . . ." George laughs as Sattelihu sits down.

"No peace pipes until we get Teedyuscung and his Indians . . . and all the Ohio Indians back inside our British camp."

Sattelihu turns to face George more privately. George looks curiously at him.

"My sister, Margaret, and her husband are in the Tioga area with some of the Indians, waiting until peace comes and she and they can return to her town. She has always favored Teedyuscung and is sympathetic to his frustration about the Valley because she . . . and all of us watched as more settlers moved onto Indian land. However, knowing Margaret, she's not involving herself with Teedyuscung's attacks. She's probably setting some of his captives free."

"And Catharine and her children? Belle? Are they with Margaret in Tioga, as well?"

George doesn't like bringing up Catharine. Sattelihu is protective of her and wants it kept private that Belle is George's daughter. He tried to tell Sattelihu once that he loved Catharine, but Sattelihu walked away from him and when he returned, he told George that he would like it if they never discussed his niece, Catharine.

"Catharine and her children are in Kah-ni-sti-oh, not far from Tioga, but far enough for Catharine to be out from beneath her mother's skirts for once."

"I've heard of this place. In fact, I stopped there with my packs and men once years back . . . Mercy, Andrew. I remember it being no man's land and quite rough. A bunch of renegades and runaway slaves living there, drunk all the time . . ."

"It's the same place, but more people live there now and maybe not as rough.. It's a place for people who want to live lives without interference. It's a village south of Seneca territory, but the Senecas keep watch over it. Only friends of the Seneca are allowed there and now mostly the angry Delaware resides there among the clutter of other disgruntled individuals. I've only been there once. Catharine has changed . . ."

"What do you mean? Did she marry again?"

George's mouth felt dry. He could use a drink, but he and Sattelihu, finished with meetings and work, weren't drinking.

"There's the old war route, George, and it goes right through Kah-ni-sti-oh. Fort Niagara has just built new earthworks and it's massive. The French haven't stopped after building forts between Lake Erie and the Forks of the Ohio River, and now this."

"What does this have to do with Catharine?"

"The old war route is a water route that travels from New France to the Atlantic with two portages, one around the Genesee and another on the Kah-ni-sti-oh River. And then it goes all the way to the Atlantic."

"I know this, Andrew . . . is Catharine traveling back and forth?"

"Travel on this route is from Fort Niagara to the eastern end of Lake Ontario and then along Ontario shores right to the Genesee River and then onto Canaseraga Creek to the Kah-ni-sti-oh River. And then westward from Tioga to the Allegheny River. A route for the Seneca, Delaware, Shawanese, Mohican, and any other Indian, to use to travel back and forth assembling, trading, and maneuvering with the French. And Catharine and her children are in the heart of this route because they live in the village. I know Teedyuscung visits Margaret in Tioga, but he also visits Catharine in Kah-ni-sti-oh. Catharine has much respect for Teedyuscung."

George is surprised because Catharine prefers quiet and to be out of the fray.

"Margaret and Catharine have always been friends with the Delaware . . . and Teedyuscung. You have always been a brother to them and I am too, a bro . . ."

"A friend, George, not a brother . . . you're a friend. But it's obvious times have changed and their loyalty has been transferred to the French. I fear my niece is sympathetic . . ."

"No, not to the French, but certainly she's loyal to the Delaware and sympathy doesn't mean she's going on raids with Teedyuscung and the others."

"Margaret assured me she's a peacemaker to bring the Christian belief to all and her daughter believes as she does, but I don't believe Catharine has ever followed the way of her mother. Catharine has her own mind, neither Indian nor French or British, but she does have her grandmother's ways to see both sides . . ."

"Like you, Andrew . . . Catharine is also very much like you. My God, she, all of you, had to get out of Wyoming Valley because of the settlers, the Indian and French attacks."

George stands up and walks back and forth near Sattelihu. It's late and there aren't any other soldiers and Indians around the fire.

"After Aughwick, we'll go to Teedyuscung and I'll ask him about Catharine, well, about everything because the governors are anxious and he's key . . . and then I'll go to this haven for runaways and renegades to see Catharine and my daughter, Belle."

The two men sleep by the dying fire as the night darkens and the calls of wildcats and wolves fill the air. Before the sun is up, they hear footsteps nearby and wake, startled. A soldier has brought them a pan of coffee and some grub. He hands Sattelihu and George tin cups and sets the pan of coffee down as he gets the fire going and places the coffee and meat on it. He pulls other utensils out of his rucksack and hands them to Sattelihu and George.

"Captain said you two need lots of refreshment and rest cause you're going to the Forks and meeting with the Delaware and Ohio Indians."

Sattelihu and George look at one another and shake their heads. Their lives aren't their own. George can't go to Aughwick and Sattelihu can't see his family in Philadelphia.

"Take yer time, boys," the soldier says, "and then get washed up and later this morning there'll be pack horses, companions, and what you need to travel."

George and Sattelihu eat as the sun rises.

"There's nothing grander than a sunrise and sunset in Pennsylvania," George says.

Later, as they drink coffee, there's a need in both to be reassured of their mission and friendship. The rose gold of the sun's rays wrap around them and as men often do when they can't speak of feelings, they remind one another and themselves of their past and recent exploits together.

Chapter Twenty-Seven

"I BRING YOU another captive, Catharine. A strong farmer to help you and the others in the village."

Teedyuscung pushes a man toward me and this time I think not paleface. His clothing is dirt colored and so is his face, tanned from working in the fields. Storm Cloud is what I'll call him and I feel the air quiver around him like what happens before a storm. Even the man's suspenders are brown. Colorless.

"What is your name?" I ask.

"Thomas Moffitt." He spits on the ground and one of Teedyuscung's men pushes him in the back with the butt of his gun. He falls to his knees.

"Get up and show honor to this woman, Catharine Montour. She and her family are respected by your people."

"Take him to the barn to meet the others and see to it he's washed and given clothing," I say. "I don't want the stench of him around me."

The men take Thomas Moffitt away and I'm left standing with Teedyuscung.

"Come into my home, my friend, and let's talk about what I'm to do with these captives."

BELLE AND I serve the chief refreshments and I wait for him to finish eating before speaking.

"Belle, bring food to Teedyuscung's friends and stay with them."

Belle gathers food in pots, some utensils, and leaves us alone.

Teedyuscung was raised in Trenton, New Jersey and like many Delawares who lived there, he was accustomed to colonial influence and dress. He likes to wear European clothing and is known as a flamboyant dresser who can combine Indian and European clothing in a flattering way, as Sattelihu is known to do. Today Teedyuscung is wearing the typical breechclout and black leggings, a ruffled shirt, and a scarlet waistcoat. He has a blue handkerchief adorned with a large silver brooch, long silver earrings, and he wears many rings and a silver arm band. His hair is long and he wears a band with elaborate feathers. On his feet are colonial boots and he carries a red broadcloth over his arm. He is dignified and his charm falls upon me like a starry night.

"You look weary, Catharine. Is this village too boisterous for you?"

I'm not used to someone asking if I'm well or weary. I'm startled by his question, but keep a calm presence.

"No, most everyone here is pleasant and we help one another . . . or mostly my family and I stay to ourselves . . ."

"My wife told me that when she visited you she suggested you marry again. Are there no suitable Delaware or Seneca Indians for you?"

I smile and recall his wife, Elizabeth, telling me I should marry. She suggested a few strong warriors. I only nodded and said nothing.

"I'm busy and trying to teach my children to read as I learned from the Moravians, but there's little time because of my my home and field work."

"And your captive, the strong woman with red in her hair. Is she behaving well?"

"She does everything I ask of her and she's quiet, but some of the British soldiers who've left the army and hide here stare at her and I fear they'll try to . . ."

"No, these men have lost their teeth and think they want to live like Indians. What about this Roger who is in mourning for the rest of his life?"

I'm surprised Teedyuscung knows so much about the people living here. He doesn't reside here except for a night or two as he travels back and forth to Fort Niagara.

"He's a kind man, someone who thinks more than he speaks, but when he talks, he has a lot on his mind."

"Do you trust him, Catharine?"

"I trust that he's a good man . . ."

"And you are interested in this good man?"

I'm flustered by this question. I'm nervous about having to take on another captive, a young man, and yes, I like Roger, but only for conversation when Elsa isn't working in the barn.

"He has my interest in conversation only, chief. Now please tell me about this captive you've brought to me. Will I have to keep him shackled in the barn?"

"He's grateful he didn't die when we captured him and he'll stay with you. We didn't even make him run the gauntlet. He has a farm north of Wyoming Valley and we brought him near your mother in Tioga. He was given to an old Mohawk who treated him kindly, like a son. Your mother, by the way, has been interpreting for us and sometime you might also like to do this. After your children are older . . ."

"No, I only wish to live away from British rule and settlers who rape Indian women, take our land, and leave us in need. I'll take captives for you to gain the attention of the British governors, but this is all for now."

TEEDYUSCUNG LEAVES AND I go to the barn to retrieve Belle. Elsa is sitting on a bale of hay and my daughter sits on her lap. Roger, Jeremy, a defected soldier, and our newcomer, Thomas Moffitt, are milking the cows and caring for the horses. It grows silent as I walk in and whatever it is they're saying, they don't want me to hear. I'll ask Belle later. She's an astute child and already knows English, French, and Indian languages. Since Elsa came to us, I've asked my children to only speak Iroquois. I know Belle slips on occasion and speaks English, but quickly stops herself. Roger and Roland speak English together and I allow this, but remind my children to speak in their own tongue. These people don't think Belle understands what they're saying. Belle jumps off Elsa's lap and comes to me. Elsa stands up nervously and immediately picks up a curry comb to work on one of my horses.

"Go to the garden, Elsa, and gather vegetables for dinner. Prepare greens from the garden and cook squash blossoms and corn with the fish Roland and John caught. There are late berries for a cake to make with dried corn flour. Mix in dried bilberries, wrap it in leaves, and bake this cake under live coals. Do you remember how to do this?"

"I make cake Swedish my way."

"You make cake Indian way, Elsa," I say to her, angry that she continues to defy me at times.

"I can show her how to do it," Belle interjects.

I look around and don't see Joseph Sweetgrass, a Seneca, who keeps his eye on the captives for me, and on everyone who lives here.

"Where is Joseph?" I ask Roger.

"He took John and Roland to play some games after they were done fishing."

"Will you find him please, Roger, and tell him to bring my boys home. I'm going to the sweat lodge when it's ready and will return just before the sun goes down and then we'll share a meal together."

Roger looks at me confused.

"I want you to come to our evening meal tonight, along with my captives and Joseph Sweetgrass and his wife."

Roger is embarrassed and I feel the same. How can I think to have a peaceful meal with this man and my unhappy captives and children.

"I always eat in my own lodge."

"I know. I'm welcoming you to my table this evening."

I want Roger with us. Joseph Sweetgrass doesn't speak English well, although he's a strong guardian and entertains my children. Elsa doesn't talk at all while we eat and I have no idea how this Thomas Moffitt will be at my table. I want Roger to help me make this shared meal interesting and relaxing. And I don't want to feed my stomach good food when it's tied in knots having to eat with people I don't have anything in common with.

Roger looks at me with interest. I wait for him to respond, knowing he's more nervous than I am.

"I haven't eaten with a body since my wife and . . ."

"I understand, but maybe it's time to join together with the people of this part of the earth, this place we call Turtle Island and . . ."

Belle, very excited, interrupts me. "And tell the story, my mother, tell the story of Turtle Island."

I have only told my children this story once and I'm ashamed for not telling them more stories of our people. Life in the Montour home had gradually become empty of stories since Grandmother went to be with the ancestors.

"Yes, Belle, I'll tell the story of Turtle Island when we're having supper."

I look at Jeremy, the toothless former soldier, who has stopped milking and sits on the stool staring at me.

"You can join us, too, Jeremy, but don't tell the other soldiers."

Storm Cloud Thomas grabs Jeremy's milk bucket and carries it and his own and sets them down before me.

"I'm not particular about my food. I'd prefer to have some grub here in this barn and sleep here, too, thank you, kindly."

"You're my captive and you'll do as I say and take supper with all of us."

Thomas shrugs. "As you please, then."

LATER, A CRIER goes through the village calling the women to the readied sweat lodge and I hurry with my kettle filled with an herb concoction Grandmother taught me to make. It is tea brewed from the leafy twigs of the Eastern hemlock and the root of the spotted coralroot. It will induce more sweating and relieve me of any foulness in my spirit. I hope this ritual will sharpen my wits and relax me. I walk to the lodge with dread about the evening meal and wonder if an evil spirit visited me in the barn. Why was I willing to offer kindness to these white people and to bring us around a table, a table made by one of the Moravian missionaries for my grandmother many years ago? I turn around to rush back to the barn to tell them I have changed my mind, but stop. How can I? My people are hospitable and my grandmother and family have always invited the stranger into our home. I continue walking to the sweat lodge, arguing with myself. These are not peaceful times, but war times, and making the white people comfortable with us might further encourage their abuse of tricking us out of our land and ways. I stop again and nearly turn around, but look up at the moon and see in her face my own. It's nearly the Full Corn Moon and Belle has reminded me of Turtle Island and I'm in love with this Turtle Island. Whether war time or peace time, I love the Great Spirit and I don't always want to be alone.

Chapter Twenty-Eight

MARY SWEETGRASS, JOSEPH'S wife, has brought in the hot stones from the fire outside the dome shaped lodge that is built by the river and made with saplings that are covered with blankets and animal skins. The woman's lodge is filled with stones and it's now ready for us. Mary is sweating and smiling as she waits for the women to enter. She'll keep bringing in stones to replenish the steam while we are here for half an hour. It isn't easy work shoveling large stones the size of turnips for up to an hour, half an hour of preparation and half an hour in keeping the stones hot. Whenever I'm assigned to this task, I will myself into a calm trance as I breathe in the steam and feel the sweat free my body and mind of maladies. The sweat lodge is used for purification, prayer, and healing and a ceremony usually takes place after the steam bathing. The men's sweat lodge is on the other side of the river to give us privacy.

Today, the sweat lodge is merely for our own private purification and cleansing. There won't be an elder grandmother reciting prayers and leading us in song after the steam bath ends. I enter the lodge and there are four other women sitting with their eyes closed. It's a custom to plunge ourselves into the river during the ceremony and this is usually done three times. We go from hot to cold, but I'll do this only once because my emotions are already going too quickly from one extreme to another.

I remove my clothing and sit cross-legged on a small blanket I have brought with me. I'm at once comforted by the rising steam from the hot rocks. I close my eyes and breathe deeply and slowly, allowing the power of water to take another form to soothe my skin and release infirmities of any kind. My thoughts release into the steam as I breathe slowly and think of water's many forms. I, too, would like to be as easeful and strong as water, but I'd especially like to be this form of water—to be like a vapor, a spirit, and to soothe and destroy the evils all around.

"It's time to go home, Catharine," Mary Sweetgrass says. "You are too long here and there will be no more water and fire. Go to the river and stop your dreams now."

SUPPER, AS IT is called by these frontiersmen and women, is served inside my home and not outside sitting on rush mats. We use wooden spoons, clay bowls, and knives. We sit at the table on twig and bark chairs made by Seneca Indian Bill after we moved here. My grandmother's table, given as a gift to her, has been admired by the Indians in Shamokin and here. We used it to assist us in food preparation and for sleeping when we had guests, but now it's used for everything. Belle has placed my kettle in the middle of the table and filled it with late summer flowers. My children, of course, bring lightness and joy into the evening. Belle, as her name depicts, is beautiful and endearing, an easy child for anyone to love. Roland is quiet and has a tempestuous spirit when thronged with too many people, but he enjoys Roger's special attention and his laughter fills our home. He'll grow out of this awkwardness, for he is between boy and man. John started stuttering when we moved and some of the other children have begun calling him Stuttering John. He stutters in French and Indian, not just in English, but he's still able to make himself understood and so he has accepted his new name. A few months ago I found him talking to an owl that sat in a tree in the middle of the day and so I gave him the name, John Wise Owl. This is what I call him, not Stuttering John. His brother and sister also call him Wise Owl and I hope this new name will be stronger than the other name the village children and men call him.

Joseph Sweetgrass, Roger, Thomas Moffitt, and my John and Roland sit around the table without speaking. Mary Sweetgrass, Elsa, Belle, and I gather the bowls of food to place on the table. Elsa and Belle stewed small pumpkins with maple sugar in a pot, I boiled smoked eel with corn, and after Mary Sweetgrass finished with her work at the sweat lodge, she and Joseph come with a bowl of chopped smoked venison and corn. And then there is the cake. Elsa kneaded corn flour with cold water, added dried berries and ground nuts, and made a big round cake that was enclosed in leaves and baked in hot ashes under live coals. There are maple sugar sprinkles and it's decorated with small flowers. She places it on the table and there are exclamations of surprise. I have never decorated my cakes. We eat certain flowers, especially squash flowers, mixing them in with our fish and meat dishes, but never have I seen them placed on a cake in a fancy way.

Elsa steps back from the table, flushed and anxious. She wipes the sweat off her face with her apron, the stained apron she had been wearing when Teedyuscung brought her to me. Although she has washed it many times in the stream, it still contains the remnants of the life she once had as a wife and mother. I haven't warmed to this woman all these months, but Belle has. Belle takes her hand and pulls her to the table to sit next to Roger.

I clear my throat and speak a little too loudly. "May we enjoy this meal now and give thanks to the Great Spirit. Roland, will you pour the special drink I made. It's a special Delaware drink made with blueberries, sugar, and water and I hope you find it agreeable. There will be no rum tonight."

I suddenly don't want to sit down with this hodgepodge. When Teedyuscung comes to Kah-ni-sti-oh with a few Indians, it's different. We are all Indian and it is Teedyuscung who regales us with stories at our meals.

"Everyone please enjoy our plentiful feast. I'll return soon."

I suspect my guests and captives think I need to go to the dug latrine down the bank behind our home. I'm sweating in my clothing that is cumbersome to have been cooking in. After the sweat lodge, I had felt so refreshed and wanted to change into my colorful clothing for our meal. Belle adores her beaded clothing, silver trinkets, and little bells around her ankles and she is always asking me to wear the same. I found my knee-length deerskin skirt that I had carefully dried and tanned years ago. This skirt, although snug around my waist after my babies, still fits. There are beads and dyed porcupine quills on it. It is mostly worn for cold weather, but the evenings are now cool and I wanted to feel youthful in wearing it. I longed to wear two braids again, but thought it best I wear one long one, as married women do, although I'm without a husband. I tied it, not with my wedding ribbon, but with a bright red ribbon George Croghan gave me. I wore leggings and put on my ankle bells.

Everyone stares as I walk across the floor with my tinkling bells. I feel foolish, as if I'm in a ceremonial dance at the wrong place. I leave and walk to the back of the house as if I'm headed to the latrine. I sit down in the field as the sun is just melting into the line of trees in the distance. Something stirs near me and I look over to see a fawn struggling to stand. Its mother rises from the field, as well as the father, a buck with a large rack. I stand up slowly and we all look at one another for what seems like minutes. We are one together in peace for a brief moment and I feel no separation from them, the field, and the sky.

Returning to my table of enemies, children, and friends, I'm calm and ready to eat. There is lively conversation between Belle and Mary and Joseph Sweetgrass in the Iroquois language. Roland is talking to Roger quietly, knowing I prefer he not speak English. He looks at me nervously and I smile and nod to indicate to him it's alright. John sits quietly eating and with his look I know he'd like to leave the table. I point to his food and smile, giving him permission to leave when he finishes. I'm surprised to see that Elsa changed her seating to be next to Thomas Moffitt and they're whispering together, but become quiet when I sit down. I stare at both of them, feeling threatened, but determined to keep my confidence.

Joseph Sweetgrass sees my concern and stands up from the table. "You two not talk now. You come sit in my place, woman. Now."

Elsa immediately picks up her bowl and sits down between Belle and me and Joseph sits next to Thomas Moffitt. Thomas buries his face into his bowl and the others continue talking and eating. I note Belle is patting Elsa's arm in sympathy.

"Tell the Turtle," Belle says in English, and then in Iroquois, "Island story, Mother."

I'm saddened to have placed my children in this situation with becoming friends with captives and demanding them to speak only their Indian language. It's too difficult for them and this is why John continues to stutter and I fear

Belle and Roland will turn against me. I look over at Roger and he is staring at me curiously.

He smiles and speaks forthrightly. "I think we would all like to forget our troubles and hear a beautiful story of creation, Catharine, but please, can you tell us in English?"

The others at the table half laugh and tension lessens.

John leaves the table and I wish he'd stay, but I had given him permission. As I ready myself to tell the story, he returns and hands me my flute. Telehemet's flute he once made for me. I rarely have time to play it and John is longing to play it himself or have one of his own. I thank him and he sits back down at the table. I'm self-conscious at first, but then I close my eyes and the image of the deer family I've just seen comes to me. I play tentatively, but then let the Great Spirit play through me and lose myself in the mystery of breath and sound. I finish, and with my eyes still closed, I begin the Turtle Island story.

Before the world was created, there was a sky world above the waters where the Great Spirit lived with many happy spirits. A giant tree of light illuminated this sky world. The light penetrated all the glowing, brilliant flowers that never stopped growing or shining. One day, a powerful wind burst through the sky world and blew the tree away. The light disappeared and all that remained was a vast hole. The Great Spirit called his daughter, Sky Woman, to look into this hole. She peered into the hole and saw through to deep waters and clouds, another world. He asked her to go into this world of darkness and gently dropped her into this hole. She fell for miles and miles and was about ready to fall into the waters, but a hawk caught her in his wings. The woman was too heavy for the hawk and they started sinking into the waters, but a great sea turtle saw them and offered his back for the woman to live on. But the woman wanted earth under her feet and she asked the animals of the waters for help, but no animals but the muskrat could dive to the very bottom of the waters. He went deep into the waters and finally touched soft mud and scooped up as much as he could and returned to Sky Woman. All the other animals helped spread this earth onto the sea turtle's back. Sky woman began to walk in circles on the turtle's back and as she walked in larger circles, the sea turtle began to grow and grow. Finally, the turtle was the size of the earth we now live on today. Together, the Sky Woman and the animals built lakes, mountains, forests, and vast plains. Sky Woman had a daughter who became the Earth Mother and she bore three daughters, Corn, Bean, and Squash. She also bore twin sons, the Good Spirit who created all the pleasant and beautiful things we have on earth. Her other son, Evil Spirit, created what was unpleasant and evil on this earth.

Everyone is quiet after I finish my story and Belle speaks in English, "Mother, do we have," and finishes in Iroquois, "both good and evil in us?"

"Belle, I give you permission to speak your question in English."

Belle repeats her question and I answer, "Yes, this is why right here we are of so many different minds and struggles."

Elsa slams her hands on the table, her face red as her hair as she speaks. "It's called sin, Belle. Sin. It's a sin to massacre and take prisoners the peoples of God. You don't believe God and his son, Jesus, who resurrected from the dead and his Holy Spirit inside us. You believe stupid turtle is the earth? It is the foolish way of believing, falling into hole and a body becoming the sun and moon . . ."

I stand up from my table and glare at Elsa. "And is it not also foolish to believe a god created the world and a spirit made a woman pregnant, not a man, but a spirit? Is it not also foolish to believe the baby born was God, is God, and was killed and rose from his death?"

Elsa squirms in her chair and stands up to clear the table.

"Sit down, Elsa."

Elsa sits down and I notice Belle again touch her arm in comfort.

"I learned of Jesus growing up in my grandmother's and mother's home. But you are here in my home and you will respect my stories and not ever call them foolish again. I might have asked for other stories to be told around this table this evening and you could have told your own Jesus story."

Roger and Thomas Moffitt sit with their heads down, as does Elsa. They must sympathize with Elsa and consider my creation story foolish, too. I'm at once very weary of this supper gathering and should have realized that after a sweat lodge visit, I needed to be alone. Joseph, Mary, and my children look at me with puzzlement, seeking to know what to do next. How do we end this unpleasant evening supper?

Roger lifts his head and smiles. "I enjoyed this story, Catharine, as well as the playing of your flute. It has brought me some peace this night."

Thomas Moffitt clears his throat. His countenance appears less angry. "There was an old Mohawk man who lived near my family. He told stories and told the story of a prophet who brought hope to the Iroquois and hope for the world. The Iroquois planted a tree of peace, a great white pine, which rises to meet the sun. Do you believe in this tree of peace?"

"It was Deganawidah who planted this tree of peace rising to meet the sun, the eye of the Great Spirit, our Creator. Its branches represent the law and its white roots extend to the four quarters of the earth so that everyone might trace peace to its source. Atop this tree is the Eagle that sees afar and watches to warn peace-loving people of approaching danger."

My grandmother taught all of us this story as children. I sense this captive is about to challenge me.

"I ask you again if you believe in this tree of peace?" Thomas Moffitt's question is angry.

"I believe in this tree of peace, as do the Iroquois who made peace with five tribes long ago called the Confederation of Five Nations, which are now Six Nations. They are called Ho-De'-No-Sau-Nee and I am also Ho-De'-No-Sau-Nee."

"But peace seems to only have come to the Iroquois, the Ho-De'-No-Sau-Nee, and not to the four quarters of the earth."

"If the four quarters of the earth do not seek peace—"

"Then the Iroquois will seek to overcome the four quarters of the earth and force them to make peace . . . so they are warring for peace, which is hardly peace at all."

Joseph Sweetgrass stands up. "Iroquois say now no one lives in the woods alone and must make new ways. It's time to thank this woman and I take you to the barn to sleep."

Elsa stands up. "Nobody eats my cake. Please have some now."

I give Elsa a knife to cut the cake, "Everyone, take some cake with you when you leave."

Roger takes a piece of cake and stands by me. He is shorter than I am, but robust and hearty in stature. I smell his milky, sweet breath and desire stirs within me. Genuine warmth, as well as sorrow, are cast in his eyes and I'm aware that both our needs are strong. We desire comfort to erase our sorrows, if only for a brief time.

My guests leave, each with a piece of cake, and my children sit at the table gobbling their pieces and asking for more. Elsa is a good baker and maybe I'll let her make a Swedish cake soon. Later, after my children are in bed, I ask Elsa to sit with me at the table for tea. We talk into the night about our childhoods and I learn that there is another woman like me who finds solace and help in the flowers of the field and trees of the forest. Elsa tells me her ancestors in Sweden were the Sami people, the native people of Northern Europe who herded reindeer. Her ancestors became Christians many years before, but her grandparents still practiced the old ways of believing that animals, plants, and even rocks, possess a soul. The Sami people know all about the stars, moon, and northern lights and have many superstitions.

"Like you, but many more superstitions."

"They are beliefs, Elsa . . . but why then were you so angry that I told a story about creation that is different from the Christian story?"

Elsa is still for a moment and then takes my hands in her own. I'm uncomfortable and start to pull away, but she's strong and holds them on her lap. I give in and let her speak.

"We lived with my grandparents in Lapland . . . very cold, very dark many months. And then my father and grandfather hurt one another with words and blows and my father said we must move to England. My father made us promise we never tell anyone we are Sami and to never talk of old ways and superstitions. My father was very strict, angry, and mean to my mother, brother, and me. We had to pray all the time to God and go to church and I have comfort only alone in my bed with prayers. I was only girl, sixteen, when I married my husband who believed in a loving God, not mean one. I begged him we come to America so I never see my father again. My sad heart grew cold to my mother and brother, too, and now I miss them and my husband is dead . . ."

Elsa grips my hands harder and cries. She stands and pulls me up with her. She shakes my arms weeping without control. I try to pull away, but the more I try, the more she clutches me.

"You. You, please Catharine, find my daughter. She is only hope I have. You have Belle. What if Belle be taken from you?"

And suddenly there is my Belle standing next to Elsa with her arms around her waist and crying out to me, "Let her go, my mother, please let Elsa go."

Belle and Elsa are crying and Elsa pulls me to her and wraps her arms around me. The three of us stand in some kind of strange circle and when Elsa finally releases me, for I hadn't embraced her back, I turn to see Roland and John standing like sentinels, one on each side of me.

"We all need to sleep and let's hope tomorrow will give us understanding."

THERE IS NO real understanding the next day or the days after this misshapen supper of good food, story, smiles, tears, and anger. The following day, I find Elsa in the barn saddling up one of my horses, preparing to leave. When she sees me, she shouts for me to stay away and let her leave.

"You are a cruel, hard woman, Catharine Montour. I kill you if you stop me going to my daughter."

And before I know what is happening, Elsa takes a gun from behind her and points it at me. I feel strangely calm, but strong.

"If you want to leave, Elsa, you can, but not with my horse. You'll have to walk. Come to my house and I'll make you a bundle of food for your long journey."

I walk slowly to Elsa who is trembling.

"Hand me my gun, Elsa. I'll give you a knife to carry on your journey, but you can't take my gun."

Elsa hands me the gun and falls to the ground, sobbing, but suddenly stands up in a fury and strikes me on the face. "I need horse to find my daughter."

I drop my gun and strike her back. She punches my arms and tries to punch my face, but I grasp both her arms as Roland comes rushing into the barn. He pulls Elsa away from me and drags her to a post as I find rope to tie her there. She is screaming and swearing in her ugly language. I've never felt this angry and now it consumes me as I tie Elsa to a post and take a whip and strike her several times. I don't strike her head, but focus on her skirts and arms. After some time, Roland pulls me away from her, telling me to stop. I throw the whip down and turn to go into the house. She can stay there all night, the white bitch who embodies all the Europeans who come to disturb our lives and take our land from us.

I can't sleep through the night and when the moon is only half finished with its shift before the sun comes to take over, I gather a basin of water, herbs, and cloth, as well as a blanket, and go to the barn. Roland had already untied Elsa and she lies in a heap next to the post. I wake her and she startles, but closes her eyes and allows me to wash and soothe her arms that I see are not bleeding. I'm relieved and place a blanket over her before I leave. I return to my home and sleep without waking until late morning to find Elsa preparing food with Belle as if nothing had happened. I wonder if I have dreamed.

IT WAS NOT only Elsa I took a whip to, but Thomas Moffitt who was becoming more belligerent each day. One day when he was in the barn with another man, an old British soldier who has no teeth in his mouth and spirit, Thomas turned to rail against me.

"I know you're French, but your white blood is weak and it's your savage Indian blood that courses through you. It's the evil, untamed, wild Indian blood that simmers beneath all your false refinement that keeps us as prisoners . . ."

I grab the whip without thinking twice about it and whip his legs and arms. And this time, I may have left some real sores on his white arms. He doesn't fight me or even try to grab the whip, for this man didn't have the savage blood of any color in him. He's not a warrior and will probably never be, except with his tongue. I leave the barn and this time I feel no remorse.

Chapter Twenty-Nine

CHIEF TEEDYUSCUNG WENT from village to village inciting Indians to put on their war paint and take up their hatchets. He is a tireless talker and persuasive, convincing all of us that the English have cast woes upon the Delaware and other Indians. I don't think we need much convincing, but had we become complacent during the peaceful times in Pennsylvania? In the exchange of furs for goods and gifts at treaties, did we really think we could live peacefully as equals upon the land of the Great Spirit? What Teedyuscung wants is a guarantee that his people will always remain in possession of the Wyoming Valley and he wants compensation for the land taken from them. My friend, Teedyuscung, had been a basket and broom maker in New Jersey and learned to speak English while living with Europeans who eventually pushed him and all the Delaware out of Trenton. In Pennsylvania, Teedyuscung soon found his voice with the Delaware who practice their ancestors' ancient rituals. He's a natural leader, but Grandmother doubted him and my uncle claims he's too changeable. My mother, however, welcomes him into friendship because he became a Christian. I see how he straddles two worlds and this makes it difficult for him to find esteem from one or the other. Most Indians seem to be caught up in these twisted and knotty times. I feel like a burl lodged in a strong oak, a distortion in a native tree.

But not all Indians want to make war with the British and many have separated from Teedyuscung and stay loyal. The Indians in Shamokin and the Wyoming Valley are against the British and these are the Indians I have known all my life. The Paximosa, Shawanese, Mohegan, Chicksaw, and yes, some of the Six Nations. And now we're being torn apart and divided by these times and this has made us weak before the white men.

A few weeks ago, my mother came from Tioga when Teedyuscung was visiting my home. At first, I was reluctant to share with her my new life, but she has also changed and we both miss inhabiting the same home. I think soon we'll live together again. She, too, has taken captives and also wishes to end this division between brothers. Her Christian way has become less harsh and this allows for the wisdom of her years. We are both convinced that captives are an advantage for the Delaware and warring Indians to force Pennsylvania and the other colonies to compensate for what they have taken and to give us a place at their tables.

And this is why I agree to take one more captive, another young man, Daniel McMullen, who was captured while at work in the woods at Minisinks. He was taken prisoner by Teedyuscung's men and taken to him in Wyoming and then was moved to Tioga.

Elsa is becoming more emotionally uncontrollable and there are times I want nothing more than to send her away. Earlier this day a messenger came to tell me Teedyuscung is on his way here and has a surprise for me. He's bringing me my new captive, I think, with disappointment. Joseph Sweetgrass and I have our days full in keeping a keen eye on these prisoners of mine. Other than being difficult at times, they are stoic in acceptance of their lot. However, we know they must be scheming to escape and Joseph and I try to keep them apart as much as possible. Belle loves them all, as she loves everyone, and John and Roland watch them, their father's strength growing in them as the years pass.

In the afternoon, I hear horses riding into the village and know Teedyuscung has arrived. I don't hear a loud whoop which means there are probably no captives. I'm filled with both dread and excitement to find out what Teedyuscung's surprise is. My days have become rote, although peaceful, even with having to be vigilant to maintain my position in this unusual household and village. None of the other Indians hold captives as I do, for most of the men are coming and going too much and their women don't wish to be burdened.

Elsa, Mary Sweetgrass, Belle, and I have cooked venison and other delicious food to welcome Teedyuscung and his party. We never know how many people will arrive with him and so we always plan for a large feast.

Belle runs to the door and when she opens it and sees George Croghan, she jumps into his arms as if she knows he is her father. I immediately feel trembling and turn my back to regain calm. I'm in dismay that this could possibly be Teedyuscung's surprise for me as he knows nothing of my past relationship with George. And then I hear Elsa's strange language strike my ears in one long wail. I turn around, pass by George and Belle who now stand in the kitchen, and walk outside to see Elsa and a young girl embrace. Both are sobbing and speaking magic words of love only they know. So this is Teedyuscung's surprise. George is not Teedyuscung's surprise for me, but yet he is. And yes, there's another captive, Daniel McMullen. And for the first time in a long time, I think peace might be possible, for this great chief in bringing Elsa's daughter here has followed his heart and not merely his pride and determination to bring justice to his people.

TEEDYUSCUNG AND I sit alone in my cabin.

"I've laid down the hatchet for good," Teedyuscung says. "Wyoming is now completely abandoned and I'll make my temporary home in Tioga and make peace between the British and the Ohio Indians. Governor Hamilton has named me a special emissary of the province and I'll be accompanied by Christopher

Post to invite the western Indians to come to Philadelphia for a treaty. Soon we'll all return to Wyoming and you, too, Catharine, and your mother, will live there again. The Governor has promised to build houses and a church for us."

Teedyuscung is his usual gregarious, handsome self, dressed in a blue broadcloth and stroud. He wears long, dangling earrings and is regal, his countenance showing no signs of being worn out from his conflictions between rampage and peace.

"What about the captives? And do you trust the British to be just and return to you the land on the Susquehanna from the Walking Purchase?"

"The captives are strategic, Catharine. We will hold them quietly and firmly as a bargaining tool to see whether we will receive compensation and our land after I bring peace with the Ohio Indians."

"I agree, but I want no more captives. Now you have brought me Elsa's daughter and this Daniel. Maybe Elsa will be still in her heart now and not give me many headaches."

"George Croghan speaks well of you, Catharine, and he is here at the bequest of Andrew . . . Sattelihu . . . your uncle does not like taking sides, but he is firmly rooted to the British and is fearful you and your mother and father are encamped with enemies of the British. He never reprimanded me for the war paint I put on, for I am his elder, but more than this, he, too, feels the loss of our Delaware lands and Wyoming being abandoned. But you must understand that your uncle has more passion for his position with the British government than for his land."

"George Croghan will tell my uncle that I have captives and . . ."

"Sattelihu will turn a blind eye from the captives, but he seeks to know if you have turned your heart away from your grandmother's vision for you to be a word maker, a go-between, and peacemaker. I think he's concerned you will go to your French family."

"I don't know my French family and he himself has met with his brother, Louis, in Ohio and has not taken me there or spoken to me about them. Grandmother never spoke of her other children to me. How could I go to them? I don't know that life and mostly I have come here to be far from bloodletting and to seek peace, willing to take captives for the cause of the Delaware and all of us.

"You are still young and you don't know where the Great Spirit will take you. Maybe back to Wyoming or maybe elsewhere."

I don't respond to Teedyuscung right away, but ponder my feelings. Do I really want to stay in this lush, but strange place? There is another land not far from here I remember and dream of, but how can I take my children from here to a place where there might not be a settlement? Roland and John like it here and have many friends and they're turning into hunters and yes, they will become warriors someday. I'm hesitant to tell Teeedyuscung the vision I keep having of Eagle Cliff Falls, but I wish to know more.

"There are many waterfalls, but do you know of one waterfall a day or two's journey from here? It's before the lake of the Seneca and the River of the Genesee?"

"The cliffs of the eagle that has left its image to watch over the sacred waters and land? You know of this place?"

"Our journey to the Genesee for me to be married to Telehemet took us by this waterfall and I have dreamed of it since that time."

"This waterfall is in Seneca territory and only a few live there. Further, closer to the River Chemung, not far from your mother in Tioga, there is a small settlement. Why would the granddaughter of Madame Montour wish to live so far from Shamokin and Wyoming where all Indians meet coming and going? We will have our land again and you will be honored among us to live there, Catharine."

"I have loved this place of spirit and beauty since visiting there . . . and I desire quiet."

"And so you don't want to stay here?"

"I don't know what I really want, but I have not stopped dreaming about this waterfall and land."

"You and I carry two faces and we are sometimes confused, daughter. You have both bloods and I, although carrying the blood of the Delaware, have spent years with Europeans."

"But we all have blood that is the same color. In this village, French, British, Indian, and even Negro blood have mixed here, separate from the rest of the world that divides blood up into different hues."

Teedyuscung is somber and his face has lost the glow of joy he had carried into my home. I want to encourage this man I have grown to care for.

"I'm going now, Catharine, and fear I'll not see you again, for your heart is in your eyes for that distant place, a place that is also covetous of keeping itself as pure as you desire. No more captives will I bring to you and your mother, and I promise to walk the road to peace for the good of our nations. I tremble not to take up the hatchet because I've believed that as we hunt the deer and bear for our nurture, so we have had to war to live."

He opens the door to leave, but turns to me.

"George Croghan loves you and you love him. Let this love flow with the currents of these times and worry not if it changes course."

So Teedyuscung knows about George Croghan and when he leaves with his warriors, George Croghan and his companion, Captain Edward Pollard, stay behind. I'm overcome with too much happening in one day and the emotion I feel for Teedyuscung. I feel nothing as I address George Croghan and his friend.

"Take some blankets to the barn and you'll be comfortable there," I say to George Croghan and this captain who keeps smiling at me, but says nothing. My bones feel heavy and I have great need to be alone. There have been too many captives, feasts, visits, and now another strange white man with George Croghan.

Chapter Thirty

I'M SITTING ON the river bank after my last invigorating dip into the icy water. I've wrapped myself in a blanket before I return to my clothes and complex life with captives and George Croghan and his friend, Edward Pollard. I watch the river as the wind carries maple, birch, and oak leaves gently on its surface. They float like tiny colorful boats down the river away from their mother trees. I, too, have fallen from my source that rooted me as a Montour and native custom. What this next life is I don't know and hope I can surrender as freely as the trees and leaves. I look up into the nearby trees and note soon they'll be as bare as I am right now. These trees are at ease in releasing and I honor them with a quiet prayer. I feel a chill and quickly dress to return to my home full of people who are every color.

EDWARD POLLARD IS of a different nature than George Croghan and I note the distinction immediately. He sits quietly with his hat in his lap smiling at George and Belle. I almost forget he's in the room. Not so George! He sits with Belle on his knee and rambunctiously regales my children and Elsa with stories of traveling into the wild, unknown territories of the west. He is careful in not describing gory details of skirmishes and death, although my children have not been isolated from these truths. Death is a guest at the longhouse of the Ho-De'-No-Sau-Nee and in our Montour home. It is accepted with tears and great ceremony, unlike the placid mourning of the English who want to bury their grief as quickly as their dead.

I sit on a willow chair near the table and cook fire, listening to George and see that Belle resembles her white, pretentious father. She has his charm and love of talk and she believes everyone will like her. I let out a ragged sigh. My passion for George Croghan has lessened. Even with all his Indian ways and love for them, he desires to be important, especially to the colonial governments. It's clear George and I traverse separate paths. I look away from his roughened, but still handsome, face. I have loved George Croghan and I love George Croghan still, but I don't want to be with him. Simple as that, I tell myself as I look at his hands and remember them touching me.

THESE TWO MEN stay for three nights and George is busy trudging through our village to find enemies of the British to convince them to return to the chain of friendship. He approached me late one night when I was viewing the stars. The sky was clear, it was very cold, and he brought a blanket to place over us. We sat on a log and talked a long time about these strange times and after he kissed me, I stood up and said it would be best if we went to our separate beds.

Edward Pollard has spoken little to me or Elsa and is shy around us, but he's been lively in conversation with my boys and Belle. The day before he and George are to leave for Philadelphia, I find him in the barn talking to Thomas Moffitt and Daniel McMullen. Thomas is brushing one of my horses and Edward Pollard and Daniel McMullen are huddled around the horse. I walk in soundlessly, as I have learned to do as a child from my father and uncle. Thomas is complaining, as usual.

"Teedyuscung tells everyone he's buried the hatchet, but he's left it in our backs and McMullen and I ain't hanging here to die at the hands of the hag . . ."

My fine stallion looks into my eyes and snorts as if to warn me that these men are up to trouble. The three men turn to see me standing in the doorway and Thomas drops the brush and leans over to pick it up. I move quickly to kick the brush out of his hand and he jumps back as the other two men move to the side nervously.

"You won't have to die at my hands, if I'm the hag you're referring to, Thomas Moffitt. But I'll consider pulling out your fingernails or cutting off some of your fingers instead. And then you can run a gauntlet stripped naked in front of this village . . ."

"And you might be even forced to sing and dance . . ." Edward Pollard interjects. I look into this quiet man's face and cannot read it. Is he laughing at me? Although I know these are Indian ways to torture prisoners of war, I doubt I could ever perform them. Or maybe I could . . .

I walk close to Thomas so he's forced to look into my eyes.

"It must be demeaning for you to be held captive by a woman, especially an Indian woman, but I'm not like your white women who lose their tongues and wits in a house full of men."

Thomas steps back from me and looks away before speaking. My stallion snorts again and nudges my arm.

"There's going to be a treaty . . . at Easton . . . Teedyuscung is bringing his people and the Ohio Indians together to unite with the British and it's only right we get released . . ."

Edward Pollard interrupts, stepping close to me. "One of the Indians who was with Teedyuscung and our party has returned. He found me first and is now looking for George and then will come to tell you there's a treaty date set for Easton. I was going to suggest to Thomas there would be no need for him to escape and then you came into the barn."

"Even if there is a treaty, we hold our captives until we're satisfied that the agreements made at treaty are carried out. Sometimes this takes a long time. So you are wrong to counsel my two prisoners, Edward Pollard."

Daniel McMullen quietly listens and watches. I don't know his ways yet to know how he feels, but I'm certain he would also like to flee. Anyone would who was being held against their will and I don't know if he has suffered loss of family members during his capture.

Joseph Sweetgrass walks in and is surprised to see me.

"I left to take Teedyuscung's Indian to George Croghan. I trusted this man to watch our prisoners," he said, pointing to Edward Pollard.

"Watch these men, Joseph, and if they try to escape, pull their fingernails out."

Joseph looks at me, startled, but quickly moves near the two prisoners, his gun at his side. I nearly laugh aloud, but maintain a stoic demeanor as I saddle up my horse and prepare to lead him out of the barn. While I'm doing so, Edward Pollard asks if I'm going to ride.

"White women ride their horses for pleasure . . . and mostly to get away from their strong husbands. I, too, ride for pleasure, to feel the certainty of the brawn of a beast made by the Great Spirit and to breathe in the whispers of trees . . . but also to get away from captives."

"Come, Wise Heart," I say, as I lead my horse out of the barn.

Edward Pollard follows, to my surprise, and walks beside us quietly as I head toward the field. After a few minutes, I turn to ask if he'd like to get his horse and ride with me.

"In time for a sunset, yes . . . yes . . . I'd be very pleased to do so."

He makes a nervous bow and quickly returns to the barn. I'm amused by this quiet man who is the first man ever to bow to me, even if it was very slight.

Edward Pollard is a fur trader who came from England many years ago. He and George Croghan, along with Sattelihu, are working for Sir William Johnson, the colonial superintendent of Indian affairs. Sir William Johnson is another Irishman, like George Croghan, and has acquired large tracts of land, mostly from the Mohawks, and is one of the wealthiest settlers in this country. Of course, like the Moravians, he encourages Christian education and also has been married to two Mohawk women. He encouraged George Croghan to marry the Mohawk woman, a friend of his second wife.

The evening after my riding out with Edward Pollard, Elsa, her daughter, Clara, Belle, and I make an evening meal. It's enjoyed by all of us, as well as George and Edward. There is no uneasiness or discussion of war and Belle tells stories I taught her that interests everyone. George pats her arm and mine, smiling at me with pride. Even her brothers become avid listeners. I allow Belle to tell the stories in English, but she uses many Iroquois names and words. While we finish eating and are sitting listening to Belle, there's a knock on the door. To my surprise, in walks Mary River Walker, a Seneca who lives on the edge of the village with a few other Indian women. These are unmarried women and known for catching the attention of British and French men traveling through the village. The Indians who live here, especially the men, don't approve of these women's lives and except for one drunken skirmish with French travelers, they're ignored. I had been asked by some of the Seneca Indians who keep watch over this village to oversee these women, but I never saw any need to interfere.

Mary is dressed in bright clothing with different patterns. She wears a tunic, a vest, leggings, and a skirt. The many necklaces hung around her neck are probably gifts from her male visitors. She's a bold young woman with high cheek bones and bright green eyes and she speaks only a little English.

"I see George Croghan. He gives gifts and money."

George's demeanor of confidence collapses when this woman enters my home. He stands up stiffly, clears his throat, and goes to Mary who grabs his hand and tries to pull him out the door.

George pulls back from her. "I will visit you after I finish my dinner, Mary."

Mary folds her arms in disgust and smirks at him. "You come or I tell uncles, the Seneca chiefs."

Mary leaves and George sits back down at the table. I'm surprised and hurt, but also feel indifferent. Did I think George only slept with his Mohawk wife and dream of me?

Elsa and Clara awkwardly stand to clear the table. I get up, too, wondering where I can go to be alone from all of this.

"Belle, please take the leftovers and corn bread and put them together in a kit for Mr. Croghan and Mr. Pollard for their journey tomorrow."

Belle doesn't know George is her father, nor does she understand the ways of men with women. Soon, I'll have to tell her, but wish for her to stay the age she is now. My boys, Roland and John, understand the relations between men and women. Elsa and Clara are quiet and do their work as if it's the most important tasks in their lives.

I look at Edward Pollard and he's flushed with anger. He stands and looks at George. "Haven't you just gotten over the clap, George Croghan, and now you . . ."

"It's none of your business . . ."

"It is my business. Getting the Indians drunk when we're trying to negotiate is one thing, but to sleep with their women will only bring trouble, not to mention disease."

I'm furious with George Croghan. And yes, I'm deflated in my opinion of him. So this is common behavior with him. I'm mostly angry that he has brought this trouble into my home in front of my children.

George leaves, Elsa and Clara go to the barn, and Belle and the boys gather in a corner to play a game. They understand I want to be alone. But I'm not alone. I stand staring at the door thinking of escape and Edward Pollard touches my arm and asks me to sit down.

"I'll make you a cup of tea, unless you'd like something stronger."

I look at him and don't know what to say. I didn't know what I wanted, except to leave this house and be by the river.

"I must walk beneath the moon for her wisdom."

"It's a cold, clear night and the moon is half its size, but you'll see well by it," Edward Pollard responds.

It isn't the time of snow yet, but Edward Pollard places a blanket over my shoulders. And just like I hadn't thought twice about asking him to ride with me, I ask if he would like to walk with me. He smiles and retrieves his hat and buckskin jacket and we walk out into the moonlight that lights the path I often take to the river. When we reach the river, we sit on a log of an old oak and Edward Pollard pulls from his jacket pocket a flask of whiskey and offers me some. Although I don't usually take strong drink, I accept and it warms my chest and calms my feelings. I look up at the sky and feel as if I've been given a big hug from Grandmother Moon.

We talk for a long time, until the moon has slow danced across the sky and the crisp air has wormed its way into our clothes and onto our skin. I'm shivering and Edward takes off his jacket and places it over me. He's a large, burly man, not heavy, but strong looking. His gentle face is fair, not swarthy, as if he hasn't spent much time outdoors. His eyes never seem to blink and are large, a deep blue, nearly violet. I hadn't noticed them before, but maybe the moonlight has changed them. He is not a young man, but neither is he old. Just the right age, I think, and laugh to myself. The right age for what?

For someone who is quiet in a room of people, he now talks candidly and freely about himself. I haven't known any men to talk so honestly about their lives. George Croghan talks non-stop, but about his exploits and dreams, not about his life as a child or his shortcomings. Edward Pollard talks to me about his childhood in England, his marriage to a Seneca woman in New York who died, and about his son who is with a guardian. I am not given to sharing my thoughts or about the days of my life as a child and marriage to Telehemet. Tonight, I'm overflowing with words and stories for this man's kind ears. And when I speak of George and our history, he already knows. Who else knows about us?

"Did he talk to you about me as if I were one of his prostitutes?"

"No, no . . . he never spoke of you until Teedyuscung planned the journey here and gave us the news of laying down his hatchet. And then George spoke of you with great respect . . . I knew from his words that he possessed more than respect for you."

"And so you know that Belle is my daughter?"

"I only surmised this when I saw her sitting on his lap. There is a likeness . . ."

"Yes, I once loved him . . . but to think he is so free with his flesh with many women."

"He doesn't frequent the Molly-Houses, as we call them in England, but yes, he has favored one or two Indian women. I know his wife, but there is no love between them . . . only respect and friendship."

I turn to Edward and without thinking before I speak, I ask him if he, too, visits these Molly-Houses.

He laughs and rubs his chin. "I had a wife I loved and now there's no time for such frivolous and dangerous behavior. And you, Catharine, do you still love George Croghan?"

I smile at him and shake my head. "I have the love of my children and the Great Spirit who resides in all of this," I say, as I sweep my arm around the vista of the river and trees. "It's enough . . . for now, it's enough."

Captain Pollard is a chivalrous man and before he leaves the village with George Croghan, he bows again and this time he bows deeply. George Croghan appears puzzled watching this, but he's too chagrined by his behavior the night before to say anything. He whispers in my ear that it is me he'll always love.

Chapter Thirty-One

WINTER BURIES US in ghost white quiet in Kah-ni-sti-oh. A few hungry groups of Indians and whites stop at our village and we feed and care for them until they leave. French, British, Indian, I don't care who they are, as long as they aren't carrying smallpox or evil intent. In the autumn, Roland, John, and the other men of the village hunted bear and other meat and we all worked hard preparing it to last for this winter. We didn't have much salt for preserving and smoke preserving is an old way and a good alternative. We also dried and pounded elk and deer into a powdery substance. Elsa, Clara, and Belle helped and after all the muscle it took to smashing, we mixed it with fat and dried berries. We keep this specialty for travelers and when going into the forest to hunt. We spent days drying vegetables to put in our clay pots and we buried the meat in bark lined storage pits just outside our homes. We have plenty of food for the heart of winter when it hardens itself against the animals in the forest.

Our home is a large cabin, but there are two long houses in the village and one is where Thomas Moffitt and Daniel McMullen live with Indian families so they can be guarded. A few scattered cabins and buildings are inhabited, mostly by whites such as Roger, who has been shy with me ever since the meal with too many strange people.

Also in autumn, Belle, Elsa, Clara, and I braided corn and hung them and a variety of squash from our ceiling. There are dried herbs and flowers that cheer us and scent our home. I welcome winter for the stillness and mystery of its ways. I watch the forest and fields relinquish its greenness and feel the lull and hum of hibernation that induces me to dream of spring and what it will bring. I had felt the winds of change while sitting on the river bank and now during this winter, my mind rests, letting the dying parts of me lay quiet beneath my wakefulness. This I accept, knowing that by the time of the Strawberry Festival, I'll be invigorated again. I hope for reconciliation with the British so I can let my captives go. I'm pleased Elsa has become like a sister and Clara is like Belle's older sister. They are at peace with me now and I wonder if they'll ever want to leave. This isn't so with Thomas and Daniel, who are often brash in their words and don't like to be in my home. They work hard and don't try to escape, so I try to ignore their unhappiness.

When I have time, I read Moravian Anna's book and a book of poems a fur trader left when he stopped here on his travels. Many words are hard for me to understand, but I get a feeling for what is written. I write with charcoal on birch bark I have taken from the forest. I try to teach my children words and writing, but Roland isn't that interested, although Belle is. John is shy and still stutters and he'd rather play my flute. Elsa knows how to write some English words and I ask her to show me more, but there is little time for her as she works and teaches Clara. We don't have much to help us with education, something Teedyuscung talked about the last time he was here. A school, he said, would be good in Kah-ni-sti-oh . . . and, of course, in Wyoming and Shamokin . . . a Christian education. I just sighed and said, yes, a school for the Indian children.

WINTER CONTINUES AND takes its time, tenacious in its grip, and I now eagerly wait for spring and movement. Movement of sun dancing over the earth bringing forth new life that climbs and reaches for warmth and blossom. In late January, there's a thaw and the earth and I both feel a rumbling. I'm expectant and full and ripe for a new experience, so I make a decision to travel in April to Telehemet's Seneca family. They can tell me if it's safe for me to settle in Eagle Cliff Falls that is in Seneca territory. Telehemet's brother is still chief in the Genesee villages and I'll be happy to be with his people. My mother will go with me, as well as my sisters, Esther and Molly, who have been staying with our mother in Tioga while their husbands and my father travel to Onondaga and go on long hunts. I don't know when I'll ever get a glimpse of my father again. My mother says he isn't as robust as he once was and claims his hunting and warring days are coming to an end. Even my high spirited mother, Margaret, looks weary, but the harsh winter and trying to be at peace during war time while caring for captives takes its toll on her. Sometimes her belief in Jesus gives her anxiety because she fears she doesn't please him enough. I tell her she's trying to please the Moravians, not Jesus, but she shakes her head at me. Roland and John will stay here in Kah-ni-sti-oh and help Joseph and Mary Sweetgrass with the captives and go on nearby hunts. I'm not pleased to leave them behind, but this desire to travel to Telehemet's family and Eagle Cliff Falls is strong and I must go. I have to find out if this place can be my home, our home. Belle wants to stay with Clara and Elsa and begs me to allow her. I desire Belle to be with me always, but I, like many Indian mothers, am too lenient, and give in to her. There will be much work for Elsa and the women in the village to do to prepare for planting and the Strawberry Festival. Belle will be needed here more than with me.

But after all my eager plans to travel in spring, an Indian arrives with a message from Teedyuscung instructing me to pack and travel with his messenger to go to Tioga and my mother and then to plan on a long journey away from Kah-ni-sti-oh. The messenger tells me that we are needed to help Teedyuscung bring peace with the Ohio Indians and other Indians. I thought I'd never see Teedyuscung again. I'm not being asked by him, but commanded to become a part of this messiness with the British and the Indians. Haven't I done my part by moving to Kah-ni-sti-oh and caring for captives? I'm angry and have no one to talk to about this, although Elsa tries to bring me relief and support. She sits with me this evening and her large, sad eyes stare into mine.

"One time I hate you, Catarine. Now I understand your story, your people's stories . . . like stories from my childhood. Like all humans' stories. You want peace. I want peace. I'm not your captive like once I was. Clara and I live with you with free hearts now. I won't run from you. I take care of Belle and this home for you. You go with the old Indian chief and make peace for all of us. I will stay here for you."

This night I dream of Eagle Cliff Falls again. I'm standing behind the long white hair of these grandmother falls when I hear gunfire and yelling. In the dream, I run to the fields and they're burning. I wake from this dream to the scent of burning corn. It takes me all morning to get rid of this stench and to forget this dream. When I was younger and dreamed, I would tell my grandmother and we could understand the dream together. But because we lived so much with the missionaries coming and going, the Montours didn't follow the rituals of the Ho-De'-No-Sau-Nee which always take heed to dreams. Indians take dreams very seriously and believe they are divinely given and must be acted upon. In an Indian village, the person who dreams a loud and persistent dream will visit each home telling this dream and everyone is to offer a meaning and say how to respond to the Great Spirit who has given this dream.

I believe I'm strong enough to say no to Teedyuscung and not go to Tioga, but I won't. Maybe I can help bring peace and stop the scorching of my sister corn that is a symbol of how the Indians have been treated. And so it is that change comes again for me and for the next two years I travel to Fort Allen and to the Easton Treaties with my mother and with a multitude of Indians from various tribes. I return many times to Kah-ni-sti-oh to visit my children in the first year and then they travel with me.

On a recent trip to Kan-ni-sti-oh, I become aware that Elsa and Roger want to marry and I'm not surprised. They have a simple ceremony on the banks of the river. It's another vibrant autumn and I watch the leaves float away again. I think of the sorrowful stories of this couple floating away and how nearly two years before, my old life floated away. I invite Roger, Elsa, and Clara to stay in my home while I'm gone. It's larger than Roger's little cabin and they'll continue to look after my horses and animals. After a joyous ceremony with Indian, Swedish, and Scottish rituals and many Indians and white settlers attending, my two prisoners, Daniel and Thomas, escape. They are merry, along with everyone at the wedding celebration and even ask me to dance. I awkwardly dance with each of them and as I watch them leave to go to the barn to tend the animals, I know they'll be gone by morning. It's a fair September day when anything is possible, including bringing together two broken-hearted people and giving freedom to young men to pursue their dreams. I spent strong money on these two men and received much work from them. I believe they left with new respect for the Indian. I, too, feel freedom in my strange, itinerant life that is giving me not only knowledge, but wisdom. I'm not an important figure as my uncle or George Croghan, but I'm adding my own color. I'm fairly content in this new life, especially now that I have my children with me, and still I dream of Eagle Cliff Falls.

My sisters, Molly and Esther, also attend the various treaties and all of us, no matter how many wampum belts are exchanged, sense the lack of sincerity on both sides.

The war with the French continues in the Ohio region until 1758 when Fort Duquesne becomes Fort Pitt. I've seen George Croghan and Sattelihu at these treaties, but other than my uncle honoring me and George Croghan tenderly addressing me, I'm busy with the work of an Indian woman. I also speak with some of the Ho-De'-No-Sau-Nee chiefs about our history, our Great Law of Peace, and learn more about the formation of our League of Six Nations. I remember the story of Dekanawidah and the Tree of Peace I told at my table in Kah-ni-sti-oh not so long ago. Now I desire to know how we can live this Tree of Peace. I don't sit in the front row at treaties as my grandmother once did, nor does my uncle ask me to. I prefer sitting in the back with the women and older children, including Roland and John. There is wisdom and wit made by the Indian chiefs and flowery and interesting words made by the colonial representatives and governors. The chiefs have much melody to their speech and it makes me proud, but both sides try to out speak one another with high-sounding, flamboyant words. George Croghan and my uncle are interpreters, but George Croghan also addresses some meetings. Teedyuscung attends the meetings in full color and at most of these treaties, he is highly respected.

Teedyuscung and the chiefs receive new saddles and many gifts at these treaties, including military hats trimmed with gold lace and regimental coats. Some of these gifts spill over to me and my children and for this, I'm thankful.

One evening after a long day of meetings, we sit around a fire. Many of the Indians are drinking rum, including Teedyuscung and a few white men who come to sit among us. I'm quiet in the evenings after Belle is sleeping and my sons are dancing or playing games with the other young men. As I watch and listen to these men interacting, I'm seeing new ways. How simple to view the vastness of the stars and feel risen far above the earth and be content, but we cannot be if we lose the ground beneath our feet. For then we'll be merely spirits and not of this earth. Is this what is intended for the Indian? Is this what the Europeans feared for themselves? Did they lose the ground beneath their feet and come to take our own? Where will we go from here? Beneath and above, but not on this earth we so love and need for sustenance of body and spirit.

Teedyuscung is feeling the rum and speaking to one of the white men named Henry sitting next to him.

Henry gets close to Teedyuscung. "There is one thing strange and for what I cannot account for. It is why the Indians get drunk so much more than the white people?"

Teedyuscung replies, "Do you think strange of that? Why it is not strange at all. The Indians think it no harm to get drunk whenever they can, but you white men say it is a sin and get drunk, notwithstanding."

Teedyuscung has failed to become a true Christian according to the Moravians. Many Indians become Christians and are given small treats and heavenly assurances for their souls, forever groveling before the white men and their god. Teedyuscung and others want to keep the sacred ways of their tribes and still receive the goodness from these people's god. Why shouldn't they?

THE SUSQUEHANNA COMPANY and the settlers from Connecticut continue to plague the lands in Wyoming, Pennsylvania with their bold building of homes and barns. They are not welcomed by the Pennsylvania governor and councilmen, but they still come. These land stealers insist they had been given a charter in the 1600s and the Ho-De'-No-Sau-Nee sold them the land. This isn't true and the Iroquois and the Pennsylvania colony have stood against it.

I'm now at a Council meeting in Easton, Pennsylvania with Teedyuscung, Indians from many tribes, and from the Six Nations. All sit before the Pennsylvania governor and the governors from New Jersey and Virginia. Sir William Johnson, the Superintendent of Indian Affairs, my uncle, George Croghan, and council members also attend. Members of the Susquehanna Company from Connecticut defiantly sit in this meeting. I have seen their greed crawling over our land like unstoppable ants who have found a bucket of maple syrup. Teedyuscung's clerk, Charles Thomson, and the Pennsylvania Governor argue because the governor declares Teedyuscung is too drunk to speak. He may have had some rum, but Teedyuscung is not drunk. And so he's relegated to the back of the room and sits silently next to me. Conochguisson, an Oneida sachem, stands up and points to Colonial John Lydius of the Susquehanna Company while he addresses Sir William Johnson.

"Brother, you promised you would keep this fire-place clear of all filth and that no snake should come into the council room. That man sitting there is a devil and he stole our lands. He takes Indians slyly by the blanket, one at a time, and when they are drunk, puts money into their bosoms and persuades them to sign deeds for our lands upon the Susquehanna, which we will not ratify, nor suffer to be settled by any means."

William Johnson agrees that Colonial Lydius is faulty and guilty of his own accord, but the meeting drones on with more talk of ill-gotten lands and there are more flowery wampum exchanges and promises. I close my eyes and am soon half asleep as I lean onto Teedyuscung.

I dream of Shamokin and see it strangely altered. I walk and walk crying out for my mother and sisters, but never find my home or them. And then Teedyuscung shakes me and I'm awake looking into his old, tired, but concerned face. The room is quiet and Teedyuscung who has become sober very quickly, makes me stand next to him.

"Catharine, granddaughter of Madame Montour, and niece of Andrew Montour, has dreamed with me the hope of our people. If you will not let me speak in this Council, let her speak for me."

Teedyuscung pulls me to the front of the room and before I can make a decision what to do, into the building walks a number of Indians painted in war paint carrying loaded guns. Everyone quickly stands and alarmed utterances fill the room. The ready for war Indians stand on each side of the room with their guns raised, looking at Teedyuscung for instruction. For long moments, nothing happens. And then Charles Thomson and the other Quakers go to each side of the room to speak to the Indians quietly. After a few minutes, Mr. Thomson and the Quakers return to their seats, gesturing for everyone to sit down. The Indians look at Teedyuscung and he gives a nod to them. They set their guns into a corner and move to the back of the Council room in silence.

Teedyuscung and I stand before Governor Denny, the other governors, and Councilmen. George Croghan's penetrating eyes look into my own and it gives me courage to speak. Teedyuscung whispers that I should speak from my heart. I hesitate, but feel inspired to finally say aloud what I have been dreaming for many years.

"I, Catharine Montour, have had visions of the land of the Great Spirit being scorched from war and have seen the disappearance of my people in these dreams. Governor and Council men, you are uncomfortable when Chief Teedyuscung asks for lands to be returned to him and to all tribes, but you urge him to make peace with you and to bring the Ohio Indians into British favor. Already the land weeps from war and the Indians are scurrying to find homes elsewhere. This land is not our land or your land, but the land of the Great Spirit. Ask the Great Spirit, ask your God, how to care for this land and how to share this land or else the Indians will be destroyed and you'll live with much guilt and confusion that your children and their children will suffer from. This guilt will alter itself and become pride. You'll not know its potency is poisonous and will continue drinking it and giving it to your children to drink."

Governor Denny casts me a stern look and tries to smile. "You have spoken well and with truth, Catharine Montour, but allow me to hear what Teedyuscung has to say, drunk or sober."

I feel dismissed and can hear shuffling and grunts from the back of the room. My Indian brothers don't approve of these men giving so little attention and respect to an Indian woman who has been acknowledged by a chief. I continue to stand next to Teedyuscung with my head held high. I think of my grandmother and feel her presence. She, too, would not have sat down. I feel empowered by her spirit and after all my struggling with her vision for me, here I am now having spoken to a Council.

Teedyuscung takes my hand and squeezes it and then speaks with his usual eloquence. "This is the time to declare our mutual friendship. Now, Brother, the Governor, to confirm what I have said in the past and that I have given you my hand, and which you were pleased to rise and take hold of, I give my hand with you now yet again. When you please, Brother, when you have anything to say as a token of confirming the peace, I shall be ready to hear and will rise up and take hold of your hand. To confirm what I have said I give you these belts."

One of the Indians from the back of the room comes forward with the belts and Teedyuscung takes them and hands them to the Governor.

Governor Denny replies with form but not substance. "We now rise and take you into our arms and embrace you with the greatest pleasure as our friends and brethren, and heartily desire we may ever hereafter look on one another as brethren and children of the same parents. As a confirmation of this we give you this belt."

The Governor gives Teedyuscung a large belt of white wampum with the figures of three men worked in it, explaining it represents His Majesty King George taking hold of the King of the Six Nations with one hand and Teedyuscung, the Delaware King, with the other.

Teedyuscung looks it over, showing it to me, and then places the belt in my hands.

"Catharine Montour and Charles Thomson are both important assistants to this Delaware King," he says to the Governor.

I have never considered myself Teedyuscung's assistant and don't wish to be so now, but I hold the belt tenderly and after the usual decorum to end a meeting, we leave the Council House. George Croghan is at my side as I walk out the door to look for my children.

"I'm proud of you, my Catharine, for you're a natural like your uncle and grandmother."

"I am my own person, George Croghan, and not a mimic of Grandmother nor my uncle, and I'm also not your Catharine."

I walk away from George Croghan and think soon we'll be lost to one another. I sigh, looking over my shoulder at his swaggering walk. We'll always need to know the other is safe and well.

Chapter Thirty-Two

AFTER TEEDYUSCUNG AND I attend more meetings and wampum exchanges at Easton, Teedyuscung declares he and his clan will settle in Wyoming, but he needs fixed boundaries to be honored. Teedyuscung asks again and again that he and his Indians will be made safe. I'm supportive because these are the stomping grounds of my young life. The Pennsylvania authorities and the Iroquois state no land was sold to the Susquehanna Company settlers from Connecticut. Who is lying? Teedyuscung tells the Governor that although this may be true, there are still settlers coming in and he wants assurance they'll be stopped. Governor Denny agrees to build a fort, a Christian school, and a church to settle the Indians in Wyoming. He designates agents to construct the work and to protect Teedyuscung's Delawares, Shawanese, Mohegans, Unamis, and others. Teedyuscung is confident that if houses are built in Wyoming, the Ohio Indians will come to live there. Governor Denny emphasizes all will be dispatched as agreed. The Ohio Indians, who resent Teedyuscung's power, say they'll move. However, they don't want to be under Teedyuscung's command. Chief Paximosa, who has never trusted the British says he'll not settle in Wyoming, but stay in Ohio, "The English pretend well and mean ill," he yells in a meeting. My mother wants our family to return to Wyoming and to Shamokin, but I tell her everything's changed and there are too many British army forts that have been built. She believes the words spoken at these treaties will be acted upon, but I don't trust these words and all I can think of is my next and, perhaps, final, move to Eagle Cliff Falls.

AND THEN THE Treaty at Easton happens in May of 1758 and there is much more confusion. The general purpose for the meeting is similar to the last and the ones before and specifies that the Indian nations will not fight on the side of the French against the British. It's supposed to finally bring Teedyuscung and his Indians who had strayed away from the British and made war on them, to an *absolute* sure and final peace. Of course, there is always the question of the sale of lands. Over the years, the Ho-De'-No-Sau-Nee have sold much Pennsylvania land to the Pennsylvania proprietors in agreement for mutual use and for Pennsylvania's protection and provision of them.

At the meetings in Easton this time, deeds are shown and eventually land is returned to the Iroquois as hunting grounds. This is in exchange for the loyalty of the Indians to the British and not to the French. British settlements from 1754 extend a little way up the Juniata River and Sherman's Creek, but at this treaty the Indians are promised there will be no further colonial settlements west of the Allegheny Mountains. And then the Delawares back down on any claims within the colony of New Jersey for the sum of one thousand Spanish dollars. I know nothing about this New Jersey, but why wouldn't these Indians want to be there? Teedyuscung was born there. In the end, the coins shine too brightly in their eyes and they agree.

There are five hundred Indians at this Treaty and I have plenty to do to keep my children nearby and follow the stories between the flowing words exchanged at the meetings. I feel impassioned to understand these treaties, the ways of our people, and the British.

Teedyuscung is acting the king he is sometimes called, and even as conflict in the meetings reigns, he becomes stronger, not weaker. He speaks eloquently of being wronged over lands in a meeting today and gives a string of wampum to the Council. And then to my happiness for Teedyuscung, Tokahayo, a Cayuga chief, rises up and commends the conduct of Teedyuscung and at the same time severely reprehends the British. He tells Teedyuscung he's obliged for his candor and openness. "You all can see this chief speaks from the heart in the same manner that was done in ancient times when we held councils together."

"We wish we could say the same for the English," Chief Tokahayo says, "but it is plain the English either do not understand Indian affairs or else don't act and speak with sincerity and in the manner they ought. When the Indians deliver belts, they are large and long, but when the English return an answer or speak, they do it on small belts and trifling little strings. And how little the English attend to what is said, for several of the belts and strings go missing. If the English know no better how to manage Indian affairs, they should not call us together. Here they invite us down to brighten the chain of peace, but instead, they spend a fortnight wrangling and disputing about lands."

The response the English gives to all of these matters is to provide a public entertainment just for the Indians, all five hundred of us. Before the new deeds are drawn up and the Indians are persuaded to sign them, there is much frivolity and celebration. As George Croghan hands me a cup of whiskey, he declares confidently, "And tonight 'tis said that it is done."

IT WAS AN important treaty and because the Ohio Indians were pacified, the French lost most of these allies. Now the British can fight the French in Canada and I can retreat with my children to Eagle Cliff Falls. It isn't over for the Indians, of course, but for me, it must be. And again, Teedyuscung promises to never take up the hatchet against the British and says he'll be true to his word until the day he dies.

It is never simple and the Indians will still be drawn into this French conflict and a couple of years later, I will learn that Sir William Johnson, with the help of the Ho-De'-No-Sau-Nee, launched a successful siege of Fort Niagara, and this victory will be because of the aid of my people. Quebec will be seized and General Jeffrey Amherst will end the French victory at the Battle of Montreal in 1760.

WANDERING FROM PLACE to place and treaty to treaty over the past two years has helped create more of a quiet place within me to settle. The miles I've traveled have been in circles, arriving back at the same beginnings and covering many miles of the same earth I've come to love as much as my own skin. The hills, fields, streams, lakes, and flowers have been as much of a companion as my family and friends. And although my travels have been confined mostly within Pennsylvania, the journey has given me world views. It started as a child with the Moravian missionaries, but now as I've trekked and lodged with many besides my own people, I've looked upon people from all over Europe and even from Africa. I may not have spoken to them during these travels, but our eyes talked about hope as we stared at one another and smiled, sometimes timidly, sometimes with boldness. Groups of one hundred to five hundred of us out numbered them and we were the ones being courted for peace.

We have been caught up in one day's mixed mood of sun and thunderstorms, all in a few years. The Iroquois, the Ho-De'-No-Sau-Nee, have had a sure confidence that wherever their feet tread, it would be home, and now there is a fear it will be no longer. And so Teedyuscung and my family and all who have been in this storm of treaties and change, have stayed together a while longer. We move as one for comfort to be sure we have one another and ourselves as we have always known before. I no longer feel different as a Montour who has had privilege other Indians haven't had.

I return with my mother to her home in Tioga with my children. Teedyuscung has been busy In Wyoming and Philadelphia. I'm very near Kah-ni-sti-oh and long to visit, but we're waiting for a visit from Teedyuscung who has revised plans for us. I'm beginning to wonder how I've become a soldier in Teeduscung's army.

Teedyuscung arrives in Tioga with his retinue of companions and we discuss many issues. Although the last treaty sealed the peace of the Indians with the British, there are still some Ohio Indians adhering to the French. So Teedyuscung, along with Christopher Post and others, are planning another journey to meet with these stray ones. Teedyuscung is everywhere, it seems. Teedyuscung and his companions lodge nearby and come to breakfast with us before leaving. Teedyuscung asks me to walk with him after we've eaten.

"I've met a great man, Catharine, a white man who doesn't wear Indian clothes and tries to be like an Indian. He respects the Indian, especially the Ho-

De'-No-Sau-Nee and their laws and constitution. I want you to meet him. Many chiefs don't want to make friendship with this man, for they feel his power is to also take land from them. He has built Fort Allen where Gnadenhuetten used to stand. He wants to protect the settlers, the Indians, and has dreams of building a new country. He wants to make certain the Christian Indians have a place to live and not be accused of siding with the French and the massacres."

"Why do you want me to meet this great man?"

"I want to know what he means by building a new country. He has big ideas to bring his people, the colonies, together like the Ho-De'-No-Sau-Nee, in one unity. He's intrigued by our laws and you, Catharine, like your grandmother, have been gathering the knowledge and importance of the Six Nations."

"If it's true this man is gleaning from our ways for the colonies, it can mean peace."

"No, Catharine, not if there are two strong powers. The English and the Ho-De'-No-Sau-Nee."

"What is this man's name?" I ask.

"Benjamin Franklin."

Chapter Thirty-Three

MY CHILDREN AND I, along with my mother and sisters, travel to Shamokin that is now called Fort Augusta. On the way there, we see homes that have been burnt by Indian raids. At one of them, there are dead bodies left unburied. My mother quietly prays and the rest of us are silent. There are no words. We fear we'll be mistaken for warring Indians by those come to bury their dead and so we hurry on. The stench follows us and the sorrowful spirits of the dead are with us as we travel. Everything has changed. Militia are present to defend the Christian Indians and white settlers from the French and Indians. Memories of my serene childhood in the woods and fields return to me, but now there are buildings and cabins where once there were none. It is mostly quiet, however, for the people have scattered to Bethlehem and Philadelphia for safety. Now that the militia is here and forts are being built, they will slowly return.

While my mother prepares to sell the rest of her cattle and cabin, Roland and I travel to Fort Allen to meet Benjamin Franklin. When Teedyuscung told me he is a diplomat, an inventor, and a printer who has written books, I remembered Anna had one of his books. She said it would help me learn English words and encourage me to live with a good and moral conscience.

Benjamin Franklin has built Fort Allen on the site of what used to be New Gnadenhutten before the massacre of the Moravians and Christian Indians. Teedyuscung asked me to learn if this white man is sincere in protecting all loyal Indians with this fort. Benjamin Franklin is the colonel in command and came months ago with many volunteer soldiers to build all the forts. But there seems to be no stopping the Connecticut settlers and others from moving into Wyoming Valley and the surrounding lands. The Pennsylvania government is unable to prevent these settlements and recently there have been outbreaks of violence against the Indians by these white settlers. It's easy to be confused with who is killing who. Will Benjamin Franklin protect the Indians, missionaries, and settlers?

I'M DRESSED IN my best Indian clothing as I walk in the ornate beaded moccasins Grandmother made for me many years ago. The sun is brilliantly shining this day and I feel uplifted and certain of myself. Besides, my mother has agreed to go to Eagle Cliff Falls with me after she visits Bethlehem and now my dream will soon become real.

The wooden fort is long and wide with a high palisade. There's a surrounding trench and three buildings for the garrison. It's a small fort, but larger than the one in Shamokin, and the British flag flies over it. There's also a large, imposing swivel gun that is mounted on one side of the stockade. I see cannon balls lying nearby as John Henry, an Indian who lives at the fort, guides me through the gate. There are many Indians and traders milling about and as we near a building where Mr. Franklin is to meet me, I hear a voice that is strangely familiar.

"Catharine Montour! Catharine!"

I turn around to see Edward Pollard striding quickly in my direction. When he is before me, he reaches out to take my hands, but steps back and makes a slight bow. He takes off his hat and perspiration dots his forehead and his long sandy colored hair hangs loosely to his shoulders. A shell necklace hangs around his neck and he's wearing a colorful Indian vest. His face is free from hair and I wonder if Edward Pollard has decided to become an Indian like George Croghan. He moves his hat to one hand and then the other and I know he is nervous before me.

"I'm surprised to see you here, Catharine. You look well. George told me you were staying with your mother and family in Tioga. How long will you be here?"

"My son, Roland, and I will be returning to Shamokin this afternoon where my mother and the rest of my children are taking care of personal matters."

"Might I accompany you and Roland to Shamokin? Have you returned to live there?" Edward laughs and swipes at flies with his hat. "Forgive me. I'm asking too many questions."

Before I can respond, a door opens behind us and we turn to see a tall, strong looking, but portly, older man. He walks down the steps wearing the common colonial clothing and a beaver hat sits atop his large head. His hair is long, curly, and light brown and as he comes near, I note his eyes are grey, full of curiosity, and his mouth is large and in a half smile. I can't help but smile at him. He bows slightly and I'm amused that in just a few minutes, I've had two white men bow to me. No wonder Grandmother liked to be admired by these colonial men.

"John Henry tells me you are Catharine Montour, a relative of Andrew Montour, one of our special Indian liaisons and interpreters. Have you come with a message from him?"

I suddenly don't know what to say. I can't tell him I'm spying on him for Teedyuscung, and he must wonder why an Indian woman is visiting him. I haven't prepared myself for this meeting. Edward Pollard must also be curious as to why I have come to see Benjamin Franklin.

"I once had a Moravian friend named Anna and she read to me from one of your books. I'm slowly learning to read and write and would like to teach my children, too."

Benjamin Franklin throws his head back and laughs. "You won't be interested in Poor Richard's Almanack. It's full of farming wisdom and weather forecasting, along with witty stories. Indian women already know how to plant and aren't pleased with our kind of farming. And I do believe Indians know how to interpret the weather. I doubt you will understand the humor, but I'm quite pleased you are interested, Catharine Montour. Certainly your uncle is quite knowledgeable of our ways and you must be also. I have time now before I leave for Philadelphia, so please come inside and I'll show you some of my books over tea."

Benjamin Franklin turns to Edward Pollard who came to stand next to me. "Oh, Mr. Pollard, are you here with some goods for the Indians? They've been waiting for you, but hopefully not for the rum, mind you. I'm declaring fastidiousness in food and drink and very little spirits are allowed to be imbibed while I'm here, except for my soldiers in moderate amounts."

"I promise you there's no rum coming from my ship. Of course, there's the usual pots and pans, guns, and glass beads. My men have unloaded the goods into the building. Is there someone in charge to supervise the sales? I'm also leaving for Philadelphia after I hope to make a short journey to Fort Augusta."

Edward faces me and smiles widely. Benjamin Franklin looks at Edward and then at me and back again at Edward.

"Yes, of course, talk to one of the militia milling around the garrison and he'll help you. There are many Christian Delawares and Mingos here and they're eager to do business."

"Pleased to do so, sir." Edward Pollard nods to Benjamin Franklin and takes my hand. "I shall do my business and wait for you here in an hour or so?"

"Yes, thank you. Roland and I will be ready."

Edward Pollard leaves and Benjamin Franklin speaks to John Henry. "Can you have your mother prepare some tea for us?"

John Henry hurries away and Benjamin Franklin swoops his arm in front of me, smiling. I have seen this done by the colonial gentlemen at the treaties and know he means for me to go ahead of him into the house. I do so, sighing with some impatience. And I'll now have to be interested in this man's books and try to find out whether he's a true friend of the Indian. I'm doing this for Teedyuscung, my dear friend, but I'm eager to leave and prepare to go to New York with my family.

"DO YOU LIKE the tea, Catharine Montour?" Benjamin Franklin asks, as we sip very strong tea.

"Yes, thank you."

"I know you and your people drink teas made with different leaves, even nut meats, so I thought you might not be familiar with our colonial tea, called Bohea, a black tea from Shanghai."

"I've had this tea when my uncle has brought it home from Philadelphia. It's a different kind of tea, not medicinal like the ones we drink."

"Indeed. Medicinal teas would benefit all of us." Mr. Franklin takes a long sip and places the delicate cup carefully in the saucer.

"And where have you been through all of this chaos with our French and Indian problem, Catharine? Are you married? And if you are, is he a Delaware, Shawnee, or an Iroquois?"

He smiles and I see his wooden teeth. I don't wish to speak of my life and hope he won't ask me if I have sided with the Delaware. I detest lying for any reason.

"My family has been caught in the middle like many Indians and because I grew up with Delawares, I understand their frustration and confusion. I was married to Telehemet, a Seneca chief who died a few years ago in battle with the Catawba. I have his children and have not married again."

Mr. Franklin's eyes widen and he blushes slightly as he takes a sip of tea. "You are an attractive woman. I would think it would be an error of your judgment not to marry again. Perhaps Edward Pollard is in line for your hand . . . or is there another chief where you live? And where do you live now? Your uncle has moved many times, as I recall."

He asks too many questions and why would this Mr. Franklin think Edward Pollard is a possible husband. It's really none of his business.

"We were living in the Shamokin area until it became too dangerous to stay. My mother and family have lived in many places attending treaties and making plans for our future."

"Have *you* attended treaties, Catharine Montour? Many of the women and children travel to the conferences. Have you sat in on the meetings?"

I'm careful in my response and hope his questions about where I live will be forgotten. "I've attended many treaties and I've learned that both the white man and the Indian have good intentions. But it seems more difficult for the white man to live up to them."

Benjamin Franklin lets out a loud sigh as he stands and goes to his desk across the room. He looks through his papers and books as I sit wondering if I have offended him. He returns with a book and hands it to me.

"Maybe you will understand the white man better if you read some of my good intentions that fill this book."

Now I have a copy of *Poor Richard's Almanack*. I thank him and think I'll probably never have time to read and understand it.

"Perhaps Mr. Pollard will have time to help you read this book, Catharine," he said, smiling widely. He is hiding his real meaning beneath the words he speaks.

Mr. Franklin again hurries to his desk, talking to himself and looking through piles of papers. I sit puzzled, wondering how I can learn of his real intentions as Teedyuscung would like me to. This man seems to waste many words and is now using up my time. I wish to return to Shamokin before dark. I look out a window and note the sun will set soon. I'm comforted knowing Edward Pollard will accompany Roland and me, although I'm capable of defending Roland and myself if I need to. I have placed my gun by the door and as I look over at it, I see someone walking back and forth. It's Edward Pollard. He's impatiently waiting for me. I stand and move around to try and get Benjamin Franklin's attention.

"I must leave, Mr. Franklin. It'll be dark soon."

He rushes to my side and hands me booklets. "These are some of the speeches at treaties and writings I've printed over the last few years. One of the speeches in the booklets is made by one of your eloquent chiefs, Canassatego, at the Lancaster Treaty in 1744."

"I was at this treaty and remember his speech," I respond, impressed that he thinks the Indian chief's words worthy to print.

Mr. Franklin sighs and looks out the door. "It's Mr. Pollard waiting eagerly for you, I'm afraid."

"He's going to accompany my son, Roland, and I back to Shamokin."

"Yes, I know . . . and you'll be in safe hands with him, I'm certain, so will you oblige me with some more of your time?"

I look toward the door and don't know what to say. I'm aware that this man is important and I can almost hear Grandmother's voice in my head telling me to stay and talk to him. I must stay, for I've come too far now not to heed her voice.

"Let me speak with Mr. Pollard for you, Catharine. In the meantime, sit down, have more tea, and if you can read a little, take a look at these booklets."

The two men stand for a few minutes on the porch. I look at one of the booklets and see Chief Canassatego's speech. I can make out his words because I remember that day, although I was young. I read the words slowly aloud . . . and stumble over many and replace them with Iroquois words.

> We heartily recommend Union and a Good Agreement between you our Brethren. Our wise Forefathers established Union and Amity between the Five Nations; this has made us formidable and this has given us great weight and Authority with our Neighboring Nations. We are a Powerful confederacy, and by your observing the same Methods our wise Forefathers have taken, you will acquire fresh Strength and Power.

I ponder these words. The Iroquois and most Indians are generous people, ready to share their wisdom. It is the spirit of the Tree of the Great Long Leaves, the Tree of the Great Peace, which has given them this desire. The prophet, the Great Peacemaker, Deganawida, counseled peace among warring tribes and to this day it's wished for all. Unfortunately, if peace doesn't come, war prevails to make that peace. It's been this way for some time. It's a peace that is flawed. I recall Deganawida's name means *two river currents flowing together.* Could it be that Chief Canassatego felt that because these Europeans have been here for some time and more are always coming, they could unite with the Indians and there would be two strong currents flowing into one powerful river?

Benjamin Franklin returns and sits down before me. "My dear, you have been gracious to an old man. I've asked Captain Pollard to wait for you and instructed him to gather some foodstuffs, blankets, and trinkets to take to your family and others in your village."

"We aren't in need, Mr. Franklin, and I've enough trinkets from my uncle's travels, but I thank you for these gifts. I shall give them to the Indians in our village."

He looks down at his papers in his lap for a moment. "Now, Mistress Montour . . . you attended the conference in 1744 and you are your uncle's protege, perhaps, or your grandmother's, Madame Montour. I never met this esteemed woman, unfortunately, but heard much about her."

"My first treaty was in Lancaster. I was young and didn't understand very much, except that the Indians and Europeans see life differently. I knew this already because many missionaries and fur traders often stayed with our family. Some of the differences I see are in courtesy and understanding. A young child is as valuable as a chief to the Indian. I don't mean to say Europeans have no desire for the same because your God teaches love for all. I believe most of us, Indian and white, are trying to live in peace. This is where we are alike."

"Might I say, Catharine, you have paler skin than most Indians . . . indeed, you are pleasing to the eye . . . and I mean no harm by this observation."

"And if I was dark as many Indians, would I still be pleasing to the eye?"

Mr. Franklin raises his eyebrows in surprise and laughs heartily. "Quite . . . yes, quite . . . you just need to smile more, my dear, but I understand these days have been most trying for all of us. Forgive me for getting off track. Now, let's see. Yes . . . I was so impressed with Chief Canassatego's speech and the many words that flowed from him that I sought him out a few times to understand this union the Six Nations have that is formidable and admirable. And then I printed his speech and have pondered it and his words and the words of your prophet over the years. In 1754 at the Albany Congress, I presented to my brethren a plan of union, a confederation of our own, similar to the Iroquois, for our British colonies. A central government with our own president and grand council, subject to the crown, of course."

Mr. Franklin sits back in his chair and sighs, looking up at the ceiling while he speaks.

"My God, what a strange thing, I told my brethren, if six nations of ignorant savages could be so capable of forming such a union and execute it for ages, why not ten or a dozen English colonies?"

Mr. Franklin rights himself up quickly and is flustered, his face red.

"I'm sorry, Mistress Montour . . . forgive me. I forget you are an Indian, for you are well spoken and refined. I am the ignorant one to call your people such, but it's not how I presented it, by all means. Or at least how I meant to speak of your people. Will you ever forgive me? Or understand? I mean to say . . . and I said this to my brethren that it be understood the meaning of ignorance is only to say the Indian is not like us in language, ways, and beliefs and still they can come together as a confederation. They are ignorant of our ways, my dear Catharine, and not ignorant in and of itself."

"And savage?" I ask.

"Savage, yes . . . savage because the Indian is also greatly feared for his warrior ways . . . thus we call him savage."

My heart beats quickly. I've heard we are ignorant savages many times, but never has a white man or woman said it to me. He forgets I'm French or maybe he doesn't know. His words don't shame me or make me cower. I'm proud of my people to have influenced the white man such as this and proud that we are feared. There's no doubt they are in confusion about us. And maybe we are also in confusion about them. Could it be possible for two strong currents to become one strong river on this land?

"You are more upset by your words than I am, Mr. Franklin. This Albany meeting was years ago you say. Are the British still considering becoming a confederation?"

"Ah, Catharine, I'm relieved you aren't upset over my *ignorant* words. This plan for union didn't transpire . . . not yet, anyway. I was asked to prepare a draft of a proposal for the confederation of the colonies. It was called the Albany Plan of Union. One of the principles was that all purchases from the Indians for the crown should be made by a single purchaser, that is, the union itself, on behalf of the Crown. This would eliminate confusion because now each colony has its own policy for trading and purchasing. And this is how it all becomes a mess. And I might add, this union would be able to regulate the demon rum."

"Mr. Franklin, although our nations and tribes have their own ways, we're more alike than we are not. Most Europeans I've met have skin color that is common to them, but their beliefs and thinking can be quite different. Our Moravian friends don't mix well with other Christians and yet most of them have the same color skin and the same God. They mix better with the Indians than with the Quakers and others. And then there are those who follow Popery, like the French, and they're even more different than the others. They are as different as a bear and a wolf, although they believe in the same God and have skin color nearly the same. We Indians have more than one creation story and are pleased even to add another, like your story, to our own. But it isn't enough for the missionaries. We have to give every belief up for your God. We don't ask other Indians to give up their creation story to believe in ours or to celebrate a festival exactly like the Ho-De'-No-Sau-Nee or another Indian tribe. The French welcome marriage with the Indian, but the British take Indian women and hide them away and if they do marry them, they make them into white women. I believe my grandmother was admired in Philadelphia because she could dress and speak as a white woman. Her skin was as light as mine. And although she was a go-between and worked for the colonial government, she could easily hide that she was an ignorant savage Indian. I ask you, Mr. Franklin, how will the colonies unite into one family when there are so many differences?"

Chapter Thirty-Four

WINDS CARESS THE sun-kissed leaves and then pull them from the limbs of their mother. Maple, beech, birch, and oak leaves release their grip from life and dance in the sky. I watch as they careen to the right and then to the left before landing on the rocks around me. A few land on my face and the waterfall near me sings softly with many voices. I'm lying on smooth warm slate that has been heated by a long day in the sun. Two autumns ago, I sat on the bank of the Susquehanna and watched colorful leaves fall away from their source. I, then, wanted to surrender to the seasons of life and be carried from one form to find another. I wanted to be like the leaves and let myself dance into more of life. And so it has happened that after years of both calm breezes and stormy winds, I've landed here at Eagle Cliff Falls. This is the place that has been in my imagination since I traveled as a young woman to marry Telehemet. I'm in the land of belonging and hope to live here until I die. There are more flowers here than anywhere I've lived. Blue-eyed grasses, cinnamon ferns, and bleeding hearts sway and dance with their tall grass partners of big blue stem, goldenrod, and switch grass. I'm reminded that this earth is Turtle Island and the heart of Turtle Island for me is right here at Eagle Cliff Falls. The marshes and swamps hiss and murmur in a chorus of praise in springtime. It is home to turtles, birds, frogs, reptiles, and many butterflies. I've sighed with so much happiness since coming here. At the end of long summer days of harvesting and cooking, I go alone to sit behind the white flowing tresses of the wise mother/grandmother waterfall. I am living in sacred rhythm with the moon times, not only in our plantings, but in our seeing and honoring. I had been out of rhythm with the Great Spirit and my tempo became uneven. I was trying to keep in step with the tempos of others who were not like me in our dances with the kin of the forest and fields.

When my children and I moved here there were no settlers or Indians on the flats by the waterfalls. Eagle Cliff Falls are sacred and there are no European or Indian settlements. Seneca Indians come to hunt and live nearby in a small village near the Chemung River, along with a few Delawares and others, but they do not live here.No settlers claim this land like the Connecticut settlers claim in Pennsylvania. This is Seneca land and it's honored and watched over as a mother who cares for her children. I do not possess this place, but it possesses me. I give thanks to the Great Spirit for my life here and for the Seneca nation who has given us permission to live on this land. When I visited my husband's family on the Genesee, they embraced me as a daughter and I recalled my wedding night and this union that gave me Roland and John. How far I've traveled from that time to here. And now I am at home and each time I walk with feet unbound, I feel my roots going deep into this bountiful place.

My mother, Margaret, my father, Katarionecha, my sisters, Molly and Esther, Joseph and Mary Sweetgrass, my children, and I journeyed to Eagle Cliff Falls. We drove our cattle, horses, and swine with us, and although the journey was long, I was sustained by my dream. After settling here, I found more waterfalls besides Eagle Cliff Falls, and there are many. There is one the Senecas call She Qua Ga Falls that is a short distance from Eagle Cliff Falls. All around us are smaller and larger waterfalls with thunderous voices in spring, lilting voices in summer, reflective voices in autumn, and serene voices in winter. All of these tumbling waters have become my family. This is my paradise.

With the help from the Indians living on the Chemung River, we built a longhouse and other buildings. We planted corn, beans, pumpkins, squash, and many vegetables. This land is lush and fertile, and although there was much work to make it our own, I've not felt such permanence and certainty since my grandmother was alive. Her scarlet blanket of love has spread over my life and this place. I feel her with me . . . and when we arrived, the terror and chaos of war became distant. Here we feel separate from Pennsylvania, Ohio, and other lands that have become embroiled in conflict. Before traveling here, my family and I stayed in Tioga and Kah-ni-sti-oh, selling some of our possessions and making arrangements to permanently move. When Tioga and some of the villages experienced a bloody flux outbreak, again my dream was postponed as we cared for the sick. My mother and Esther became ill and my children and I somehow escaped this horrible condition. When everyone in the family was well again, we traveled away from the travails, confusion, and raids.

My mother is my elder and so we call this village Margaret's Town. I'm pleased to be here with my family and although I miss my uncle, he's busy in pursuit of the enemies of the British. George Croghan is with him and there are messages back and forth. My mother is at peace with this beautiful land, but she is restless and doesn't like to be cut off from the Moravian missionaries and Christian Indians. My father is happy to go on long hunting journeys with the Seneca Indians near the Chemung and as much as he loves my mother, his preference is to be with other Indians. His warring days are over and I'm relieved, for he and my mother are becoming the age of sages who sit before the fire and tell the younger ones stories of their ancestors.

For a long time, we live like this and I want it to be forever, but it's a tender gift that will change as the seasons. My children are growing, my mother and father will go to the ancestors, and my dreams tell me I'll speak for this land and its glorious lakes that are the fingers of the Great Spirit.

MY MOTHER TRAVELS each month to Tioga with a few Indians from Chemung to visit the smithy and trade for supplies. This day, she returns with white captives in her custody. I'm angry and disappointed. It's the first change to come to Eagle Cliff Falls and I ask this eagle who imprints her wings upon the rocks by the water to protect us. This eagle has always been the protector of the Ho-De'-No-Sau-Nee. She lives atop our Tree of Peace and alerts us if danger is about. I feel danger has now come.

"These two men were brought to me by Teedyuscung's Indians, Catrine. They built homes and buildings in Wyoming where Teedyuscung was promised a church and school would be built."

I look at the two young men and think of Daniel McMullen and Thomas Moffitt. They look to be the same age and possess the same defiant and hateful demeanor. It'll take time to tame them and I have no stomach for it. No one else will do it. Esther has reunited with her husband and they live in a village at the junction of the Chemung and Susquehanna. Molly is going to be married and wants to live near Esther.

My voice is angry when I question my mother. "How many scalps did Teedyuscung's Indians take? He promised to lay down the hatchet for good."

"Teedyuscung has laid down the hatchet. Ohio Indians who had returned to live in Wyoming raided because the settlers from Connecticut continue to come. Even after the governor promised they wouldn't. These Indians decided not to listen to Teedyuscung telling them to keep peace."

"How many were killed?"

The two prisoners get off their horses and turn their backs to us. I want to scold them, but hold my tongue.

"None . . . the warriors told them to leave their homes and after they were emptied, they burnt them and took these two men. Jessie Smith and Peter Schmidt will help us with our livestock and work. And until these governors keep their promise to Teedyuscung and all Indians, we'll keep captives until they do."

I speak to the young men of our ways and warn them that if they try to leave with our horses or on foot, there were many Indians surrounding our small village who would find them and pull their fingernails out and do worse. They don't know there aren't many Indians living near us, although I have confidence the Chemung Indians will come to our aid if we need them. Two Delaware from the Chemung have journeyed with my mother and these prisoners. They look startled by my strong words and when I look at my mother, she tries not to laugh. My father will be home soon and his presence will bring more assurance. For now, these young men will live with Joseph and Mary Sweetgrass and because Mary and Joseph don't have children, they'll be the grandparents of these men.

Joseph is pleased as he enjoys having white captives to teach them of Indian ways, whether they like it or not. And Mary is most happy making food and feeding others. I'm not at peace with this intrusion into our new life here. I sense in these young men something more than hostility and later I tell Joseph Sweetgrass to be vigilant with his guns. For now, these young men will not go hunting with Roland, John, or any of the Indians from Chemung.

TIME PASSES WITHOUT any incidents, but melancholy visits me after one of my monthly moons and it doesn't leave. With this outflow of blood, I've lost strength and it's difficult for me to participate in our village life. Belle has had her first moon and her girl's body has become womanly. Her strength is intact and she's a great help to me. My father doesn't hunt again one early winter when the Chemung Indians come for him. It's sorrowful to see his strength weakening, but his stately, wise manner and love for my mother who has become an old moccasin in a short time, warms my heart.

My distrust of Jesse Smith and Peter Schmidt lessens as they work hard and try to learn our way of life. Joseph and Mary speak well of them and I speak as little as possible to them. Since they arrived, I've not felt at ease as when we first moved here. My melancholy is a surprise and I wonder if there is sickness in my body as I've always had robust health. My mother makes special medicinal teas and I go alone to visit the waterfalls nearby, packing food and riding my horse on trails the Seneca Indians and Indians at Chemung have made. I have never feared being alone, even after Tom Miller attacked me long ago. There are no white men here, except our captives, and my own Indian brothers would not harm me. The wild animals have their own ways and I'm not in fear of them. In the last year, I've hunted with my sons and I've become an able user of the spear to catch trout and other fish in the lakes and streams. And I take my gun with me all the time now.

Each waterfall has its own distinctive voice and seasonal mood. The rocks surrounding the falls are chiseled and sculpted into patterns that often glisten from the droplets of water filled with sun rays. I call them sun drops when they sparkle and dance around me. When my sisters and I were children, Grandmother would tell stories about the Jogah, nature spirits that come in many different forms. As we grew older, these stories disappeared with the visits from the Moravians and fur traders. And now here sequestered from the influence of many voices and concerns, my eyes and spirit are open to see Grandmother's little people and remember her stories. What I see dancing about me must be the Gahongas, the stone throwers and rollers who live in rocky places and riverbeds. I wonder if they have created these rock designs and decorations. Do they live in the tiny forests of the moss that climb and cover the rocks? I let my imagination run wild at these waterfalls.

I continue to visit these places, even in winter when there are ice designs in the falls that speak of being still and remembering. When I return to our village refreshed, I share with no one about my reveries with the Jogah and the Great Spirit.

As my strength returns, I become inspired to make preparations for a Strawberry Festival in May. We don't have Keepers of the Faith for the festivals because the Indians at the Chemung come from different nations and many have not been here long. Because my father was a Keeper of the Faith in Pennsylvania, he chooses three others from Chemung and they become the speech makers. Many of the women from Chemung visit and move to our village with their husbands. In May, we'll do the Great Feather Dance that I've not done since a child.

Our Planting Festival this year was very heartwarming, an invocation to bless the seeds. There were many seeds this year and we planted apple and peach orchards. I remember Chief Shikellamy being concerned many years ago about the Indians planting orchards. He imagined we'd lose our Indian ways and take on too many European ways. We're not afraid of this now, for there are many things we've learned from the Europeans that are good and we can still keep our Indian customs and discard the rest we don't like, especially here in my paradise. Haven't we also given to the Europeans some of our gifts? Give and take. As we watch the earth do the same, shall we not also be this way with one another?

The strawberries are plentiful and we're grateful for their medicinal healing tonic and for being the first fruit from the earth. We thank the Great Spirit for being kind to us, in sparing our lives, and giving us peace. We celebrate with thanksgiving and the children eat berries and we dance to the music. Na-ho! I help prepare the berries with maple syrup and put them in big bark trays in a form of a jelly. Oh, what a day it is, full of sunshine, fluffy clouds, and a breeze that cools us as we gather before the She-O-Qua-Ga waterfalls. The Keepers of the Faith decide there's more room here than at Eagle Cliff Falls. We have many more people participating and so I'm pleased to keep Eagle Cliff Falls for my own thanksgiving ceremony I'll do later before the sun sets. At the end of this happy day, Mary Sweetgrass, my sisters, and the women from Chemung carry food back to the village. I look around for Belle and don't see her. She's been moody and wasn't excited about the festival today. I'm concerned, but eager to go to the falls before the sun sets. I find Roland and John and tell them to look for her while I'm gone.

I walk to the falls and I'm full of peace and contentment for all that has become my life here. As I climb the rocks to get to the falls, I step around the dark purple violets and daisies growing between rocks and moss. They are delicate and strong and remind me to live the same. I don't have my flute, but I sing as

I walk close to the waterfalls. When I'm finally before these grandmother falls, I see Belle behind them, but she is not alone. Jesse Smith is with her and they're entwined in an embrace that I think Grandmother would approve of.

"Belle!" I yell over the cascading falls.

The two lovers look over at me and jump into the water to swim to where I stand. Belle walks out of the water with Jesse timidly following her. He hides behind her as she stands before me, her eyes soft with love. The eyes of George Croghan's who had the same expression when he looked into mine. She is silent, respectful, and waits for me to speak. I hear Jesse behind her sigh.

"Our thanksgiving festivals are celebrated as one people. You missed out on our village thanksgiving. We don't think our own thoughts and go our own ways during this time, Belle. You and Jesse should not be here, but in our village helping with cleaning and evening work."

"I helped with the bark trays, Mother, and made food. I cared for the children and danced with the women. And then, like you, I wanted to come here to Eagle Cliff . . ."

Jesse interrupts as he shyly comes from behind Belle and stands before me. "I asked Belle to walk with me, Mistress Montour. I should have asked for permission."

"Belle does not need my permission. She knows our ways and what is required of her. You, however, are not free to go where you want to go. You do need my permission."

I look at these two young, eager faces and I'm reminded of when I longed for Telehemet to return and found it easy to love George Croghan.

"Return to the village, Jesse, and care for the animals. Don't ask Belle to go on walks again."

Jesse nods and quickly leaves. Belle and I stand looking at one another for a few moments. I sit down on a rock and ask her to sit next to me.

"Your name is from a French word, bel, meaning beautiful and fair. It's a form of the name, Isabelle, your great grandmother's name. You've lived up to your name and are much like your grandmother who spoke her mind and was unconfined in her living. I'm pleased you are like her . . . and also like your father, George Croghan."

Belle stands up and looks at me, confusion on her face. "He's my father?"

"Telehemet was my husband and we always loved one another. But he was away more than he was home with me and his sons. He eventually took another wife far from us and this I accepted. While he was gone, I was lonely and because I'd always known George Croghan since I was a child, for he was Sattelihu's friend, it was natural for us to love one another. You were born out of this love George Croghan and I have had together."

Belle sits back down and I turn to cup her face in my hands.

"I don't want you to have this kind of love that your father and I have had, Belle. It had to be separate from my family, my village, and was very confusing."

Belle's eyes fill with tears and I hug her close to me. She weeps for a few moments and I think how strange it is that I seldom hold my daughter. The air was growing cold and the light dim and I didn't want us to stumble over the rocks back to the village.

Belle pulls away from me and smiles. "I always wanted the company of George Croghan when he visited. I thought he was great fun with his stories. Irish stories . . . remember?"

I smile, remembering how he amused us all.

"Does he know I'm his daughter?"

"Yes, and he offered to provide for you and will always know where you and I are."

"So now I have French and Irish blood."

We stand up to leave and hold hands as we walk to steady ourselves in the oncoming dark.

Chapter Thirty-Five

IT'S ONLY NATURAL for Belle to experience love and the pleasures of her body, but I don't want her to do so with Jesse Smith or any other white man. It's time for my captives to be returned to their people so I can be free to live in my paradise and Belle can be married to someone of her own kind.

"Jesse is my kind," Belle says, putting her face close to mine. "Look at my pale skin. My great grandfather was French and my father is Irish."

"French and Irish may be white, daughter, but they're different. If you measured out your blood, you are more Indian and this is the blood we are honoring in our lives."

"You are untrue then, Mother, for you have said that no blood is better than another's."

Belle leaves me at the cook fire, slamming the door behind her. I hope she returns to the field to work and not to the barn where Jesse is. Yes, these young men need to leave for many reasons. Esther and Molly moved from our village and they've also taken captives in Pennsylvania. The Montours have always been in good friendship with the British and taking captives is increasing tension between us. Messengers have come to tell us that Governor Hamilton is pleading for the return of all captives. I find my mother working in the garden and tell her it's time to return the captives. She is bent over and when she stands, she groans, telling me she needs rest. My strong mother, Margaret, has been growing weaker by the day. We walk to the cabin and I make her tea and tell her she must lie down. She doesn't resist, nor does she object to me returning our captives.

Molly visits and we talk about our captives and both of us are eager to release them. She says Esther won't give up her captives and there's been no word from Teedyuscung to encourage or discourage us in returning them. I send a message and a string of wampum with Molly and her husband to take to Governor Hamilton in Philadelphia saying I'll release my prisoners in autumn. I apologize to him for the indisposition of my family who has long prevented me from complying with the request for the release of our prisoners.

In the summer, Belle delivers a stillborn baby and our small village grieves. We hold a condolence ceremony and the pain of this loss causes Belle and Jesse to dissolve their love. My mother asks for the Moravians to come and baptize this dead baby, but they don't. I think how I might have lost Belle this way and I'm empathetic and attentive to her. I consider telling her father, but I don't. If this baby had been born, I would have given him the news of a grandchild. But it isn't necessary and Belle doesn't speak of her father. Belle is solemn for a long time, but she, like me, finds solace in the forest and waterfalls. Both of us spend much time at Eagle Cliff Falls together and are close again. I tell Jesse Smith and Peter Schmidt they are being released from captivity and will be taken to Philadelphia. Belle is relieved by the news, for Jesse's sorrowful, long face has been a constant reminder of her loss.

Roland and John accompany me to Philadelphia with our prisoners. It's a long journey and we set up camp along the way. When I sit by the water, I watch vibrant leaves falling from the limbs of trees. Here it is another autumn and change is on the horizon for me yet again. My boys are grown men and desire to travel and hunt. They are forming their own opinions about the French and British, and like Sattelihu, they are inclined to be loyal to the British. They had encouraged me to return our prisoners long ago. Their simple talk of entering this war against the French frightens me, but I know this is natural for their youth, although I've always encouraged diplomacy before fighting. They're fierce hunters, but are they warriors? I say nothing and only encourage peace. We, in our village, are not at war with anyone.

Roland and John will travel to Wyoming to meet with friends, to visit with Chief Teedyuscung, and to hunt and trade furs, but there are other reasons for their flight away from me. I see tenderness in their eyes that tells me they're interested in marriage. They are very young, only seventeen and eighteen. I tried to teach them to read and to learn from the few books I had, but they were not ready. I want them to be happy, so I tell them I will welcome an introduction with the daughters and their mothers they're interested in. Mothers have this obligation, but have my boys chosen already? Are we not abiding by our Ho-De'-No-Sau-Nee ways? Much has changed in the Indian ways of life and some things I accept, but as a Montour, was there ever strict adherence? I give John my flute and know he'll woo a young woman the way his father wooed me. I look forward to their marriages, but hope their wives' families don't live too far from Eagle Cliff Falls.

BY SPRING, THERE are two marriage celebrations and the promise of another in the Montour family. Roland and John, my handsome and strong sons, marry according to their hearts and not merely because of the choice of the mothers. In Ho-De'-No-Sau-Nee custom, my children could marry into any clan but their own. Roland marries Sarah whose mother is from the Cayuga nation and her father, Sayengueraghta, is a highly respected Seneca chief. Sarah, I know, will require many baubles from Roland, but her eyes brim with love for my son and this pleases me. At their wedding ceremony, she dresses in the Indian manner and shines in gold lace and silver jewelry. John, my Wise Owl, who is still called Stuttering John at times, marries a quiet woman. Her name is Dyani, meaning deer, and she's also from the Cayuga clan. She is pleasing to the eye and gentle in heart and I think she's perfect for my sweet John. Belle, with her pale skin and sudden interest in dressing in colonial cloth, catches the eye and heart of many men, but mostly the white men. She is flirtatious and demure, but makes no commitment to any of them. She has lived only sixteen years and has time to make a good choice. After we delivered our prisoners to Governor Hamilton, my sons and I decided to stay in Philadelphia for a period of time. I sent a message for Belle to come to us and was pleased she agreed. I wasn't content to be without my daughter.

While in Philadelphia, we were encircled by people of all nations, Indians, Quakers, traders, and soldiers. Philadelphia, called the city of love, has tried to create tolerance and respect between Indians and Europeans. And so it was in Philadelphia where love awash with the golden yellows and apple reds of autumn slipped into our lives. Belle and I were invited to a home of a wealthy white woman for tea and were sweet talked by many women, including Governor Hamilton's wife. I felt Grandmother smiling over my shoulder, for she had been regarded highly at teas given in Philadelphia. Although there was some talk of war, Philadelphia was like one big festival for dances, teas, and yes, romance.

The promise of another marriage was my own. I loved two men in my life and thought there was no room in my heart for more. Passion didn't course through me as it once did, but friendship with one man aroused a buried well of desire. Edward Pollard and I met again in Philadelphia. Hadn't I known when we were together last, a seed of affection had been planted in my heart? I had been resting from dancing at a gathering of Indian dances one evening when the moon was nearly full, but not quite. He said my name, bowed, and I knew. In a few days, both the moon and our hearts were full of love for one another. The following year, Edward Pollard and I married by Eagle Cliff Falls on an autumn day. We were surrounded by my sons, their spouses, his son from his marriage to his deceased Seneca wife, my mother, father, sisters, and a few Chemung Indians and others in our village. The leaves danced freely in the air, for Sister Wind played her song for us, swirling our hair, our skirts, and blessing our union. John played my flute and there was merriment, dance, delicious harvest food, and venison from the hunt. And then after two weeks of much lovemaking and happiness, my husband left to continue his business as a fur trader headquartered at Niagara. He is a man of business and when he first arrived from England, he had a company of other young men. He continues to thrive in his business. He has to travel, and this I accept, and by the time he left, Edward and my sons and daughter had created a bond. Edward is delighted to have one big family and is quite at ease living with us in our Indian village. He has encouraged John and

Roland to learn to read and is going to arrange for them to go to school near Albany. They thanked him, but they're now men, not children. I know they wish to honor my new husband and please him.

Edward will be gone from me often, not as Telehemet in the hunt and with his other family, but as an important trader. Love has come for me this time when I have learned to be content with love for myself . . . in my paradise. Our marriage becomes a union of deep friendship and respect, although our times together are sparse.

IN 1763, MY mother, Margaret, and my father, Katarionecha, went to be with the ancestors. My mourning was difficult, especially with my husband being gone at the time. My mother had asked that she be buried in Otsonwakin, near Shamokin, where she had been born and my father wanted to be buried next to her. After my mother died, we traveled with her body and my ailing father to Pennsylvania to bury her. Molly, Esther, and their families, as well as Sattelihu, came to the ceremony and left afterward. While my children and their spouses, my father, and I stayed in Pennsylvania to visit my old friend, Chief Teedyuscung, my father, longing to be with my mother, breathed his last breath. My sisters returned to bury him, but Sattelihu was unable to come. He's under constraint by General Amherst to help quell the rebellion that has been started by the Ottawa Chief Pontiac and many Indians from nations who are dissatisfied with British rule.

The French and Indian war is finally over, but the Indians know it will never be over for them. There are new lands for the white colonists to settle as the French scurry away. But this land has always been our land, Indian land, and there is a desire to keep it, especially with the French gone. The king proclaims the lands west of the Appalachians are only for Indian use. How did this come to be that a king across the ocean tells us we can have what we already had? I know this has gone on longer than I have been alive. The king forbids colonists to settle in the west and more garrisons are built, but the Indians wonder. We see how the colonists are taxed by this father king and they feel burdened and angry. This land reserved for us by the British king is merely a folly. And the king's children are becoming more irate and will not be told what they can or cannot do on this side of the sea with land they've already determined to be their own.

As the fire of one war hisses and dies, I'm here in Shamokin, but will return to Eagle Cliff Falls soon. For any other rebellion and oncoming war, I will stay tucked away in my paradise. I will not go against the British as long as they don't take my paradise away from me. I cannot help Chief Pontiac, but I'm sympathetic, but I *am* married to a British trader.

The Moravians are still in Wyoming Valley true to their mission to a few Christian Indians who stay with them, but most of the Indians have left. The

Indians' disillusionment is felt everywhere. The battle between the Pennsylvania proprietors and the Connecticut settlers of the Susquehanna Company continues, but the settlers seem to be winning. Teedyuscung stubbornly clings to his ideals for his people to live in the Wyoming Valley and continues to plead with the Pennsylvania authorities for help. They build houses, but don't come through with all of their assurances to him and his people. Promises are as forthcoming as flowers in winter and the settlers are as forthcoming as a large flock of crows scattered over a ripened field of corn.

THIS DAY I'M sitting in Teedyuscung's newly built home and can smell the spirit of the tree who has given its life for his new home. Teedyuscung is eager to talk to me.

"The governor says to break the Susquehanna Company's deed to Wyoming land, but it was given falsely and the Six Nations must destroy it, not me or the Delaware."

"Teedyuscung, you never give up, but at least now you know your uncles, the Ho-De'-No-Sau-Nee, agree with you that the settlers from Connecticut must leave. You have not always been on good terms with your uncles."

I laugh because Chief Teedyuscung has been his own person and has not cowered in fear before the Ho-De'-No-Sau-Nee or the governor of Pennsylvania. Or before anyone else. He speaks to me in a low tone, as if someone is listening. I look around. His windows are open, but there is no one nearby.

"I told the Governor that my people and I would settle in Wyoming with certain boundaries fixed and we wanted help building more houses. We needed a fort and then the Indians from Tioga can move here, too. And I asked for Christian teaching."

"Did you ask for Christian teaching so they would find it easier to give you your other requests?"

Teedyuscung doesn't answer me. He has struggled in following the ways of the Moravian Christians. He is disquieted and needs to talk.

"Pennsylvania doesn't like the Connecticut settlers declaring they have a right to this land and so they want me here. They say my presence will keep them out. It isn't working. I promised I would force the Ohio Indians to be on the side of the British, but first let all the houses be built and then the Ohio Indians would come. The cabins for the Indians have been built. More captives were given up, but the Ohio Indians under Paximosa don't want to be in Wyoming, as they have no trust in the English."

"You're here now after another treaty in Easton and you and the Indians received many gifts. And the new homes you all received."

"I've done as much as I can. The Delawares and Mohegans are here, too, and helped build the cabins. I pleaded with the Ohio Indians and they gave their word they would be true to the English. We will see . . . we will see. But I have gone back and forth, back and forth . . . doing the bidding of both my people and the governor. And the settlers from Connecticut claim not just that the king gave them a charter, but that Mohawks sold them the land. The Iroquois say this land was not sold by the Mohawks or any of the Six Nations. Maybe sold by staggering Indians . . . drunk Indians who did this without approval of the Council. The chiefs came here, Catrine . . . they came and confronted the Susquehanna Company and protested against the settlement and asked them to leave. They agreed, but said they would seek another conference with the Six Nations. I told the governor that I could have taken up the hatchet against these settlers, but I didn't. And I haven't. I wanted to, but I didn't. I was angry at him and said that all the pains he and I have taken will die away if these settlements continue. And now these settlers are slowly returning."

I don't know what to say to my friend. He has his home, his wife, his sons, and there are other Indians nearby, as well as the Moravians, but the sound of building and the arrogance of the settlers disturbs him . . . as it does me. I'm so happy I can leave and return to Eagle Cliff Falls. I sigh, sit back in my chair, and close my eyes for a moment. And then my heart quickens and I sit up frightened. How do I know that this won't happen in Eagle Cliff Falls?

"Catrine, daughter . . . are you alright?"

"I was thinking maybe you and Elizabeth could come to Eagle Cliff Falls and stay with us for a rest. It is most pleasant and our corn will be ripe soon and we'll have a thanksgiving feast and ceremony . . ."

"No, no . . . I cannot go. The Moravians and David Zeisberger have asked me to go with them to Bethlehem. And then I'll return and stay the winter here. Governor Hamilton asked me to report to him of the settlers and to keep watch. He has written General Amherst, Sir William Johnson, and the governor of Connecticut about them. It will soon change. There are too many good people who know the Susquehanna Company is not on the side of justice. There are more of us than them and soon we'll only have our people here with the missionaries and then there will be peace. And you will come to visit me, Catrine, with your new husband, this Edward Pollard."

I remember once when Teedyuscung was in Kah-ni-sti-oh I feared I'd never see him again when we said goodbye. I was wrong. Teedyuscung is indestructible and is a symbol to me of the fortitude and sincerity of my people. But now saying goodbye to him, I feel the same foreboding and my tears flow onto his gold trimmed regimental coat he wore just for me today. I leave, reminding myself I'm grieving over my mother and father and this makes me very tender.

Chapter Thirty-Six

IN APRIL OF 1763, after Teedyuscung's travels with David Zeisberger and the Moravians to Bethlehem, they returned to Wyoming and a bloody flux raged in the valley. Abraham, the Mohegan, Teedyuscung's wife, Elizabeth, and many other Mohegans and Delawares die. I long to go to Teedyuscung during this time of sorrow, but he tells me not to and he'll come for a visit. He says there is a new Christian school Rev. Eleazer Wheelock has built in Wyoming. Teedyuscung says he was pleased at first, but now he's irate that the children of his people are made to dress and act like white children. He also tells me there are over two hundred settlers from Connecticut. *But Catrine, the valley has become even more important as a stopping place, a half-way station for all Indians traveling from the headwaters of the Susquehanna to Philadelphia, Easton, or Shamokin. I still believe the Indians can prevail here and the governor and my uncles, the Ho-De'-No-Sau-Nee, will remove these settlers. Until then, maybe I will come to visit you in your peaceful paradise.*

AND THEN A few months later, I receive the message that my dear friend, Teedyuscung, died in a fire in his new home in the village of Wyoming. If only he and Elizabeth had come to stay with me long ago. My grief for Teedyuscung is unlike what I hold for my mother and father. It is not a soft wind that blows memories into my mind, but like the fire that killed him, anger consumes me.

Other lodges of Teedyuscung's warriors also went up in flames, but he was the only Indian who died. Many Indians leave Wyoming in grief and weariness. Andrew, the Delaware messenger of this news, tells me it is said that a few traveling Indians had stopped at Teedyuscung's house and became drunk on firewater. The traveling Indians left and a fire not tended started the blaze. I tremble receiving this message from Andrew and ask him what he is going to do. He doesn't know and I invite him and his family to live in our village.

"You are welcome here. You and your family, and any other families from Wyoming who need a new home."

Andrew bows his head, nodding, and big tears fall onto his moccasins. He also loved this old chief. This prompts the flow of my own tears.

"What about his body?" I ask.

Andrew lifts his head, his tattooed face dark and brooding. "No body. Gone in the flames."

"We'll have a ritual with fasting and wakefulness to release his spirit from his duties on this earth. We'll burn tobacco and he'll go to the Sky World, to the ancestors, and he'll no longer be in dismay and struggle . . . where are his bones? Can his bones be brought here by his sons?"

"His bones will be carried by his son in a mourning war soon to come."

I sit down on one of the chairs my son, John, made for me. I motion for Andrew to sit next to me.

"People were seen outside his house and me and some of the others saw no traveling Indians visiting him. We were with him late that night and none of us drank much rum. The Connecticut settlers had left a few months before because the Six Nation chiefs came to tell them to leave. But they returned, one by one, and then many."

"Did these settlers burn Teedyuscung's home?"

"No one believes this, but the Indians."

I'm enraged. My children are grown and except for Belle, are married. I want to stay here in Eagle Cliff Falls, but I also want revenge for my friend . . . and for the land that is taken from my people by these settlers.

"I will go with his son on this raid to avenge Teedyuscung's death, Andrew. Where is he and his warriors now?"

What are these words coming from my mouth? Can I kill and scalp? I shudder and think of Grandmother. She was a peacemaker, but no one crossed her and no one would cross me. White settlers have interfered with our Indian lives in Wyoming Valley . . . and everywhere. And now they have killed Chief Teedyuscung. His death needs to be avenged.

"There have been many raids because of Chief Pontiac. Presqu'Isle, LeBoeuf, and Venango have been captured and there are many scalping parties attacking settlements in Pennsylvania and Maryland. But Teedyuscung's son, Captain Bull, will lead a band of warriors to avenge his father in raids in Pennsylvania and New York in July."

"It's only May now. I'll make plans and you can give my message to Captain Bull, but say nothing to my villagers or to my children."

I remember that my husband will return next month and he'll be angry if I tell him I'm going with Teedyuscung's son to avenge his father's death. And so I won't tell him.

Andrew stands and smiles at me. "I'm honored to be invited to live here in this quiet place. I'll stay for a few nights and then go to Wyoming to bring my family here. We'll be happy here living with you, the mother of this village, now that your mother is gone to the ancestors. We will call you Queen Catharine. The English like their kings and queens and we, too, have our own."

"I am only Catharine Montour, Andrew, and that is enough."

The months pass and I don't go on the raids with Teedyuscung's son, Captain Bull, in July, but stay in my village. And no one, but the Delaware Andrew and Captain Bull knew of this desire I had to avenge Teedyuscung's death. My anger lessens because I hear the old chief's voice speak to me in dreams, right along with my grandmother's. One night they come to sit at the end of my bed and look at me with fondness and concern. They tell me to keep my heart free from the fire of raging anger, this anger that consumes both Indian and white people. In this dream, Teedyuscung tells me that the fire that burned his body has purified him and he is resurrected, but the fire of anger that is in me can bring destruction. Grandmother tells me to build a large bonfire and invite the ancestors to visit and there will be purification for me and my village. It will purify me and bring renewal so I may endure another fire that is coming. I wake and sit up shaking, looking around the room for Grandmother and Teedyuscung. Edward lies next to me on our mattress stuffed with hay and straw that rests on a pine four post bedstead. I curl up next to him and slowly return to sleep, but wonder what fire is coming?

My anger for justice subsides and peace returns as our village harvests large crops of squash, beans, and pumpkins. Edward helps me buy more horses and I breed them to sell. They become my closest companions, except for Belle and Edward. My horses listen and answer with their ancient eyes. I know they carry many souls that have lived before. We also have cattle and swine and are a very busy and contented small village. I've come to love the people in this village now called Catharine's Town. Here lives mostly the Seneca, but others from different nations dwell here . . . we live like wildflowers swaying and dancing together in the winds of change. We are in a dream world of all the good that had always been in our lives as Indians. We are not ignorant about human fighting and killing, but we weed out the news of hopelessness. We live differently here, and although some of the men go to war along with the Chemung Indians, they know that when they return they must purify themselves and not speak of scalps, honor, and loss. Edward knows this, too, but he is a trader, not a warring man, and tells me it is my gentle, strong spirit that has created this sacred place. I tell him this place was already sacred before I came and we have only been invited to treat it as such and give thanks in it. It has humbled me to live here, especially after my eagerness to avenge my friend's death. The waterfalls and my dreams have returned me to peace.

While we live in serenity at Eagle Cliff Falls, we are surrounded by rampages. When we receive news from travelers about raids, I insist we make a bonfire to purify ourselves and to pray for our brothers who have taken up the hatchet against the British. Some of the Delaware who had followed Pontiac into war come here, as if our prayers have brought them. All of us see the injustice and are angry, but here I insist we not take up the hatchet.

My sons live near the Genesee with their families and believe, like me, that diplomacy and treaties are the way to solve these tensions. They greatly admire Sattelihu and his position in the British army as captain.

It is 1764 and Chief Pontiac's war rages along with hostile Delawares and others. Sir William Johnson sends Six Nations Indians and a few Rangers under the command of Sattelihu, Captain Montour. My young sons, Roland and John, join the Rangers. I always knew they would become warriors, but I never thought they would be warriors against the Delawares. They join Sattelihu in the middle of February and help seize a party of forty Delawares who have been under the command of Captain Bull. When I hear this news, I'm in dismay, yes, for what has happened, but also for what might have been. If I had gone with Captain Bull to avenge Teedyuscung's death, my sons and uncle would have captured me. Some of their prisoners are sent to Fort Stanwix and then to Johnson Hall. Captain Bull and thirteen of his warriors are sent to Albany and are in jail. The rest of the prisoners are distributed among the friendly Indians aligned with the British to replace lost relations.

I send a message for my sons to visit me after I learn this news. When they arrive, I don't offend their manhood as warriors or speak ill of Sattelihu, but I ask if they will lay down the hatchet against these Indians who have gone astray and are against the British. I tell them to do this for me because many of the Delawares and others have been friends and are still my friends. They go home to their wives and go to school (at Edward's expense), or try to, and don't take up the hatchet for a few years. As for my uncle, I'm disappointed, but not surprised. The lure of the white man's glory is understandable.

My life is at peace here, but news continues to come like hail on a summer day that threatens to destroy our crops. A few months pass quietly and I receive news that my uncle, Captain Montour, along with 140 Indians and Rangers, attack Kah-ni-sti-oh. Sixty houses and many cattle are destroyed and this place of refuge that had once been mine is now no more. My uncle has done Sir William Johnson's bidding to bring the murderers and outlaws, Indian and white, to justice. Kah-ni-sti-oh did not only shelter murderers and outlaws, it sheltered me and others of all tribes and skin colors. They were people who hadn't been able to live with hypocrisy and lies who had committed crimes they were sorry for and could not find a place among their own clan or kin. I had once been one of them who lived in Kah-ni-sti-oh. And now I seek to find those that fled from my uncle's righteous rampage and bring them to live in my paradise.

If my sons had participated in this raid and destruction, I might not have been able to forgive them for many years. They respect Sattelihu and being young and needing honor, they might have followed him there. Instead, they heeded the voice of their mother and received my honor. They will go to war soon enough.

I'm relieved Elsa, Roger, and Clara had already left Kah-ni-sti-oh for England the year before this rampage. Some of the others I had known had left by the time my uncle destroyed the village. A few Delaware and Seneca Indians from Kah-ni-sti-oh come to live with us and the longhouse grows larger. How do I know who should live here in my place of peace and who should not? How have I come to be queen of this town and been given the respect of many? Edward Pollard is not the chief of this town, but I'm the queen. Eagle Cliff Falls was once created by the Great Spirit and maybe it was made with me in mind. I will always dwell here, even after I leave.

THE YEARS BECOME rife with turmoil as the children of the king gradually divide and become two. And the Indians are caught in the middle. The rebels of the king boldly thrust themselves onto the land in the west and feel the lure of a body ripe with fertility. The Indians know what these men don't know, that this land is not to be taken with force, but treated with tenderness. The patriots are emboldened like young bucks who want to be free of their mother and no one can hold them back. As they feel the collar of their mother country tightening around their necks, they not only sniff out what is ours, they dream dreams that are bigger than who they are. Dreams that come from the purest part of themselves. Dreams that we already know as Ho-De'-No-Sau-Nee and have awakened in them. Dekanawidah's dream to bring peace that is always being torn apart. Our Ho-De'-No-Sau-Nee dreams have not become as pure as they were intended and all of us, European and Indian, are full of withered spirits.

We at Eagle Cliff Falls continue to live separate from the rest of the world and although news creeps in and there are battle worn Indians who come to stay with us, we try to live in peace. We, the Ho-De'-No-Sau-Nee, who are dependent on the British for trade and goods, what do we do? Our Oneida brothers are in sympathy with the rebels, but our chiefs, including Roland's father-in-law, Seneca Chief Sayengueraghta, encourages the Six Nations to stay neutral.

The years pass and my Belle marries in Philadelphia, quietly and sweetly, by the busy waterfront. A spectacle we were, a small gathering of Indians and colonials engaged in a unique wedding ceremony. Before this marriage, I had agreed to travel with Chief Sayengueraghta to Philadelphia to state the neutrality of the Ho-De'-No-Sau-Nee. Tensions were high, but an official war had not begun, although many skirmishes with deadly results were taking place. Belle begged me to take her with us and, of course, I did, not wishing her to ever be far from me. Later, I would be angry that the spirit of my grandmother had not warned me not to take her.

We were invited to tea and asked to attend a ball by wealthy Philadelphia ladies. Belle wore a gown and accessories one of the ladies insisted on giving to her and I wore my Indian clothing shimmering in beads and fine fancywork only an Indian woman can create. I would not become a British plaything and, at first, I hoped Belle would become the *belle of the ball* in her blue gown and pale skin. Instead, all attention was upon me in my Indian clothing. And where was Edward, my husband? In England again. Although the ball was mostly attended by those loyal to their king, I was told there was a meeting elsewhere in the city attended by the rebels.

The fascination with my Indian self I understand, but the awkward attention Walter Butler, the son of Lt. Colonel John Butler, gave my daughter was confusing. I knew of Lt. Colonel John Butler through my uncle because he had also been an interpreter. He had worked as a captain in the Indian Department under Sir William Johnson, along with my uncle. He knew many Indian languages and customs and after his command at the Battle of Fort Niagara in 1760, he became wealthy and recognized by the British government. My Belle was like Cinderella at the ball, a story Moravian Anna once told me. But Belle was an Indian woman and even in her luxurious gown, she could never be one of them. It would have been better if she had worn Indian clothing like her mother and been given the attention I was given. I watched her, embarrassed for her as I listened to whispers. I was angry and uncomfortable. *Best to be bold as an Indian and not pretend to be someone you are not, daughter.* But when Walter Butler asked her to dance and she fumbled in his arms and lost both shoes that didn't fit her small feet, she gained the love of this young man. At the time, I was neither pleased nor displeased, but later would come to regret having gone to Philadelphia that year.

Chapter Thirty-Seven

EDWARD POLLOCK LOVES me and I love Eagle Cliff Falls more. After the thirteen colonies declare their independence from Great Britain, I declare mine from him. He pleads with me to go with him to Fort Niagara.

"My son is there and trading has to go on, Catrine. And your sons, my adoptive sons, Roland and John and their families, have moved close to Niagara. Your daughter, Belle, is nearby with Walter Butler. It makes sense that you come with me to live where we'll all be safe."

"This is my home. Here I can pray to the Great Spirit for my children's safety. The Ho-De'-No-Sau-Nee once stood strong and refused to take part in this conflict, but now they've changed their minds. Each nation must decide for itself. Look at us now. We're divided for the first time since the prophet, Deganawidah, brought us together. Our Oneida and Tuscarora brothers have sided with the rebel patriots. I don't want to side with anyone, Edward. But my sons and son-in-law are in John Butler's Rangers and they war against these rebels. I'll stay here with my people and be safe."

"As my wife, I want you to come with me. I've heard rumors that a large campaign designed by George Washington to destroy Iroquois villages is being planned. Do you think they'd show mercy to you or to anyone in this village?"

"My sister, Esther, is in her village in Pennsylvania, as is Molly. I will stay here in mine. I've heard from Belle that she is coming to stay with me while Walter is away and she is pregnant with their first baby."

We are sitting in chairs in front of our small cabin. I'm working bead work into new clothing for Belle. I hope she will prefer it to the clothing of her husband's family. Over the years, Edward has asked why I don't build a larger home, one like many Indians are now building. I've told him I don't need a large home. "I'm more at home outside than inside so why do I need to expand my inside dwelling?"

Edward stands and walks back and forth in front of me. He clenches his fists as he walks and then abruptly stops to face me, his face pinched and sullen.

"When I walked into your home in Kah-ni-sti-oh all those years ago, my heart was beholden to you. I waited patiently until you were ready and God Almighty brought us together. And now am I to lose you?"

Edward, the man who has bowed many times before me, falls to his knees and places his head onto my lap and weeps. I stroke his head and my tears fall upon his soft silk corn hair. I promise I'll go to Fort Niagara if it becomes too dangerous. I promise I will always love him. And this is true, for no man, not even Telehemet or George Croghan, has had my heart as Edward has. But for me to love him as I love this place is impossible. Worship should only be given to the Great Spirit, not to man.

IN THE END, Sattelihu, my uncle, was neither Indian nor white. Once when he was living at Sherman's Creek in Pennsylvania, he was supposed to drive off colonial settlers. Instead, he invited them to live there. Of course, he was given payment by them, but that wasn't his only motive. I remember this well and thought that he and I were of the same cloth as Grandmother. He had dreamed Sherman's Creek could be a place, perhaps like we once had, where neighbors were all different peoples living together. It was Conrad Weiser who went to the Six Nations and purchased this very land beneath Sattelihu's feet. Weiser promised the Ho-De'-No-Sau-Nee he would keep the colonists at bay, unlike my uncle who had invited them in peace. I think Weiser and many of the Ho-De'-No-Sau-Nee believe this country should be a land of lines that divide Indians from whites, not a place of shared meals and lives. Weiser, who had been a friend and mentor to my uncle had done this behind his back and my uncle never forgave him. I think of this now as I recall the last time I saw Sattelihu where he lived not far from Fort Augusta on a tract of six hundred acres near Chillisquaque Creek. After commanding raiding parties in Ohio during Pontiac's Rebellion, he bought this home. His second wife had left him, his children were grown, educated, and living in New York. And one son, John, is now a soldier . . . for the rebels! My uncle, like me, had wanted to live in peace on his land.

I'm sitting in front of my cabin and remember how eventually I forgave Sattelihu for attacking Kah-ni-sti-oh. A sudden sob gets stuck in my throat as I think of his untimely death at his own home in 1772. A Seneca Indian, a man he had entertained at his house for days had struck him down. Over the years rum had become more of a companion to my uncle than his wife or George Croghan. It was George Croghan who wrote to tell me of my uncle's death. George sorrowed so heavily, I feared for him who, unlike me, could not find contentment in one place. He told me he trusted no one, but would continue to take care of the Indians and keep them neutral during this war. Was he neutral? He had been sold 127,000 acres from the Six Nations in 1768, of which he had given to various friends. But things hadn't gone well for him. He was hounded by his creditors and he watched as the settlers poured into the Ohio Country that he considered his. Even George Washington sought land from George Croghan he believed was rightfully his. There was never good blood between those two. George Croghan had resigned from the Indian Department after my uncle died and then Great Britain agreed for George to start a new colony called Vandalia, which is not working out well. And then after purchasing more land from the Six Nations and William Johnson died, he tried to regain his position as an agent, but was rejected. He came to visit Belle who is now staying with me, and complained about the war, his debts, and his gout. He is no longer the swashbuckling man I knew as a young woman.

Belle is nearing the time to deliver her baby and her husband, Walter, is with the Rangers, as are my sons. We haven't heard anything about George Washington coming to destroy our Seneca village. It was probably a rumor Edward heard. Although the division between the Ho-De'-No-Sau-Nee brothers and the loyalists and rebels continues, I feel this chaotic warring can't continue and eventually all of us will have to live differently. I have no fear living in Eagle Cliff Falls, but I'm concerned for my daughter, son-in-law, sons, and their families. My daughter is very large and cries daily for her husband. The timing of George Croghan's visit is good because Belle warms in her spirit to see her father. He tells her he now has two beautiful daughters. George left his Mohawk wife and married a white woman and has had children. I can hardly keep up with his life and escapades. He is still full of promises.

"One day, soon, Belle, after this war is over, you and Susannah will meet and be close. I just know it."

"And I can stay at Croghan's Hall and this new Vandalia? And will you entertain and will there be balls?"

"Yes, I will host a grand ball in honor of Belle and Susannah."

George Croghan, always the talker, left us that day and handed me a wad of money for Belle and me. I shoved the money into his coat pocket and shook my head no. I didn't need his money. I had my horses and cattle, Edward gives me money, and Belle . . . she had married well. He felt guilty for not being involved in Belle's life and as always, he confused love with money and possessions.

Kissing Belle's cheeks and hand, as well as mine, George Croghan left for Williamsburg where he was then suspected of collaborating with the enemy by his friend, also from Ireland, General Edward Hand. General Hand had fought with the British army, retired, and later joined the rebels. When he saw George in Williamsburg, he said there was a loyalist conspiracy and many of George's friends were now imprisoned. General Hand forced him to go to Philadelphia and after the British evacuated, they left him there only for General Hand to return and accuse him of collaborating with the enemy. George finally convinced him he was not a collaborator. I don't believe George was for one side or the other, but was for his side, and yes, for the side of the Indians, but always for himself first. He sent me letters saying he was paying off his debts and was sick in bed, but paying off his debts was most important. And he wrote that when the war was over, I must bring Belle to Croghan's Hall.

MY BELLE WILL never go to Croghan's Hall or attend a ball again. I listen, my sore eyes closed, to the words of Chief Sayengueraghta address the funeral for Belle and her baby boy. The springtime creek is running high and singing Belle's name. Edward is in England, George Croghan is in bed in Pennsylvania with gout, my sons are warring with Butler's Rangers, and Belle's husband, Walter, is with them, not here. I sent Delaware Andrew with a message to take to Fort Niagara and he returned with condolence gifts from a British general. It is not known when the message to Walter and my sons will be relayed. The war is escalating and in my dreams, I hear canons being fired and see cornfields being destroyed, although we hear nothing here.

The war in Belle's womb finally ended after two days trying to birth a baby boy who had no desire to become a warrior on this earth. He took a look around for a few hours and left. I'm angry he took my Belle with him and I cannot help but think her body could not withstand the mixing of Indian and white blood. As soon as I think these thoughts, I hear Belle's voice, "My mother, you are being dishonest with your beliefs again. You birthed me with vigor." Everyone in our village is at this funeral, loving Belle to the end, her mothering of their children having made her endearing to them. They, too, grieve strongly. The chief recites this funeral prayer to her:

"Now we become reconciled as you start away. You were once a woman in the flower of life and the bloom is now withered away. You once held a sacred position as a mother of the nation. Looking after your family was a sacred duty and you were faithful."

Belle looked after her family and our village family while she waited for her own. Over the baby, the chief prays, "Now we become reconciled as you start away. You were a tender bud just born, feeling the caress of many, before you left us. Now the bloom has withered away. Let none of the things that transpired on earth while you were here for a few hours hinder you."

Belle and Baby Walter are put into the earth and we all try to keep our sobs silent so we can hear the words of the chief. "Now we release you for it is true that it is no longer possible for us to be together on the earth. We lay your bodies here and we say to you to persevere onward to the place where the Creator dwells in peace."

Chief Sayengueraghta turns to me and the villagers, and says, "I bid you all here in Catharine's Town to cheer your minds once again and rekindle the hearth fires in peace, put your houses in order and once again be in brightness, for darkness has covered you. The black clouds shall fall away and the bright blue sky will be visible once more. Be in peace and sunshine will come again."

Mourning will be for ten days and we will cease most of our work to do this. A funeral feast is being prepared and I wonder how it will be possible for the black clouds to roll away and how I'll ever be in peace. My daughter who has always been at my side has left me.

A few hours later, I collapse by Belle's and Baby Walter's grave, unable to release the birds from their cage to signify the setting free of their souls. Mary Sweetgrass and three women from our village carry me on bearskins attached to poles to Eagle Cliff Falls. They know I require the thundering voice of the falls and the protection of the eagle over my spirit. It is here I rinse the bloody clothing and cloths from the birth and deaths of Belle and Baby Walter. I do this as an offering of their blood to the sacred Spirit who reigns in this place.

I'M UNABLE TO greet the lush season with any hope. My boys and Walter visit in late spring. Roland and John possess the hardened faces of warriors, but they weep over Belle's and Baby Walter's grave. Walter's face is shadowed, his feelings lost within himself. He doesn't weep or say Belle's name, but sits silently at their graves for many hours. When these three warriors announce they have orders to go with Butler's Rangers and Chief Sayengueraghta to Wyoming, Pennsylvania, I tell them I will go with them to visit my sister, Esther. I feel again seeds of vengeance sprouting within me as I tell them my plans. Teedyuscung is dead and the Indians there have been driven away. In all of the Pennsylvania colony, there are only a few Indians left, like Esther and Molly. The Connecticut settlers have built homes, farms, and forts. And they have become more than the enemy of Pennsylvania and the Indians. They are now enemies of the British. I will go because I need to be near my family who still breathe on this earth. The Chief and Roland beg me not to go and to go instead to visit Sarah who is carrying Roland's baby. But I cannot be generous and care for a daughter who is not my own.

Chapter Thirty-Eight

IT IS NOW July 1778 and I listen to Andrew's plaintive voice tell of his journey to Wyoming, Pennsylvania. He accompanied Roland, John, Walter, and Chief Sayengueraghta to meet Lt. Colonel John Butler and the Rangers. Once again, I had been forbidden to travel because of a dream. This time, it was Belle who came to me and pleaded for me not to leave her. I couldn't leave my daughter, for although she had been released through prayers to live another life, her spirit is still in Eagle Cliff Falls.

"Your sister, Esther, was seen wearing a scarlet cloak and carrying a string of fresh scalps as she rode on a white horse. Her son is dead, killed by an American devil. She bashed out the brains of rebel Americans at Forty Fort. Colonel John Butler and a thousand loyalists with many Ho-De'-No-Sau-Nee allies led the attack, but your sister took out her own revenge."

"This news you bring to me, Andrew, is untrue. Brainwashing. Brainwashing it is, not brain bashing. The rebels are stirring up grievous trouble. They and their greedy forefathers over many years pushed my family and other Indians off the land. And now they fight their own brothers and we are caught between them. Why do you speak these lies, Andrew? Esther and my family are faithful to our covenant chain with the British, but neither of us would kill for them. My sons fight, but no, not Esther. And we in this village must not be caught in the cross-fire between the British and their rebellious brothers. There are too many Seneca, Cayuga, Onondaga, and Mohawk taking up the hatchet with the British, but no one in this town must do so. My sons are grown men who have chosen to be warriors for the British, but we will not be warriors here. Now tell me no more lies about my sister, but speak clear to me of her whereabouts."

"Cornplanter has taken her away, but he'll not say where," Andrew replies, tugging at the pouch that carries gun powder. He's tired and dreaded delivering this message to Catharine.

Andrew leaves Catharine, his shoulders heavy with the knowledge that not only has Queen Esther slaughtered white prisoners, there have been over three hundred people killed in this recent battle. And it was Catharine's step-son, Captain Pollard, who led the massacre, along with her sons, Roland and John. Andrew cannot tell Catharine this, for although this son of her second husband is a warrior, he is oftentimes not a wise one. Most of the dead are American patriots and Colonel Butler is heaping some blame on the Ho-De'-No-Sau-Nee. The patriots killed were the settlers from Connecticut. Andrew didn't fight, but secretly believed this massacre was an eye for an eye and just. He didn't explain all of this to Catharine, for she is fatigued from the loss of her daughter, Belle, and also from what is to come. He has heard she has been having dreams, but she won't share them with her village. The Seneca and Ho-De'-No-Sau-Nee have always lived with the threat of war, but for a long time before the British splintered into two groups, there had been relative peace. This peace Andrew wishes and prays for. Peace for himself, his family and his people, and for this mother, Catharine, who is their queen. She is loved as their Seneca queen, but she claims she belongs to no one, but the Great Spirit and the tumbling waters.

AFTER ANDREW LEAVES, I sit down behind the thundering voice of Eagle Cliff Falls and wonder what the birds, trees, and waterfalls think about scalping and murder? I close my eyes, shut off my mind's talking, and listen only to the song of the waters. And then I walk down the steep path from the waterfall and amble between the sturdy golden stalks of corn that are becoming as tall as my people. I stretch out my arms and delicately touch each green cloak that sheaths my sister corn who stand as strong sentinels in the golden field next to the stream. In my thankfulness to them, I beseech their guidance and strength. And then I let the veil fall from my mind and there's revelation that Esther, my flesh sister, has fiendishly become the embodiment of the heartache and wrath of the Ho-De'-No-Sau-Nee, the Shawnee, Delaware, and all Indians. *How have we endured the endless European conquest for our land and our allegiance that strips us of our dignity while dressing us in new clothing?* The reality about Esther comes to me as I caress the hair of my sister corn . . . this sister who cannot strike back but who will soon be slashed and burned by the colonial rebels. I've dreamed this and must act soon to save my people. But how? *I will stand as Catharine Montour, neither for the British or for the rebels, and offer Catharine's Town as a place of peace and rest.* As I walk into my village, I see an owl feather on the ground and mindlessly pick it up and stick it behind my ear.

Chapter Thirty-Nine

THERE ARE RUMORS now that not only Esther and my sons killed and slaughtered many rebels who hid in Forty Fort, but I myself was there. I did not strike them, except in my heart, for am I not a woman of peace? Did I condone Esther scalping and murdering patriots? Esther's son and my son-in-law, Walter, are both dead now from all this warring. After Walter died, Belle's spirit left Eagle Cliff Falls. I believe my sister, Esther, had become the rage and wrath of every Indian mother, past and present. I forgave her. And myself.

By the time my son, John, brought me the captive, Luke Swetland, who had survived the massacre at Wyoming, my wrath, like a snake, had slithered away and waited silently in the rocky place of my heart. A heart still tender with loss. John said Luke had been abused on the journey and had just been through a gauntlet in Chemung.

"They were gentle with him in Chemung, Mother, because of your influence, but he has been tormented and battered as we encountered other Tories and Indians along the way from Wyoming. He is to be taken to Candawhaes and given to an old squaw as a grandson."

"Place him with Joseph and Mary Sweetgrass for now, but when will you take him? I don't want any captives here. If the rebels come, they must know we are at peace here in this town. And tell me, is it true Esther has killed many patriots?"

John and I look at Luke Swetland who is a few feet away lying on the ground and looking as if he is praying to the moon.

"I didn't see Esther. I left with this captive and others, but rumors are flying she scalped many after the patriots surrendered. If she did this murderous deed, it wasn't ordered by Colonel Butler."

In the morning, I feel sorry for this captive. I tell him what is going to happen to him and he's pleased to hear me speak good English like himself. He begins to tell me about his family he left behind and I stop him and ask John to put him on horseback and take him to the Cayuga village. He'll not be too far from me, but far enough so I don't have to hear his pleas and be a part of his loss. Hopefully, he'll settle in living as an Indian because if he tries to escape, he'll meet some of the Tories and Indians who will be merciless. I cannot think any further about him, for he's not my responsibility. I say goodbye to John who will meet up with Roland and some of the Rangers who are in Cayuga before going on to Niagara. I seal my heart with strength so as not to let in fear. The Cayuga Indians have been my good neighbors, but they are involved in all of this warring, as are my sons.

The Indians in Catharine's Town are anxious over what is happening around us and fear they must be called to war, too. Which side shall they take? The agreement of neutrality in 1776 between the Ho-De'-No-Sau-Nee and General Schuyler has fallen apart. The Ho-De'-No-Sau-Nee are falling apart. I stand daily behind Eagle Cliff Falls and let my grief fall away because it's harvest time and there is thanksgiving to be had and much work to be done for our winter storage. And my horses need me as much as I need them. I become renewed by this season that has always brought significant change to my life. I resolve that if the rebels come to Catharine's Town, I will make peace with them and share our corn and sustenance. They will see we are not for one side or the other. I lay aside my concerns and feel new vigor for this bountiful harvest.

A few weeks later, a message comes from Candawhaes that Luke Swetland is ill and has asked for the French Queen at Catharine's Town. Joseph Sweetgrass and I go on horseback to visit him and after we'll go on to Niagara. I've received a message that Butler's Rangers are in reprieve there and I expect Edward will have returned from England. I miss him and wonder if we'll ever have a good life together again.

When I visit Luke, he weeps and fears he won't see his family again. This makes me weep, as well.

"My child, you will be well. They will treat you kindly because I'll tell them to do so."

"They are kind to me and bring me milk and buttermilk. My Indian sister goes to a special spring that she says has medicinal qualities and walks a long way for it. I'm grateful, but I miss my family . . ."

I give him sweet flag root to steep in water for drinking and tell him I'll check back on him after I return from Niagara.

He cries again and then sits up and earnestly looks into my face. "You call me child, but we must be the same age. How is it you speak so well and are different from the other squaws?"

"It's a long story, Luke Swetland, and one that requires many fires to sit by. If you can become an Indian and learn our ways, someday I will tell you."

ALONG OUR WAY to Niagara, I see Tories and Indians with many prisoners and there is only talk of war. When we arrive, I'm received into the camps with much kindness, for they know I'm a Montour who has always been loyal to the British. I'm very disappointed my husband is not here. My sons and I embrace and they plead with me to stay in Niagara where I will be safe, for they say the rebels will eventually attack our village. Their wives and families are here, too, and I will be with my family.

"Catharine's Town is not fighting. We are at peace and will not take sides."

"You've always been loyal to the British," John says, "and they will know this."

"My husband is not here and my people, our harvest, and my horses are waiting for my return. I cannot stay here."

I leave, weeping, not only for my sons who I bore to become warriors, but also for Edward who is not returning from England. He has lost his money, his courage, and me.

I RETURN TO Catharine's Town safely and we live through another glorious autumn and share some of our harvest with Fort Niagara and have plenty for our winter storage. And then a message arrives that Esther's Town has been destroyed by the rebels in retaliation for the Wyoming Massacre. Esther had a settlement near Athens, Pennsylvania at the junction of the Chemung and Susquehanna Rivers. She had a large house that was a long, low building, constructed of logs and a porch she liked to sit on. Her village had seventy houses. Everyone loved Esther in this valley, but after Wyoming and the rumors, their love grew murderous. Her home and town were set on fire by the rebels and she fled with Molly and eventually came to me. She warned me there were stories that I had been with her at Wyoming and the rebels would come here to destroy my town. I didn't ask her if she slaughtered rebels. I could see in her countenance she was changed. How many did she scalp? I don't know, nor care to know. Killing is all around us now. I sent her and Molly, whose husband is fighting with the Rangers, to Cayuga up the lake from me. I don't want them here and I don't want to be associated with this retaliation. I hope that my name will not be tied to the Wyoming Massacre.

The Senecas went on a rampage, feeling falsely accused for Wyoming and to avenge the burning of Esther's Town. Cherry Valley Massacre takes place in November and my sons take prisoners to Niagara. John told me he saved an old man from being scalped and then dragged him to Fort Niagara as a prisoner. I told him he was foolish and should have let the old man be killed. I become as dark as a moonless night and as icy as the waters of Eagle Cliff Falls that freeze in winter. The Great Spirit is silent and my heart doesn't thaw until spring with the return of the flow of thundering falls. And then there is a planting season right through to another robust autumn.

Chapter Forty

WE AREN'T VISITED by rebels, but the war continues and it's difficult to know who is winning. My sons visit once in the summer and when they aren't fighting with Butler's Rangers, they're with their families at Fort Niagara. They continue to ask me to move there, but my home is here. Esther and Molly live quietly in the hills north of here in Cayuga country. I see them when I visit, but don't invite them here. I want to be certain that our village doesn't have attachment to this war.

And then I hear word that my son, John, was injured at the Battle of Fort Freeland and is traveling to Fort Niagara with captives. I take Andrew, Joseph Sweetgrass, and a scout to go ahead of us to find out where they are. My John will make light of an injury and I want to bring him home to Eagle Cliff Falls and keep him safe.

The next day, we find John and a unit of Butler's Rangers resting at a Tory home on the Genesee. He has a shot gun wound to his lower back and is fortunate the ball didn't lodge deep. I'm able to remove it and apply my healing herbs to his wound. We are sitting outside a barn where his captive is being held and there are spirits of death and war all around us.

"Come home with me and stay until your wound is healed," I tell John.

"I will not leave Butler or Roland. You need to go to Fort Niagara with me to be safe and not ask me to go with you to Eagle Cliff Falls."

My head is sore from too much thinking and worry. I can't leave Eagle Cliff Falls and my people, but I also don't want to leave my son, John. What if John and Roland are killed in this war? I need to walk because I can't think clearly about what I'm supposed to do. I stand and turn to see that John's captive is behind us ready to lunge at John. I pull my tomahawk from my belt and raise it to strike him before he strikes John.

"You devil! Stand back or I'll scalp you right here."

John jumps up and the captive drops his knife and raises his hands in surrender. John leads him back into the barn and I walk quickly around the property, trying to keep up with the beats of my heart. I would have killed the man without any hesitation. Should I stay with John and Roland and fight with them as my sister Esther did? I'm not afraid. I clench my fists and release them, praying for Grandmother's wisdom. Finally, I realize that I'd be fighting only for my sons, not for one side or another. And this would be disrespectful to the manhood of my sons.

I leave the next day, knowing there is nothing I can do to protect my sons. They are warriors and like all Indian women, didn't I know I'd be birthing warriors if I had sons? But never did I believe they would be fighting white men in a war like this, one that will change us forever.

SOON ENOUGH, AUTUMN is here and there is more talk that George Washington is going to invade our Ho-De'-No-Sau-Nee country and destroy all settlements. I would like to believe it's another rumor, but feel this time we may be in danger. Andrew, Joseph Sweetgrass, and other chiefs say we must leave. I spend much time at Eagle Cliff Falls to comfort my fears and to ask the Great Spirit what we must do. The maple, hickory, and oak have especially revealed their splendor this year as I again watch the leaves float down the creek and away from their source. What will this autumn mean for me, for Catharine's Town? I sell a few horses to Indians who come to visit and talk of this war. These Indians don't wish to fight and instead want to fight the Cherokee. When our prophet, Deganawida, founded our great confederacy, he cast the weapons of war into a pit and planted over this pit the Tree of Peace. Nations and allies were to sit beneath the shade of this tree on this turtle island of earth. The British and now the Americans are promising they wish to sit down under the same Tree of Peace with us, but can they sit together? There will always be war, it seems. I would like to declare my independence.

Onondaga, the place of the Ho-De'-No-Sau-Nee Council Fire, was destroyed by the rebels. I have only heard this news now. They had declared neutrality, but who can be so when there is a stench of burning flesh and blood flowing into the earth. The Council Fire is temporarily being held in the Seneca village of Canadasaga, Chief Sayengueraghta, Old Smoke's home, Roland's father-in-law, on Seneca Lake. I'm surrounded by the fires of war, but try to maintain peace in our village and carry on with our life here. Roland sends a message asking if we can provide them with some of our corn again this season. Butler's Rangers are camped out there and are hungry. They are so close. We planted more corn this year and my sister corn is as tall as our tallest Indian and is breaking open with sustenance that will feed us. It's nearly time to pick and harvest this corn, along with other vegetables and fruit when Butler, his Rangers, and six hundred Indians arrive here in Catharine's Town, along with John and Roland.

"We're fourteen miles from Sullivan's army and we'll harass this enemy as they approach," Roland says, his countenance hardly recognizable after months of being on the war path, hungry, with his hands swollen and sore from killing and scalping.

What a sight to behold in my town. I cannot help but feel proud of my sons among the Rangers, the Seneca army being led by Old Smoke, and Blacksnake leading the Delawares. The great Cornplanter is here, Farmer's Brother, Little Beard, Handsome Lake, and Red Jacket. They stay only two nights before leaving to fight General Sullivan's army who is advancing toward us. Sullivan has a devouring army planning to destroy all villages and then going to Fort Niagara. It will be a new country, these rebels say, an America that will be a place of freedom and justice. My sons and most of my Indian brothers are now fighting against this new freedom. And so must I, but in my own way.

Chapter Forty-One

THIS TIME THE sound of guns and war whoops is not only in my dreams, but is as real as the quick beats of my heart. I hear thunderous sounds that have never been in my imagination or dreams. Retreating Indians from Chemung come to alert me to leave as quickly as possible for Fort Niagara. They send a message from my sons who are safe, but still fighting. They describe the terrifying devastation of cannon fire. So men have taken thunder from the Sky Mother to make war on earth. I have no time to think, but my heart does it for me. I have to make my own thunder to gather my people together so we can leave as quickly as possible.

Flutes, drums, rattles, and other festival things are stored in a log cabin for our ceremonies. I run quickly to retrieve a drum that makes the loudest noise. It's my favorite because the hide of an old horse I had favored is stretched over it. Filled with a little water, it sounds out the heartbeat of Mother Earth. I run through the town of fifty log homes, pounding this drum and proclaiming a retreat to Fort Niagara. People were already alerted to danger when the armies stopped here, but now they hear the sounds of battle and are eager to make haste to safety. I instruct the women to take one basket for each family and quickly go to the corn field and fill them with our sister corn. The men are by my side waiting for my direction and already painted with black paint for war.

"We'll ride horses to the lake and we'll fill every canoe and bateaux. We'll cross the Seneca and travel to the mouth of the Genesee. Stay together. Hurry, there's a command by Washington to destroy and devastate all settlements. Our crops will be burned and prisoners will be taken. Hurry!"

I don't have time to visit my beloved falls. I don't have time to take any garments or the bead work I've been creating and I don't have time to visit Belle and Baby Walter's grave. I know they are with Sky Mother and the Great Spirit and I whisper Belle's name to assist us as I glance at my field of horses with sorrow. Our cattle and swine. These rebels will feast on our abundance and destroy the rest. Shall I stay and confront these rebels? Will being a Montour help me now, granddaughter of Isabelle Couc, Madame Montour? No . . . of course not, these soldiers have already forgotten they are the same as their British brothers and if they remember the Montours, we will be remembered for our loyalty to the British. But then I remember Sattelihu's son, John, is fighting with the rebels. Maybe I can tell them . . .

Suddenly an old woman stands before me, her face a picture of serenity. Old Moccasin Spirit Water and she reminds me of Grandmother.

"You must leave, Catharine. Don't try to make peace with men who want war, not peace. I'm too old to journey and it's my time to go with the ancestors. I'm not afraid. The Great Spirit and angels are here."

"You must go with us. You can ride with me . . ."

"No, daughter, I will not go. Go quickly with your people. Take this crown I made for our thanksgiving harvest festival we'll not have this year. It will ensure you of your return to this home you love."

Old Moccasin places a crown made of birch twigs and leaves on my head, the colors vibrant and hopeful, in contrast to the dark fear I feel. Soon, we are fleeing Eagle Cliff Falls, my heart broken, and as we pass by the field of corn, I reach down to caress my sister corn.

MONTHS HAVE PASSED since our escape from Sullivan's army that brought terror and destruction. My sons fought valiantly against them and survived, as did Old Smoke. And now I'm huddled in a camp at Fort Niagara that stretches for miles. Winter is merciless and I derive no comfort from its pure stillness. It has turned against me and all of us. I don't ever recall such a winter as this in my life. We're hungry, cold, living in squalor, and the snow is as high as two men and it continues to fall. Deer and animals perish and I believe the Great Spirit is sickened by this turtle island and is washing away hate and bloodshed. There is too much heartbreak and confusion and I'm unable to return to Eagle Cliff Falls. It is no more and I'll never live there again, but die here with so many of my people who are dying.

General Sullivan destroyed our town and over forty others. Our livestock were driven away or killed. Our horses . . . my horses . . . Bushels of corn were slashed and burned. Cabbages, watermelons, carrots, squashes, parsnips . . . my mouth waters and I become sick just thinking of the abundance we once had. We call General Washington the Town Destroyer and none of us want to live in his new world of liberty for all. This kind of freedom will forever carry the stench of death. Our homes were burned and there is nothing left. They took bear skins, kettles, plates, knives, furniture, feather beds, and even the masks of our False Face Society. And how surprised they were that we lived so well in our homes, villages, and towns, not as the savages they call us.

Savages. I think of Benjamin Franklin's blundering comment in describing the Ho-De'-No-Sau-Nee as savages who are capable of living in unity, forgetting that I who sat before him was an Indian. What savagery the rebel Americans have caused. Roland described the rebels' brutality that Indians would never do. And as fierce as our warriors can be in scalping and killing the enemy, what they say about us is exaggerated.

"After Freeland," Roland said, "we went back to look for two of our Indians. They were dead and skinned from their waist down to make leggings for their major and lieutenant. Another time, we were reconnoitering and saw a crippled Indian and his mother locked in a house that was set on fire. We tried to save them, but it was too late. Shall I tell you more, Mother?"

I thought of the Old Moccasin woman I left behind and feared her end was as atrocious.

"Tell me if there was mercy, Roland. Did you return to Eagle Cliff Falls?"

"Mercy? What is it, Mother? After Sullivan ended his murderous campaign, we advanced to attack some of the rebel towns. We stopped at Eagle Cliff Falls and found one old woman. She wasn't harmed and was left with food and warmth."

"That is a small touch of mercy," I said, wondering if Old Moccasin died in peace with the coming of the winter.

There are thousands of us here. Onondagas, Senecas, and Cayugas. Most of the Oneidas still fight for the rebels, but a few came here to negotiate and surrender, but were locked up. An old Oneida chief I once knew died and I couldn't help him in his withering state in prison, for I'm in my own captivity with much suffering in my body and spirit. And what do the British generals say to our people after so many have given their lives to fight for their cause?

"Stay in the settlements and go into the wilderness to hunt and gather, for we do not have the resources to feed five thousand Indians," one general announced to all of us gathered at the Fort in early November.

Many of my friends from Eagle Cliff Falls die the slow death of starvation and our British brothers can do nothing. They do not have evil intentions, only human weakness. Our warriors, including my sons, are valuable to them if they continue to fight. And fight our warriors do, for not all the villages were destroyed and they left us as birds on the wing, as one of them was heard to say. Now I seek to stay alive for my sons and to return to Eagle Cliff Falls, but we are told to not consider returning and to make do on reservations they preserve for us in Canada.

My sons continue to battle and are reckless as well as courageous, loyal to Butler's Rangers. Not long ago, they took captive a family from Pennsylvania. The Gilberts are a large, peaceful, and respected family who owned a grist mill. None, but one, died of natural causes on the journey to Fort Niagara and Montreal. I wanted to question my sons why they would take prisoner a quiet family who were not for one side or another. A family like me. I'm relieved my sons were not brutal and only tested the merit of the captives. One daughter was given to my daughter-in-law who had lost her baby in childbirth. I'm glad my sons are gone most of the time from this wretched Fort Niagara and when they raid a farm, they take food to eat. They bring enough to keep me alive and I share it with

Joseph, Mary, and Andrew who stay with me in a poorly built cabin where we sleep huddled together to stay warm at night.

Raids continue in response to Washington's plan to have every one of our villages pillaged and laid waste. Sir John Johnson, Handsome Lake, Brant, Red Jacket, and my sons with Butler's Rangers attack the Schoharie Valley and wipe out all white settlements in the Mohawk Valley. They're hungry for justice and food. By the time this war ends, miles and miles of colonial territory is ruined and there is deprivation, hopelessness, hundreds of widows and thousands of orphaned children.

The Delawares I had known all my life, in their confusion we all felt, had agreed to take up the hatchet against the Seneca with General Brodhead, but then quickly changed their minds and turned to the British. General Brodhead took out revenge with his squaw campaign and destroyed Delaware towns, burning, killing cattle, murdering their prisoners, and taking eighty thousand pounds of plunder. My brothers, the Delaware, have suffered more than any of us.

I receive letters from Edward Pollard begging me to come to England. Although he has lost all of his money, he writes that he will borrow money to bring me to him. I miss him, but feel a gulf between us that is greater than the sea that separates us. He has not lived through this war. He hasn't seen Turtle Island turned inside out and humans skinned like the animals he hunted. I write to him expressing my love, but tell him I won't ever leave my sons.

And then my son, Roland, is killed and the voice of the Great Spirit and my grandmother that had grown dim, is drowned out by my sorrow and anger. He dies in September when the leaves are falling and more change comes to my life. Will I ever love this season of autumn again?

"WAKE, MOTHER! IT'S John!"

It's late in the day and I haven't risen from my bed to find food and water. I'm used to the stench of myself, the dirt crusted between my toes and fingers. I feel no more hunger, but know I must eat. I want to sleep and not wake. Joseph and Mary Sweetgrass are thin and dying and are probably out looking for food. Andrew left to live on a reservation somewhere near here. I'm ignored by a British general when I ask where my son's body is and where John is. And now I hear John's voice, but is it in my dream? My clothing has worn thin and my body is unrecognizable when I look at the lower half of myself. Mary Sweetgrass tries to wash and comb my hair the best she can, but she can hardly take care of herself. I begin to drift to sleep again when I hear John's voice.

"The war is over and we must leave. The Americans have won. There are rumors the British are feeding the Indians poisoned flour. They have abandoned us and we're now the conquered British allies. They don't care for us because they cannot save themselves."

I look into John's face full of scars and small ruts. He hardly looks like himself, but is still dignified and handsome. I note that his stutter has left him.

"Hold me, my son, hold me," I cry, as he lifts me to my feet.

John cradles me in his arms and I hear one deep sob come from him and then it stops. I am crying like a river, long and loud. John, my son, is all I have.

"Come live with my wife and me on the Genesee. We'll live on the Big Tree Reservation. Cornplanter and Red Jacket will also live in this new America, but many of our brothers will stay in Canada."

I unfold myself from John's strong arms and step back to look at him.

"Do you still have your father's flute he made for me, John?"

"Yes, Mother, I've kept it safe through every battle and I've brought it back to you."

"Then I will take it with me to Eagle Cliff Falls.

Chapter Forty-Two

MY WISE OWL John shed his warrior husk and became a gentle medicine man who helped mold me back into the strong woman I had once been. He said he was poisoned by British flour. Was this a slap in the face for his loyalty? A slap that altered his face, for he had an ulceration of his upper lip that was eaten away that left his teeth and jaw exposed. Was this flour ruined when it was transported across the sea or did the British deliberately poison us? Our people are bitter and believe this is true. I don't know. John's eyes and the rest of him make his disfigurement unnoticeable to me and to all who love him.

For a time, I live in Big Tree Village with John and his family. It's a village the Americans forgot to include on their maps. Big Tree is a reservation near the Genesee River which means pleasant banks in our language. Big Tree Village is a small patch for John and other Indians, but it's big in the spirit of our people. There are waterfall cliffs nearby that have the rugged, dignified faces of our people naturally carved in the rocks. You can see them only if you look with your spirit. You will see us in all the rocks of the gorges in this land! We cannot be banished! We'll always be here and reveal ourselves through the landscape where our blood was shed, mixing in with the blood of those who conquered us. It is in the landscape where we will triumph. We were here before those who sought freedom to live with our faces in the rocks, our spirits in the waters, and the entwining love of the Three Sisters.

Most of the time, I'm glad I survived and still live in the bountiful land of the Great Spirit. But there are times I wish I'd gone to be with the ancestors and my children. Our traditional homelands in New York are being settled by the patriots who were soldiers in the war between brothers. Only one small Indian village remains in Pennsylvania, owned by Cornplanter who has stood up for the rights we always had. We are dispossessed and Turtle Island is broken up into smaller and smaller pieces where the Indian lives in the corners. Will we fall off and be no more? We sell and give up our land to live where they tell us to live, but some of us still negotiate and just as Grandmother imagined for me, I'm a frequent visitor to Philadelphia with Ho-De'-No-Sau-Nee chiefs to represent my people. I'm as formidable as the rock faces of my people, but also gentle as the autumn leaves that float away from the mother trees. I abandon myself to change and will eventually become one with the earth, this Turtle Island.

BUT BEFORE I shed this life, I float away on the Genesee River to Lake Seneca and onto the creek near Eagle Cliff Falls. I arrive in autumn and renew my love for this season and the tumbling waters. The rains and winters have washed away some of the marks of the desolation in 1779. There are remains of the charred long house, cabins, and cook fires . . . bones . . . whose? Old Moccasin? I conduct a ritual and thank her for her wisdom and life and tell her I'm now the Old Moccasin. I bury them next to Belle, Walter, and my grandchild.

Edward Pollard no longer asks me to go to England and so we love one another in our dreams. George Croghan is bed ridden and his daughter, Suzannah, died in childbirth. Suzannah and Belle are together in the heavens and maybe there is a ball they attend that is grander than any ball on earth. Esther and Molly live quietly a few miles from me by Lake Cayuga and Esther likes her rum too much. Both talk about moving to a reservation because settlers are gradually moving to Cayuga and they know more will come. The soldiers from Sullivan's army remember our sister corn taller than men and how lush and fertile our land was. Their payment for destroying our lives is our land. I remember a time long ago when we lived peaceably with the Europeans in Pennsylvania, but now this new country wishes us to disappear. They remember us as savages and see themselves as victorious white settlers. The Treaty of Fort Stanwix in 1784 officially establishes peace with us, the Ho-De'-Ne-No-Sau-Nee, the Six Nations, but we are dissatisfied with the terms and so there are a few trips to Philadelphia with Cornplanter, Red Jacket, and other chiefs. Grandmother's spirit always accompanies me on these trips. Red Jacket and I became friends when we met in Eagle Cliff Falls when John and Roland's army stopped before confronting Sullivan's army. Red Jacket despised being a warrior and tried to hide it, but all is forgiven because of his eloquent oratory skills. I'm pleased he has developed these skills practicing at She-O-Qua-Ga Falls. He was at the Treaty of Fort Stanwix and made a great speech in opposition to the terms. And I was proud of him when he spoke strongly to the missionaries who called him a pagan.

"The Great Spirit will not punish for what we do not know. These black coats talk to the Great Spirit and ask for light that we may see as they do, when they are blind themselves, and quarrel about the light that guides them. These things we do not understand."

THE LARGE BALD eagle sits atop the tallest tree at the waterfall when I am there. Other birds flit here and there, but this eagle is still and quiet, watching me. Does she see her imprint in the rocks? She has become my protector and friend. Sometimes she follows me back to my cabin where I live alone, content with occasional visits from John and his family, as well as Esther and Molly. My sisters and some of the Cayuga and Chemung Indians who still linger in the area helped me build this new home and establish my gardens. They also brought the bones of those who were slain in Newtown and those who died near here. We created a burial ground surrounding the graves of Belle, Walter, and my grandchild. I harvest my food, fish, and live simply, as I've always wanted to do. I am home now and will be pleased to lay my bones down here when I die.

The Great Spirit is in the wings of my eagle, whom I name, Spirit Wings. She has a large wing span and is always alone when she visits me. Spirit Wings flies higher than any other bird and brings me messages from the heavens that lodge into my heart as she flaps her enormous wings over my cabin. One day she brings me a gift and drops a rainbow trout in front of my door. I ponder its beautiful colors that shine on its skin in the sun and give thanks and cook it. That night, I dream again the dream of long ago just before Grandmother died. I remember having no understanding of this dream where strange people rose from the water and sat on the rocks as I swam among them at the waterfall. In the dream, I'm invisible to these people of many colors. I wake in a sweat, although it's cool in my cabin. I remember Grandmother telling me I didn't need to understand this dream. "The sun gives light at the beginning of the day's journey, but doesn't instruct us how to live the day. The light is enough to see where to walk and you, Catharine, will walk where the light is the strongest. "

In late summer, the first white settlers arrive at Eagle Cliff Falls and although my first intention is to shoot them right off their horses and wagons, I don't. I remember more of what Grandmother said about this place and know now that Spirit Wings warned me of this danger. "Your spirit will always dwell here, Catharine. Different colors will come to this place and will have difficulty seeing or hearing the ways of the ancient ones."

What color is this that comes, Spirit Wings? I ask aloud to the sky for Spirit Wings is nowhere in sight. Did she leave me alone with these pale faced men? Thomas, William, and John McClure come from the Wyoming Valley to Eagle Cliff Falls. Wyoming Valley. Was it not enough for them to scatter the Indians away from Wyoming Valley and Pennsylvania, but now they must have Eagle Cliff Falls, too? Grandmother's words return to me once again and for the last time. "I want you to bring understanding between people who don't know the language of the Great Spirit." I still have Grandmother's scarlet blanket she placed over me before she died. When I meet these men, their wives, and other families, as well as the postmaster who comes to visit and drink tea with me, I always place it over my shoulders. Mostly, I am invisible to these settlers, but soon they begin to call me Queen Catharine and accept that Eagle Cliff Falls will always be my home.

Chapter Forty-Three

I WALK THROUGH the Philadelphia streets with Cornplanter on one side and Red Jacket on the other. Behind us, twenty-five dignified chiefs and their families follow. It is August 1787 and the large, brick buildings are saturated with the heat of the sun that reflect back into the streets. Our blankets are folded in our leather satchels and all of us envision the cool streams, waterfalls, and lakes we are eager to return to. It is for these sacred places we have come here again to plead for. As I look up at the State House and the giant clock that men have made to replace the movement of the sun and moon, my heart beats out of time for a few moments. Just as these white men have placed the days and nights within a large wooden box to keep order to their lives, we are being placed on reservations to keep us in order. This will be my last visit to Philadelphia. I have listened to the call of the Great Spirit and heeded Grandmother's words. We have planted the words and ways of our people into the rich tapestry of these men's minds who are full of ideas and hopes for their new country.

Women buried in layers of petticoats and skirts stop to stare and flutter their handkerchiefs at us. I don't want to be invited to their teas or balls, although each time we visit this city, we mingle among all of them. I'm tired from this journey and wonder how long we will stay, for already I miss Eagle Cliff Falls and my cabin and gardens. I only want to live a simple life. I have only ever wanted to live a simple life.

I look up to see that between the flounces of skirts, an old man with snow covered hair emerges, his cheeks wrinkled puffs of pink and his eyes shining through small spectacles. He walks toward me with a slight limp, wiping his brow with a handkerchief, and when he is near, we all stop walking.

Benjamin Franklin bows before me and I almost wish to extend my hand for him to kiss, but never have I done this odd gesture I've seen many colonial women do. He shakes hands with Cornplanter and Red Jacket and turns to me with earnestness.

"Catharine Montour! I'm pleased you are here. I've heard of your visits, but have always missed them and now you are here at a very auspicious time. We have been months long in a sweltering convention trying to steer ourselves into one nation."

Mr. Franklin looks away from me and stands somberly before the chiefs behind me.

"There are gifts and refreshment for all of you. Please continue on into the State House and you will be well accommodated."

He turns to me again and says awkwardly, "Catharine Montour, I'm on a short break from these grueling meetings. Might you accept an old gentleman's offer to go to a coffee house?"

I smile. I have only tried coffee once and spit it out. Edward gave me some and it had tasted like the ashes of a fire.

"I will go with you, Mr. Franklin."

WE SIT IN the London Coffee House on Front and Market Streets in a building with a large window facing the street.

Mr. Franklin tells me it is a very popular coffee house, but one he will not frequent on market days. "Out this very window on market days, my dear, one not only sees barrels of rum being sold to the Indians, but enslaved Africans being auctioned and sold. It is something I detest . . . slavery. But one step at a time . . . one foot in front of the other, I say."

He removes his spectacles and dabs at his eyes with his handkerchief. I don't know if he is crying or he has the eyes of the old ones that often run. I believe it is because the old ones have lived so long with grief that it overflows without consent. Our bodies know our stories and try to care for them for us. But has Benjamin Franklin known grief?

"I'm sorry, my dear . . . I am old and seem to have no control over these eyes . . . or the rest of my body, for that matter."

He laughs and then looks into my face with gravity. I see then he has known sorrow.

"Chief Canassatego said that many arrows cannot be broken as easily as one and right now we're trying to bundle the many arrows of our thirteen colonies together into our new country."

"Your new country . . ."

"Our new country, Catharine. You and your people are also of this new country."

"I liked the old country, Mr. Franklin, and have had no say in this new country. What Indian has? What woman has? What African has that you are in sympathy with?"

Mr. Franklin gulps his coffee and wipes the corners of his mouth. "A few years ago, I invited the chiefs here in Philadelphia to tell them that the advice of Chief Canassatego over thirty years ago had been taken. The Tree of Peace and your constitution we have studied. Why, everyone here at the convention has had personal experience with Indians. How could they not, or you, influence us? Our formidable John Adams has written about different types of government and this includes philosophers from Europe, the Iroquois Confederacy, and other native governments. The visits you and your people have made here to Philadelphia have been important, not only in making certain there is land for you to always live on, but for much more."

Benjamin Franklin takes my hands that are folded loosely around the coffee cup I haven't put to my mouth and holds them in his old knotty ones.

"Catharine, my meeting with you long ago gave me new eyes to see your people and later, I made the resolve to work to abolish slavery. And now in Philadelphia you are here when wisdom from many will be formed into a new government for all people. You, my dear, as well as your people, have become an integral part of this."

I gently pull my hands away from his and take a sip of the coffee that is cold, but I like it this time. I take another sip and think maybe there will be other things I'll try before I lay down to sleep with the ancestors in Eagle Cliff Falls.

LATER, I HEAR about the signing of this new constitution and learn that Benjamin Franklin was in such poor health, he needed help with his pen, and as he signed, tears streamed from his eyes. He and the signers of the constitution took a light from our Ho-De'-No-Sau-Nee fire and carried it over to light their own fire to make their nation. The prophet, Deganawida's name means two rivers flowing together. I pray to the Great Spirit that our two rivers can flow in peace and meet up with other waters to nurture this great Turtle Island.

NEW YORK

SHE-QUA-GA
"TUMBLING WATERS"
A SKETCH NOW IN THE LOUVRE
MADE ABOUT 1820 BY
LOUIS PHILIPPE
LATER KING OF FRANCE

STATE EDUCATION
DEPARTMENT 1932

Afterword

Catharine, Queen of the Tumbling Waters, is inspired by real history, a real woman of history, but is also a work of imagination. The following is documentation which provided some of the fabric for weaving a tapestry of Catharine's story upon.

Madame Montour
(Isabelle Couc, Catharine Montour's grandmother)

Madame Montour and the Fur Trade (Simone Vincens)—page 41-44— Witham Marshe, a secretary for the Lancaster Conference and Treaty of 1744 writes in his journal about meeting Madame Montour. He describes her as a famous woman who claims her father had been governor of French Canada until she was taken captive by the Iroquois. Thereafter, she married a great chief of the Iroquois nation and had several children. Marshe writes she had been a beautiful woman, genteel, and of polite address, and had visited Philadelphia for renewal of friendship treaties with the Iroquois and English. He journals that Madame Montour is esteemed by the whites of quality and always treated by them with the greatest politeness. Simone Vincens writes that Marsh was captivated by Madame Montour who was at ease being in a bark hut or at a stylish Philadelphia home. She states he reported everything she told him, but without questioning her complexity. Vincens writes, "After further study, it turns out that Madame Montour was not the daughter of a governor, that her name was not Montour, that she had several husbands before she married the great Iroquois chief, and that she was seventeen years older than she claimed. And adventurer then? Certainly, and why not?"

Madame Montour and the Fur Trade (Simone Vincens)—page 47-27— Vincens describes the birth of Isabelle Couc (Madame Montour) in 1667 in a small Jesuit community near Trois-Riviere on the St. Lawrence. Her mother, Marie Metiouamegoukoue, was Algonquian and her father, Pierre Couc, was French. Pierre Couc came from France in 1651 when Trois-Riviere was a large settlement of Jesuits, Algonquians, and Hurons that contained a large fort. Ongoing battles with the Iroquois over fur trading led to two other forts in Quebec and Montreal. Pierre Couc became a farmer and a soldier and fought against the Iroquois. He married at a time when government policy encouraged assimilation with Native American women. The French attempted to make the young native women into good Catholic women, but mostly it backfired. The Algonquian women were repulsed by French men and their body hair and they had relative freedom before marriage. But by the time the Iroquois attacked Trois-Riviere and the French were holed up in a fort with the natives, Pierre Couc and Marie fell in love. A short-lived peace treaty was signed between the Iroquois and the French. Vincens writes, "This particular birth (of Isabelle Couc/Madame Montour) at this particular place is an irony of destiny: in the same year that the Five Nations (Iroquois) renounced their domination of the St. Lawrence, the woman who would later become known as the queen of the Iroquois appeared on the banks of the same river."

Pierre Couc had a home, large family, and climbed the rungs of the social ladder as Trois-Riviere doubled in size. His first-born, Louis, was intelligent and also would do well. His daughters were much sought after in marriage. A tragic rape and murder of one daughter went unpunished and shook the family's foundation. Isabelle Couc (Madame Montour) was twelve and her mother must have stated that Algonquians never heard of rape. Vincens writes, "The comparison between the two cultures did not favor the French. Elizabeth (Isabelle) who later became Madame Montour, would never forget it."

And then in 1684, Pierre Couc's son Louis, has a son who was baptized and given the name Jacques Montour. It is the first time the surname Montour appears on an official document regarding the Couc family. Louis also chooses that name for himself, as well. Isabelle Couc marries Joachim Germano and thereafter, will come to have three more marriages and two lovers, her fourth marriage to the Oneida Chief, Carondowana. From this chief, she will have her daughter, Margaret, and son, Andrew. Margaret would marry and birth Catharine Montour who would become Queen Catharine Montour.

Louis Montour (Madame Montour's brother) becomes a coureur de bois, an independent trader, who exchanges various French goods for furs from the Indians. As the Iroquois attacks continue and the English and French fight over fur trading and eventually land, the fur traders continue traveling to the Western Great Lakes and trading. Eventually, the supply of beaver pelts greatly exceeds the demand and the government forbids licenses to trade, although there were many contradictions and higher ups in government were still allowed to trade. Louis continues to trade, eventually with the Iroquois and English, working outside French law. Many Indian nations leave the Detroit to go to Iroquoia and the New York colony and Louis helps them. And his sister, Isabelle, becomes his interpreter. According to Vincens, Louis had no other way of earning a living and had spent his life trading and living like an Indian. The governor of Nouvelle-France, Vaudreuil attacks New England and the English plan a defensive. The French ask the Iroquois to be on their side, but all except the Seneca, side with the English. Louis Montour, caught in the crossfire as a trader, is murdered by the French army soldier and interpreter, Joncaire. Vincens writes, "In Louis's absence, it was his sister Isabelle who, with aching heart, brought the party of Mississauga immigrants to Albany…In continuing the work of her brother, Isabelle brought purpose to her desultory life. At forty-two years of age, she found herself in a strange land. She had no family near her other than Louis's widow…Having burned her bridges to Nouvelle-France, she probably had little choice other than to become Iroquois."

Catharine Montour, Children
—John, Roland, and Belle Montour; Captain Pollard

John Dochstader's Third Wife (Charles Julian/Genealogy.com)—"The branch of the Montour family that John Dochstader most probably married into is that of Roland and John Montour who served in Butler's Rangers and the Indian Department. Cruikshanks "Butler's Rangers" contains numerous references to these brothers. A critical piece of information for the placement of this branch comes from a 1779 letter from Francis Goring to Edward Pollard which gives Roland, John and Belle Montour as children of Edward Pollard. Pollard was head trader at Fort Niagara following the end of the French and Indian Wars and married Telenemut's widow Catharine Montour, from whom his children inherited their surname. Pollard apparently also fathered Captain Pollard, head chief of the Seneca at Buffalo Creek, by another Seneca woman, but had returned to London by 1780. In the letter of 1779 given below, Goring, who was at this time employed as Pollard's clerk, mentions that the widower of Pollard's daughter Belle Montour has been killed on the Ohio River, and oddly enough the person who has reported this incident to him is none other than a Lt. Docksteder."

Portions of a letter from Francis Goring to Edward Pollard on Newton battle Niagara, Sept. 12th, 1779

Dear Sir,

Yesterday came in Captain Powell from Canawagoris, where he left Col. Butler two days before in perfect health and spirits. He informs me their first attack with the Rebels was about fifteen miles from Shimango, where Col. Butler made a breast-work, which the Rebels observed, and with two six and four three pounders and small mortars, in half an hour, obliged Col. Butler to retreat. On the same day, a few miles from this, Col. Butler attempted again to stop them, but in vain. In this attack, the Colonel lost four rangers killed, two taken prisoners and seven wounded;—three Senecas and one Cyugo (Cayuga) killed. Your son John Montour, (not Roland) was shot in the back, and the ball lodges in him; however, he is likely to do well, for in a few days after, he, with twenty Indians, stopped the pass of the advanced guard of the Rebels, which was upwards of one thousand, and obliged them to retreat. In this action Col. Butler and all his people was surrounded, and was very near being taken prisoners. The Indians here all run away, being struck with a panic, and has not been able to gather till very lately . . . The Indians are determined, to a man, to dye with Col. Butler . . . Docksteder writes from the Ohio that a party of Rebels has destroyed several Indian villages, with all the corn. He also informs me that a party of Indians going on a scout in three canoes, was fired on by a scout of Rebels from the shore, which killed three, among which was a son of yours, the eldest and handsomest of the white boys, that was formerly married to your daughter, Belle Montour.

Published source: "The History of Buffalo", p. 346 (incomplete citation)
Kindly submitted [to http://www.nyhistory.net/~drums/goring_to_pollard_newtown_091279.htm
http://www.nyhistory.net/~drums/goring_to_pollard_newtown_091279.htm] by Maggie Parnall
The background of the Montour brothers is given as follows:

"The names of these Indians, with their respective tribes, are as follows: Rowland Monteur, 1ˢᵗ captain; John Monteur, second in command, who was also styled captain. These two were Mohawks, descended of a French woman.

The Gilbert family, who were taken prisoner by Montour's company, were ultimately led back to Fort Niagara to run the gauntlet and then be adopted by families (including Roland Montour's) who had lost family members. Mention is made of Roland's Cayuga wife, the daughter of a Seneca Chief Siangorochti, alias Grahta or Old Smoke . . .

Catharine Montour

A History of Wilkes-Barre, Luzerne County, Pennsylvania Volume I (Oscar Jewell Harvey, A.M)—page 205-207. One requires a magnifying glass to decipher the writing. Madame Montour is mistakenly referred to as Catharine. The Moravian Count Zinzendorf calls Ostonwakin, a French town . . ." a promiscuous population of French Indians, who are yet under the protection of the English . . . In 1760, Margaret, Catharine, other family members living at "Margaret Town"—New York (see PA Colonial Records VIII 499). This, no doubt is the village, after the death of Margaret, was known as Catharine Town."
Page 207—"Catharine Montour, daughter of 'French Margaret,' became the wife of Thomas Hutson, or Hudson, called by the Indians 'Telenemut.' He was

a Seneca and his brother John was head-chief of Caneada a Seneca village on the Genesee River in what is now Alleghany New York. Thomas Hudson died early-certainly prior to 1760. Some years later . . . the widow Catharine was married to an Englishman who was then or had been an Indian trader with headquarters at Niagara and had been married to a Seneca squaw who having born him several children, died."

"For many years Catharine was known as 'Queen Catharine' and during the Indian depredations in 1755-56 several white prisoners taken by the Indians were sold to her at her home in New York. She was then living in Canisteo previously mentioned but sometime before its destruction by her brother (sic), Andrew she removed to a village on a beautiful flat near the present town of Havana, New York about three miles from the southern extremity of Seneca Lake. The Indian name of this village was Shequaga (sic) but it soon became known as Catharine's Town . . . in 1779 when it was destroyed by General Sullivan's army (see Chapter VVVIII) it was a village of fifty log houses, 'in general very good and the country near it very excellent. Having been driven from this locality, Catharine Montour and her family and followers removed to the vicinity of Fort Niagara, where they continued to live for some years. Subsequently to 1788—probably in 1790 or 92 'Queen Catharine' visited Philadelphia with a delegation of Indian chiefs from New York State. She is said to be a woman of considerable ability and intelligence and some refinement."

A History of Wilkes-Barre, Luzerne County, Pennsylvania Volume I (Oscar Jewell Harvey, A.M)—page 332-335—" . . . McMullen was kept . . . in captivity until the following Spring, when he was sold to French Margaret's daughter at Canisteo, 40 miles northwest from Tioga. From there, he escaped in Sept. 1757 . . . Thomas Moffitt, 26 taken prisoner by 9 Indians near Poughkeepsie, NY and brought to Wyoming . . . One party removed to the Allegheny River region, and the other, including Moffitt was sold to Queen Catharine. In the following September he escaped in company with Daniel McMullen."

*A History of Wilkes-Barre, Luzerne County, Pennsylvania Volume I (Oscar Jewell Harvey, A.M)—page 341—*Teedyuscung, after his homeward journey from Fort Niagara . . . stopped at Canisteo, where according to the testimony of Thomas Moffitt, the King boasted, in a drunken frolic at the house of Queen Catharine that the Indians could make peace, and the Indians could also break peace when made. Moffitt also stated that when Teedyuscung left Catharine's house, he sold an English female prisoner for a horse . . ."

Luke Swetland's Captivity and Rescue from the Indians (An early settler of the Wyoming Valley and a soldier of the American Revolution) (Edward Merrifield)— Luke Swetland was one of the Connecticut settlers in 1769, the very same settlers Chief Teedyuscung and Queen Catharine (my conjecture), amongst other tribes, despised for settling on their land. Swetland had a narrative of his captivity printed at Hartford in 1778. It is amazing to me that he meets Catharine after he's been taken captive and she is very kind and empathetic to him.

Page 20—"We went on and came to French Catharine's, a squaw so-called. This place was Catharine's town, and the residence of the famous Catharine Montour . . . She spoke good English and told what they were going to do with me. Next day she sent two Indians to carry me on horseback toward Appletown, to a place named Candawhaes . . . Page 23-24—"About the 10th of September, I was taken sick with a fever and ague . . . During this time of my sickness, French Catharine came to see me. She spoke in English, and said, 'How do you do, my child.' I could not forbear weeping, it was so agreeable to hear English words again. She wept and so did the old grandmother and sister. French Catharine told them to be kind to me. She went to Niagara, and on her return gave me sweet flag root to steep in water for drinking, and it helped me."

Battle of Wyoming and Massacre, Queen Esther, French Margaret, and Catharine

Indians in Pennsylvania (Paul A. W. Wallace)—page 165—"It is doubtful if Queen Esther was present at the massacre although tradition identifies her as the Indian woman who killed the prisoners at what is now known as 'Queen Esther's Rock.' The tradition is out of key with her known character. She treated the Strope family, who had been her prisoners since May of that year, with great kindness. The 'Narrative' of Mrs. Whitaker (Jane Strope) makes that clear. It is possible that at the time of the massacre Queen Esther may have been confused with Catharine Montour (wife of a Seneca chief), who, it is commonly thought, was her sister. Catharine's name, instead of Esther's, appears in several early accounts of the massacre as that of the 'priestess' who presided at it. On the other hand, we know that Queen Esther, whatever her normal character, may have been inflamed to avenge the death of her son, who had been killed by American scouts the day before the battle."

Indians in Pennsylvania (Paul A. W. Wallace)—page 174-175—"FRENCH MARGARET . . . When the upper Susquehanna was vacated by the Indians in 1755, Margaret moved to the Chemung River, near present Elmira, New York, and her family are last mentioned there in 1763. Margaret had two daughters, Mary (Molly) and Catharine (Kate) and a son, Nicholas Quebec. Another Indian woman, Queen Esther, has also been identified as a daughter, but on rather weak evidence."

George Washington, George Croghan, and Andrew Montour

The Indian Wars of Pennsylvania (C. Hale Snipe)—page 168-171—" . . . it will be well to devote a few paragraphs to three noted characters whom we have met a number of times thus far in this history and who assisted Washington in his campaign of 1754—George Croghan, Andrew Montour, and Christopher Gist. Croghan was born in Ireland and educated in Dublin. He came to America somewhere between the years 1740-1744. He engaged in the Indian trade and appears to have been first licensed as an Indian trader in Pennsylvania, in 1744 . . . he was made a counsellor of the Six Nations at Onondaga . . . in March 1749, he was appointed by the Governor and Council of Pennsylvania one of the justices of the peace . . . he had a trading house at Logstown, which was made the headquarters of Weiser upon his visit to the Indians of that place . . . He had also branch trading establishments at the principal Indian towns in the valleys of the Ohio and Allegheny . . . Croghan's abilities and influence among the Indians soon attracted the attention of Conrad Weiser, who, in 1747, recommended him to the Pennsylvania Authorities, and, in this way, he entered the service of the Province . . . His part in Washington's campaign consisted in furnishing the Virginia forces with flour and ammunition . . . Much of the powder and lead used by Washington at Fort Necessity was furnished by Croghan and Captain William Trent . . . However, Croghan was so much delayed in furnishing flour that, as we have seen, Washington's forces suffered greatly from hunger in the later days of the campaign . . . The outbreak of the French and Indian War ruined Croghan's prosperous trading business. He was brought to the verge of bankruptcy and threatened with imprisonment for debt. Then the Pennsylvania Assembly passed an act giving him immunity from arrest for ten years, in order that the Province might have the benefit of his services and influence among the Indians . . . Early in 1756, Croghan resigned from the Pennsylvania service and went to New York, where his distant relative, Sir William Johnson, chose him deputy Indian agent . . . he had purchased a tract on the Allegheny, about four miles above the mouth of the Monongahela, where he entertained George Washington in 1770. When the Revolutionary War came on, it seems he embarked in the patriotic cause, and later was an object of suspicion, and then Pennsylvania proclaimed him a public enemy . . . and died at Passayunk on August 31, 1782 . . . Croghan's Mohawk daughter became the third wife of the celebrated Mohawk Chief, Joseph Brant."

People of the American Frontier (Walter S. Dunn, Jr.)—page 179—Dunn writes, "Prostitution was not common on the frontier. The practice in the 18th-century required a large market of unmarried males and was usually confined to cities and seaports. Venereal disease was not easily cured. George Croghan, the Indian agent, had such a serious case that at one point he was forced to wear a kilt to avoid discomfort. A few Indian women were used as prostitutes by the white traders and soldiers.

The Indian Wars of Pennsylvania (C. Hale Snipe)—page 168-171 "Andrew Montour, the 'Half Indian,' whose Indian name was Sattelihu, was the eldest and most noted of the children of Madam Montour. He is one of the most picturesque Indian characters in the early history of Pennsylvania, and accompanied George Croghan on many of his missions to the Indians of the Ohio and Allegheny valleys. Governor Dinwiddie gave him a captain's commission . . . Montour and his forces assisted Washington in the battle of Fort Necessity . . . In the spring of 1755, Montour and Croghan, with about fifty Indian braves, joined Braddock's army at Cumberland . . . Throughout the French and Indian War, he took part as interpreter in many Indian councils with the Pennsylvania and New York authorities, and was on a number of important missions . . . A town, a creek, an island, a county, a mountain range—all in Pennsylvania—are named for him and his mother."

A History of Wilkes-Barre, Luzerne County, Pennsylvania Volume I (Oscar Jewell Harvey, A.M)—page 205-207—there are wonderful descriptions of Andrew Montour and some of his activities.

Wyoming Valley, PA, Susquehanna Company, Chief Teedyuscung

A History of Wilkes-Barre, Luzerne County, Pennsylvania Volume I (Oscar Jewell Harvey, A.M)—page 239-451—I used this resource (and others) to include in my novel which has the history of the Susquehanna Company, a land company formed in 1753 in Connecticut for the purpose of developing the Wyoming Valley in Pennsylvania. They claimed the land was purchased from the Iroquois in 1754, but also claimed immigrants from London who settled the Colony of New Haven in 1638 had been given a charter for the right to settle in Wyoming Valley. These pages also describe Chief Teedyuscung's battle for the Delawares and other tribes in Wyoming Valley who were being threatened by these settlers and eventually pushed off the land. Later, the settlers were embroiled in troubles with the rival settlers from Pennsylvania, which lead to the Pennamite Wars. There is also material leading up to the French and Indian War, the Treaty of Easton (more than one), Pontiac's Rebellion, and many other treaties, including the Fort Stanwix Treaty in 1768.

Catharine Montour Family Tree

Primary Source from *Madame Montour and the Fur Trade (1667-1752)* by Simone Vincens; journals and diaries

Pierre Couc (1627) (French fur trader) married to **Marie Miteouamigoukoue** (Algonquin) in Trois-Rivieres, Quebec, Canada
> **Children:** Jeanne, Louis, Angelique, Marguerite, **Elizabeth/Isabelle Couc**, Madeleine, Jean-Baptiste

Elizabeth/Isabelle Couc Montour (1667-1753 – aka Madame Montour) (interpreter, diplomatic consultant for New York and Pennsylvania) married her 4th husband,

Carondawana (Oneida Chief) – Madame Montour's brother, Louis, assumed the name Montour and Madame Montour, also assumed it after his death. Madame Montour moved from Canada to New York and after marriage to Carondawana, moved to Pennsylvania
> **Children:** Madame Montour had children from previous marriages. Offspring from her marriage to Carondawana (aka Robert Hunter): **Andrew and Margaret** (possibly more)

Andrew Montour (1720-1772 - aka Sattellieu and Henry) – interpreter and negotiator in Pennsylvania, Virginia, and Ohio in the 1700s (married twice and had children; he was Catharine Montour's uncle)

Margaret Montour (1711 - aka French Margaret) married **Katarionecha** (aka Peter Quebec) (Mohawk) in 1728
> **Children**: Esther Montour, **Catharine Montour**, Mary (aka Molly), Nicholas, Karontase

Catharine Montour (1729? - aka Queen Catharine) married **Telehemet** (Seneca chief) and **Edward Pollard** (English fur trader)
> **Children**: Roland, Belle, John (aka Stuttering John), step son, Captain Pollard

Character Index

Queen Alliquippa – (died 1754) a Seneca woman known as the head of an Indian community near present day Pittsburgh. George Washington in 1753 called on her and Conrad Weiser visited her often.

Jack Armstrong – a Pennsylvania fur trader who was killed by the Delaware, Mushemeelin, in 1744. The two men had known each for years and Mushemeelin owed Armstrong a debt in furs and Armstrong took his horse. Later, Mushemeelin killed him and his servants.

Chief Allumpapes (aka Sassoonan) – (1675-1747) a Delaware chief whose people went to Ohio country and he stayed in Shamokin as a representative of the Iroquois.

General Edward Braddock – (1695-1755) a British officer and commander-in-chief for the Thirteen Colonies during the start of the French and Indian War. He commanded British forces in the unsuccessful 1755 campaign to expel the French from the Ohio Valley.

Chief Bull aka (Captain Bull, Honest John) (mid-1700s) – the son of the great Teedyuscung, King of the Delawares. After he believed his father was murdered, he avenged his death when he and his warriors murdered more than fifty white settlers.

Lt. Colonel John Butler – (1728-1796) a Loyalist who led a militia known as Butler's Rangers during the American Revolutionary War. He learned several Iroquoian languages and worked as an interpreter in the fur trade.

General Walter Butler – (1752-1781) the son of Lt. Colonel John Butler and a British Loyalist officer during the American Revolution. He led the raid on the settlement in Cherry Valley which became known as a massacre.

Butler's Rangers – a Loyalist military unit of the American Revolutionary War, established by American loyalist, John Butler. Most were Loyalists from New York who recruited Indians from the Six Nations to fight the Americans. Catharine Montour's two sons, John and Roland were part of this unit.

Chief Canassatego – (1684-1750) Onondago chief, member of the Six Nations (Iroquois) Great Council. He attended conferences and spoke for the Iroquois in Philadelphia.

Cornplanter – (1732-1836) an influential Seneca leader. His mother was a Seneca woman and his father was a Dutch trader from Albany. He fought for the British during the American Revolution, but urged reconciliation after the war.

George Croghan – (1718-1782) a prominent trader, Indian agent, frontiersman, land speculator who learned native languages, an Onondaga Council sachem, and eventually appointed Deputy Superintendant of Indian Affairs. He was born in Ireland and emigrated to Pennsylvania in 1741. Within a few years, he became a successful fur trader, was quick-witted and a brilliant negotiator and intermediary.

Deganawidah – (died 15th century?) The Great Peacemaker and prophet, who, with the Mohawk orator, Hiawatha, founded the League of the Iroquois (Iroquois) and had a vision of bringing peace to his people. It is believed he established this League of Five Nations (Seneca, Cayuga, Onondaga, Oneida, Mohawk) and later, Six (Tuscarora) (Haudenosaunee – People of the Long House). He envisioned a great pine tree whose roots were five powerful nations. From these roots, the tree grew so high that its tip pierced through the sky and on top there was an eagle watching to help keep peace. His desire was to bring all people beneath this Tree of Peace. Various sources indicate he was born a Huron in the 15th century and his story is epic and symbolic, having a powerful impact on the unity of the Haudenosaunee and the beginnings of the United States.

Benjamin Franklin – (1706-1790) a writer, diplomat, printer, publisher, scientist, inventor, statesman, and political philosopher in Colonial America.

Christopher Gist – (1706-1759) a frontiersman, surveyor, explorer active in Colonial America.

William Johnson – Superintendent of Indian Affairs in 1755; born in Ireland in the 1740s and was quick to accumulate wealth in Mohawk territory of New York as a trader with the Indians. He assimilated Indian culture into his business with them. He was adopted into the Mohawk Nation and took Molly Brant as a second wife. He worked tirelessly during the American Revolution to ally the Six Nations with England, but overstepped his position in breaking a boundary line established between the Six Nations, England, and other tribes. His relationship with the Mohawks influenced them to support England during the war.

Martin and Jeanette Mack – (mid-1700s) the first Moravian missionaries at Shamokin, PA. They were linguists and lived with Madame Montour while building their mission.

William and John McClure – came from Wyoming Valley, PA and were the first white settlers in 1787 in Catharine's Landing, what later became known as Havana and then Montour Falls, NY in honor of Catharine Montour. Eagle Cliff Falls is the name used in *Catharine, Queen of the Tumbling Waters.*

Daniel McMullen – (mid-1700s) a white captive from PA taken prisoner by Chief Teedyuscung and sold to Catharine Montour at Canisteo, NY in 1757. He escaped with Thomas Moffitt sometime later.

Thomas Moffitt – (mid-1700s) a white captive taken prisoner near Poughkeepsie, NY and brought to Wyoming Valley, and then to Tioga and sold to Catharine Montour. He escaped with Daniel McMullen sometime later.

Moravian Missionaries – the first large-scale Protestant missionary movement, dating to the Bohemian Reformation with origins in ancient Bohemia and Moravia (present day Czech (Czechia) Republic) of the 15th century. In the 1700s, a small group of Moravian dissenters in Germany made Bethlehem, Pennsylvania their center and were known for communal living and global missions, including missions to Native Americans. They lived among the natives and planted, sang, prayed, fed, and healed and only shared the gospel if the moment was right.

Mushmeelin – (mid-1700s) a Delaware who lived in Shamokin, PA and killed a Pennsylvania fur trader, Jack Armstrong. They had known one another a long time and there was conflict over debt.

Anna Nitschmann – (died 1760) a Moravian missionary, lyrical poet, and the second wife of Count Nicolaus Ludwig Zinzendorf.

The Ohio Company – known as the Ohio Company of Virginia, was a land speculation company organized by wealthy Virginians (including George Washington). The British government granted the Ohio Company land near the headwaters of the Ohio River. The goal was to promote trade with American Indians and to secure British control of the Ohio River Valley.

Edward Pollard – (1700s) an English trader with headquarters at Fort Niagara who had been married to a Seneca woman and to Catharine Montour.

Captain Pollard (Big Tree) – (died 1841) son of Edward Pollard and a Seneca woman. Catharine Montour was his stepmother. He participated in the American Revolution and was a war captain in the War of 1812.

General John Sullivan – (1740-1795) John Sullivan was an early political leader and officer in the American Revolution who won distinction for the campaign initiated by General George Washington against Loyalists and the allied Iroquois nations. Under Sullivan, the Continental Army carried out a destruction of the lands and homes of the Iroquois Confederacy (Haudenosaunee). More than forty Iroquois villages and their stores of winter crops were destroyed. Five thousand Iroquois were driven to Fort Niagara seeking British protection. Although considered successful, the expedition didn't fully destroy the Iroquois and later there was devastating retribution by the Iroquois.

Susquehanna Company – a land company formed in 1753 in Connecticut for the purpose of developing the Wyoming Valley, Pennsylvania. The company claimed King Charles II of England had granted a charter to them in 1662, however, there were already settlers there claiming they had a charter. And, of course, Native Americans had lived there for thousands of years. Delawares, the Iroquois, and other tribes were initially opposed to the settlements. The Pennamite Wars ensued and in 1782 a Continental Congress granted the land in favor of Pennsylvania, but the Connecticut settlers refused to leave. After the second war, there was a Compromise Act of 1799 and the Pennsylvania legislature secured a means of settlement with the Connecticut settlers.

Luke Swetland – (1729-1823) a soldier in the American Revolutionary War who was taken as a captive from Wyoming Valley, PA by Seneca Indians loyal to the British in 1778. He was given to an old Seneca woman in New York State near what is Romulus, NY today. Luke Swetland was originally from Connecticut and part of the Susquehanna Company's land company's settlement in the Wyoming Valley. He was kept as a captive for close to two years, escaped, and, returned to Pennsylvania. His account is recorded in an old journal that includes him meeting Catharine Montour.

Chief Teedyuscung – (1700-1763 aka King of the Delawares; Honest John) baptized by the Moravians, he left their mission, and settled in the Wyoming Valley, Pennsylvania to become a spokesman for making peace for the displaced Delawares, Shawnees, Mahicans, and Munsees. He was controversial, sincere, and demanded respect.

Conrad Weiser – (1696-1760) a German pioneer who served as an interpreter and diplomat between the Pennsylvania Colony and Native American nations. He migrated with his family in 1710 and at the age of fifteen, decided to live among the Mohawk tribe of the Iroquois. He worked with Andrew Montour and helped secure him a position as an interpreter for the Pennsylvania Colony.

Rev. Eleazer Wheelock – (1711-1779) Yale educated Congregational minister and educator who started colonial boarding schools to train colonial and Indian boys to become schoolteachers and missionaries. He fervently pursued the conversion of all Indians to Protestant Christianity, including starting a school in the controversial Wyoming Valley in Pennsylvania. He became the founder of Dartmouth College that was intended to educate the Indians of New England. Wheelock depicted the Indians as brutes that required conversion to civilization and was zealous in this pursuit. Ultimately, most of Wheelock's missionary endeavors with the Indians faltered and failed, but Dartmouth College did not.

Nikolaus Ludwig Zinzendorf – (1700-1760) a religious and social reformer and later, leader of the Moravian church in Pennsylvania, whose headquarters was in Bethlehem, Pennsylvania. He desired to unite all Pietistic groups, such as Lutherans, Reformed, Dunkers, Quakers, Mennonites and other sects. Although sincere, he failed in this unity, but established Indian missions that were notable.

Bibliography

Anderson, Chad L. *The Storied Landscape of Iroquoia, History, Conquest, and Memory in the Native Northeast*. Lincoln, Nebraska: University of Nebraska Press, 2020.

Aquila, Richard. *The Iroquois Restoration, Iroquois Diplomacy on the Colonial Frontier, 1701-1754*. Lincoln, Nebraska: University of Nebraska Press, 1997.

Buffalo Historical Society. *Red Jacket, Transactions of the Buffalo Historical Society, Volume 3*. Buffalo: Order of the Society, 1885. (Captain Pollard; Catharine Montour, page 83)

Cleaver, Mary Louise Catlin. *The History of the Town of Catharine, Schuyler County, N.Y.* Vermont: Tuttle Publishing, 1945.

Cruikshank, E. *Butler's Rangers, The Revolutionary Period*. Forgotten London Books, 2012, originally published by Lundy's Lane Historical Society, 1893.

Dunn, Walter, S. Jr. *People of the American Frontier, The Coming of the American Revolution*. Westport, CT: Praeger Publishers, 2005.

Graymont, Barbara. *The Iroquois in the American Revolution*. Syracuse, New York: Syracuse University Press, 1972.

Harvey, Oscar Jewell, Smith, Ernest Gray. *A History of Wilkes-Barre, Luzerne County, Pennsylvania, Volume 1*. Wilkes-Barre, Pennsylvania: The Wyoming Historical and Geological Society, 1909. (Catharine, page 205-206, 332-334, 341; Andrew Montour, page 207-208.

Harvey, Oscar Jewell. *A History of Wilkes-Barre Luzerne County, Pennsylvania, Volume II*. Wilkes-Barre: The Wyoming Historical and Geological Society, 1909. (Catharine, page 984-985, 1027, 1041, 1084; Esther Montour, page 913, 1917, 984-985, 989, 1015, 1018, 1019, 1027, 1032-1034, 1092.

Hinderaker, Eric, Mancall, Peter C. *At the Edge of the Empire, The Backcountry in British North America*. Baltimore: The Johns Hopkins University Press, 2003.

Hubert, Archer Butler, Schwarze, William Nathaniel, Editors. *David Zeisberger's History of the Northern American Indians in 18th Century Ohio, New York & Pennsylvania*. Lewisburg, PA: Wennawoods Publishing, 1999.

Lloyd, Herbert M., Morgan, Lewis H. *League of the Ho-De'-No-Sau-Nee or Iroquois*. New York: University Press, 1922.

Ketchum, William. *History of Buffalo, Volume 2*. Buffalo, NY: Rockwell, Baker & Hill, Printers, 1865. (John and Roland Montour, page 122-127).

Merrifield, Edward. *Luke Swetland's Captivity and Rescue from the Indians*. Scranton PA: 1915, Wennawoods Publishing, 2000. (Catharine, page 20, 23-24.

Merrell, James H. *Into the American Woods, Negotiators on the Pennsylvania Frontier*. New York: W.W. Norton & Company Ltd., 1999.

Sipe, C. Hale. *The Indian Wars of Pennsylvania, Book One*. Westminster, MD: Heritage Books, 1929. (George Washington, Andrew Montour, George Croghan, page 159, 162, 168-172).

Schoolcraft, Henry R. *Notes on the Iroquois*. East Lansing, Michigan: Michigan State University Press, 2002, originally published in 1847.

Taylor, Alan. *The Divided Grounds, Indians, Settlers, and the Northern Borderland of the American Revolution*. New York: Alfred A. Knopf, 2006.

Thwaites, Reuben Gold. *Early Western Journals 1748-1765*. Cleveland, OH: The Arthur H. Clark Company, 1904.

Vincens, Simone. *Madame Montour & The Fur Trade* (1667-1752). Xlibris, Corp., 2011.

Volwiler, Albert T. *George Croghan and the Westward Movement, 1741-1782*. Andesite Press, Imprint of Creative Media Partners, "Reprint from The Pennsylvania Magazines of History and Biography," October 1922.

Wallace, F.C. Anthony. *The Death and Rebirth of the Seneca*. New York: Vintage Books, 1969.

Williams, Benjamin, as told to by Chainbreaker (Governor Blacksnake). Edited and Notes by Thomas S. Abler. *Chainbreaker, The Revolutionary War Memoirs of Governor Blacksnake*. Nebraska: University of Nebraska Press, 1989.

Online Resources

Franklin B. and Hall D., *Minutes of Conferences held at Easton, October, 1758*. University of Pittsburg, digital.library.pitt.edu.

Faull, Katherine. Dr. *The Shamokin Diaries 1745-1755*, Bucknell University, Pennsylvania: https://shamokindiary.blogs.bucknell.edu.

Gist, Christopher. *Christopher Gist's Journals*. U.S. GenWeb Archives Pennsylvania, usgwarchives.net.

Hays, John. *John Hays Diary and Journal of 1760*. https://www.familysearch.org.

Charles, Julian. *John Dochstader's Third Wife*. www.genealogy.com, 2006.

Marshe, Witham. *Journal of the Treaty at Lancaster in 1744 with the Six Nations*. Internet Archive: www.archive.org.

Pauff, Georgie. *Teedyuscung: Chief of 10 Tribes was Respected Warrior, Diplomat Called Gideon by Christian, He Negotiated Treaties for His People*. The Morning Call, www.mcall.com, 1999.

Catharine, Queen of the Tumbling Waters

by Cynthia G. Neale   **ISBN 978-1-960373-02-1**

"I'm not like your white women who lose their tongues and wits in a house full of men."

So says Catharine Montour to her white captive during the Indian depredations of the 1750s. Catharine Montour, a métis, born during Pennsylvania's Long Peace, is nurtured by her grandmother, the celebrated Madame Montour, an interpreter for the British colonies. Her uncle, Andrew Montour, is also an interpreter and sits on the Council of the Iroquois. The Montours are an unconventional, yet highly regarded family who host diverse and fascinating assemblies of fur traders, missionaries, Indians, and colonial leaders in their home.

As the Long Peace ends and the French and Indian War, and eventually the American Revolution occur, Catharine, desiring only to live quietly by a waterfall in New York, becomes a fearless, determined, and passionate leader who demands loyalty to peace in her village and for all. And then in 1779 when General John Sullivan leads the campaign to destroy all Iroquois villages, Queen Catharine, heroically guides her people to Fort Niagara.

Today as American exceptionalism prevails against the recognition of indigenous peoples, Catharine's relevant and fact-based story spans two wars and enlightens and makes visible the unwritten truths of early American history.

From the Author

I've often said my writing career includes working with the dead and although this sounds morbid, it is not. We all carry the blood and stories of our ancestors and there's a thin line between here and there if we attune our hearts to listen. I wanted to be a writer at a young age, but it took years to learn to listen.

I grew up in the Montour Falls, New York vicinity and was intrigued by Queen Catharine, but there was little known information. Historians have puzzled over Queen Catharine Montour and the Montour family for years. The Montours were elusive, famous, but obscure, and have been difficult to track down. Historians have disagreed over the life of Catharine Montour and her various

family members for years. It was Simone Vincens, author of
the wonderful biography, Madame Montour and the Fur Trade,
who encouraged me to learn about Isabel Montour and her son,
Andrew Montour, if I wanted to know Catharine Montour. After
uncanny and astounding Catharine nudges and reading local
history articles, I delved into Simone Vincens' book and it became
the skeleton that eventually led me into fleshing out Catharine's
life.

Discussion Questions

l. Prior to reading this novel, how many famous Native American
women of history did you know about (besides Sacajawea and
Pocahontas)? Do you think Catharine Montour should be famous?
If so, why?

2. In Chapter Seven, Catharine and her children are living on the
renegade reservation in Kah-ni-sti-oh and Catharine invites her
captives and others to supper. She tells the story of the prophet
peacemaker, Deganawidah, who, along with Hiawatha, brought
the warring tribes into the Iroquois Confederacy. In this history/
legend/myth/story, the five tribes were brought together in peace
and together they planted the Great Tree of Peace, which is a
metaphor for how peace can grow if nurtured. A white captive
challenges Catharine by asking what kind of peace is it if when
other tribes refuse to come under this Tree of Peace, the Iroquois
then war against them. Later, during the American Revolution, in
1775, the Continental Congress in a meeting in Albany, asked the
Iroquois Confederacy to remain neutral in the war between the
colonists and Great Britain. "Brothers . . . We desire to sit down
under the same tree of peace with you; let us water its roots and
cherish its growth till the large leaves and flourishing branches
shall extend to the setting sun and reach the skies."

Catharine does not have an answer for the captive. Indeed,
there is some hypocrisy here and also in the message of the
Continental Congress. And yet clearly, the establishment of
the Confederacy united the five and later, six, tribes together
in peace and unity for hundreds of years. It is evident that all
humans are united as flawed human beings.

  a. Do you think human beings are capable of being united in
  peace and do you think the Iroquois Tree of Peace is possible
  today for America? How?
  b. Discuss Catharine and this chapter and how this is relevant
  today.

3. Catharine clearly loved all three of the men in her life.

    a. Discuss the relationships and their positive, as well as, unhealthy attributes and how they help develop her as a strong woman.

4. Overall, Catharine believes in the equality of all people, but decides to fight for her Indian people and takes captives. And she didn't want Belle to marry a white man.

    a. Do you think Catharine has high ideals that she couldn't live up to?
    b. Should she have whipped Elsa and Thomas Moffit, her captives?
    c. Do you think she gave her blessing to the Wyoming Massacre and could she have been there herself condoning the slaughter?
    d. Do you think she was neutral during the war, especially at the end?

5. The British Empire tightened control over the colonies at the end of the French and Indian War with the Proclamation of 1763, declaring all lands west of Appalachia off limits to settlers and private citizens, and colonial governments were forbidden to buy land or make agreements with natives. Only licensed traders could use the trade routes, which the British Empire desired. They felt they couldn't control their subjects and it would be too costly to regulate. The colonists defied the proclamation, resented it, and it failed to stem the tide of westward expansion. The French had given up the land after the war, but were still there. The British Empire didn't want the colonists crossing into Appalachia and creating problems with the French and Native Americans there. And there were already American colonists who had settled there prior to the proclamation. The colonists rebelled against the proclamation and this became one of the many battles the Americans had with their mother country that led to the revolution.

    a. Do you think the rights of the colonists were wronged or do you think the rights of the Native Americans were wronged?
    b. Do you think the British Empire was unjust to its subjects?
    c. Does this part of history make you re-think the American Revolution?

6. In Chapter Thirty-Two, Benjamin Franklin and Catharine Montour meet and he tells Catharine how he has sought to bring together the disparate colonies into a confederacy under

Great Britain, similar to the great Iroquois Confederacy. He had printed the great Onondago Chief Canassatego's speech. This speech proposed the British colonies do likewise as the Iroquois Confederacy and be united and in agreement. He said that many arrows cannot be broken as easily as one. This inspired the bundle of thirteen arrows held by an eagle on the Great Seal of the United States. Benjamin Franklin told Catharine that at the 1754 Albany Congress he had said that if ignorant savages could form such a union, why not twelve colonies. In 1988, a Senate Resolution was passed to acknowledge the contribution of the Iroquois Confederacy in the development of the United States Constitution. This is not widely known and there are many who refute their contribution, believing it was only European influences that helped shape our Constitution.

The Iroquois Confederacy is believed to have been founded anywhere from the 1200s to the 1400s, and it might be the oldest living democracy. The Iroquois constitution is an elaborate, complex, and functioning constitution that, unless you are a Native American scholar, would probably not know about.

a. Do you believe the Iroquois Confederacy and their great law of peace helped shape our democracy?
b. If such a powerful people influenced America, why is it not widely known and celebrated?
c. Do you think it is American exceptionalism and that we have been enculturated in the belief that the United States is more unique and special than other nations?
d. Do you believe that we are in a time of reconciliation and that we can still be patriotic and proud to be Americans without revising history?
e. What do you think of this quote, "All of us are asleep" a Jewish saying goes, "By telling stories, we are awakened. Has this novel awakened you?

7. Catharine respects, honors, and communes with nature. It was a view and a custom for Native Americans to give thanks for the animal in the hunt before killing it. They viewed nature as brothers and sisters and the land belonging to the Great Spirit. The European view was that of nature being a resource and having ownership. They would refer to the Biblical passage in Genesis, "Be fruitful and multiply and fill the earth and subdue it." This led to misunderstanding between Native Americans and the colonists in the treaties and land sales. The Native Americans did not see the land as a commodity and initially thought they had sold land to be shared.

a. Do you believe that the view of the land as a commodity and one to be subdued contributed to pollution and climate change?

b. Can you imagine a different country if the Europeans had listened and implemented the Native American spirit in caring for the earth?

c. How could they have combined both views and is there still time?

d. What do you know about today's indigenous peoples who are on the forefront of environmental battles?

Cynthia G. Neale is the author of *The Irish Dresser, A Story of Hope during The Great Hunger (An Gorta Mor, 1845-1850)*; *Hope in New York City, The Continuing Story of The Irish Dresser*; *Norah: The Making of an Irish-American Woman in 19th-Century New York*; *The Irish Milliner*. Ms. Neale has also written a dessert and essay book, *Pavlova in a Hat Box, Sweet Memories & Desserts*. In addition to these works, Ms. Neale writes plays, screenplays, short stories, and essays. A screenplay, *The Irish Dresser Series*, adapted from her four novels is currently being pitched to producers. She holds a B.A. in Writing and Literature from Vermont College. Ms. Neale enjoys Irish set dancing, ballroom dancing, reading, painting, hiking, and kayaking. An accomplished baker, she also enjoys creating events for food, dance, and fund raising.

Printed in the USA
CPSIA information can be obtained
at www.ICGtesting.com
JSHW082130201223
53997JS00001B/41